THE LEGENDS OF THE ROAD

A STORY OF TWO AMERICAN RACES

BACK TO BACK

THE RACE ACROSS AMERICA

THE PIKES PEAK INTERNATIONAL HILL CLIMB

By MICKY DYMOND

Xtrema Publishing

Torrance, California

1

MICKY DYMOND

Written account of the 2014 RAAM and 2014 PPIHC.

Cover Design: Dale Galford
Cover photos::Dymond, Rushton, Tollett
Editor: Vic Armijo
Title ID: 7247645
ISBN-10: 1548022381
ISBN-13: 978-1548022389

Interior photographs by Legends crew, Ducati, Faulkner and Livingston, John Rushton, Brian Manley, Michael Larkin, Joe Lawwill, Vic Armijo. Mandy Newman, Travis Tollett, Michael Robson, Brian Bishop, Tage Plantell, Painting by Chris Wooley, Maps from RAAM and PPIHC.

Acknowledgments

This book was a swing for the fence in many ways. I cannot thank everyone who offered advice or guidance because there were so many. First I want to thank Vic Armijo you are the man, thank you for making me readable. Brenda Lyons, my muse, best friend and confidant, Love you. Thanks for putting up with all my rants of anger and frustrations. Special thanks to Thomas Mueller for all your guidance to get this book published. Ben Bostrom, David Zabriskie, and Dave Mirra you are all awesome, Men above men, thank you. Rick and Fred Boethling and the RAAM, Brian Bishop from who it started, Tage Plantell, Michael Robson, Wayne Dowd, Laura Kindregan, and the Legends crew of 2014 (Brian, Meg, Paige, Rick, Danny, Rush, Dave, Scott, Will, Stephen) for actions, thoughts, photos and memories. Joe Lawwill, Steven Cassar, Erik Eastland, Jennifer Davies, Ray and Bev Dymond, Amy Snyder, Jimmy Mac, Carl Harris, Paul and Becca Livingston, Rod Faulkner, Gary and Greg Trachy, Don Canet, Jeremy Toye, Fabrice Lambert, Megan Leatham, Tom Osbourne, The Riggles, and all the people of the Pikes Peak International Hill Climb, Michael Larkin, Paul Thede, Mike Mason, Chris Wooley, Liz and Gary, The Mecca, Tracy and Daniel Ainslie, Jure Robic,

Chris Ragsdale, Billy Edwards, Julie Lyons, and everyone else who gave me time, listened and spoke about this amazing adventure.

To my family, Mom and Dad, my kids, Hunter, Trevor, and Ronni. Love you

To Dave Mirra

LEGENDS OF THE ROAD

INTRO FROM DAVID BAILEY:

My first memory of Micky Dymond was in Cycle News, a weekly paper that covered all types of motorcycle racing. Dreaming of being a top motocross racer, I would keep an eye on races and results and riders in other parts of the country, especially southern California. I lived in Virginia so I was always interested in what was happening in California and would study the race reports and photos. One time I saw this guy with a cool name riding a big bike and his style got my attention. I remembered him and had a feeling one-day our racing paths would cross.

As I made my way up the ranks, eventually picked up by the Honda factory team, I watched Micky on his Husqvarna making progress as well. There were certain riders I would watch for ideas and Micky was in that group of riders. Even though the bike seemed to be holding him back, he made the most of it and kept pace with the lead pack. It was just a matter of time before he would land on one of the dominant Japanese brands and be a front-runner. I wasn't threatened by him as a competitor, more intrigued because of how he rode and that he seemed like a sharp and interesting person. I was too busy doing my own thing to introduce myself and talk to him. Then during the off-season of 1985 I got a call from one our managers at Honda. Honda was restructuring the team and they needed a 125cc rider. I listened to all the names he was considering and then I said, what about Micky Dymond? There was a pause, followed by the realization like, hmmm…Micky Dymond huh? The next thing I knew he signed with Honda and would be my new teammate along with Rick Johnson from El Cajon, California.

Honda dominated the 1986 season with Rick Johnson taking both the indoor Supercross and outdoor 250cc titles. I won the 500cc title and Micky won the 125cc title. Rick wrapped up his titles earlier, but Micky and I wrapped up ours the same day. I was happy to cap off the year with a title and really happy to see him get his first!

Since Honda restructured again at the end of 1986, that meant my longtime teammate, training partner and best friend Johnny O'Mara was leaving to ride Suzuki for 1987. In the back of my mind I thought Micky and I might be doing some riding and training and elevate each other's skill and fitness the way Johnny and I did. Since Rick came to Honda and won titles right away, titles I wanted to win, I was somewhat threatened by him and didn't plan on sharing too much information. With Micky, since he would defend his title in 1987 in a different class, I was already considering how teaming up and doing some riding and training together might benefit us both.

Then everything changed. At a pre-season race near Fresno, California I crashed and broke my back and my career came to an abrupt halt. The last thing on my mind was Team Honda or titles, I was wrestling with the reality that I would never walk again and had just learned that my new wife Gina was pregnant.

In the months that followed, I tried to stay positive, but the loss was so intense, so life changing that things just kind of got dark. I followed motocross a little bit, enough to know that Micky won the championship again, but our lives went separate directions. I had an early exit from motocross and became a husband and a father. Micky, despite being a 2-time national champion, was dropped from Honda in another one of their restructures. That didn't seem right, but I was in my own hell.

Fast forward to 2013. Gina and I had two children, a boy and a girl, and I had found training to be the most effective at keeping my head right and my body in good health. It seemed Micky had done the same. Word on the street was that he was cycling a lot and eyeing the Race across America (RAAM). I was instantly intrigued and again he was on my radar! He had been interested in the race since the early 80's the same as I was, but I never thought about actually doing it…that's just crazy!

By 2014, Micky had assembled an incredible 4-man team comprised of the legendary Dave Mirra, motorcycle road racing's fine specimen Ben Bostrom, and former Tour de France specialist and National Time Trial champion Dave Zabriskie! I didn't know Micky was that caliber of a cyclist, but then again, there was a lot I didn't know about him. A lot of years had passed. I just knew him to be a natural on a motorcycle, where he also won a Supermoto title – a hybrid of motocross and road racing – and was instrumental in the birth of freestyle motocross. Utilizing both his creativity and riding skill he was once the record holder on a Ducati for the fastest ascent of Pikes Peak. He was about to take on both RAAM and the Pikes Peak challenge!

I sat in front of my computer looking for any updates while visualizing where he was. First the desert, then the Rockies, then the windy plains and then the steep Appalachians. I was hooked!

He and I have since ridden together. We have both been through allot and have grown. He is sharp and interesting. He's also an excellent storyteller. I'm not alone in saying I could listen to him talk for hours! I just didn't realize he was such a bad ass on a bicycle. Then again, he is a champion and he has that spark. I recognized that from looking at a picture of him in Cycle News! When he makes up his mind to do something, he does it, and he intends to do it well. It's inspiring and usually surprising, much like his story telling. "So I had this alligator once…" he said out of the blue. You never know where he is going with things. You think you do, but then he takes it someplace else.

As you read this book, it will inspire, humor and move you. It will also in a subtle, yet surprising way make you take a good look at how you are living your life, what you are living it for, and if you are doing your best. Is there anything you could do to be happier and more effective and more aware of others? The book motivated me to reevaluate my approach to life. I didn't expect that. Our paths did in fact cross in motocross and again in cycling and a little bit in life. I sensed that they would and I'm glad they did

LEGENDS OF THE ROAD

LEGENDS OF THE ROAD INTRO
RAAM.
June 19th 2014

Its daybreak and the rain has finally stopped. Up ahead the road is a series of rolling hills and deep valleys weaving through Virginia's heavy, green canopy. But, there is no time to take this all in right now; there are only painful efforts to maintain the insane race pace, as is my duty. At this moment the pace is dictated by Team Innovation Africa. They have three riders switching out every 15 minutes while Ben Bostrom and I, one half of the Legends of the Road Team, are riding closer to 18-minute shifts. I am both physically and mentally beat down to ruin. I am starting day five of RAAM. My body is exhausted. My chest cold has gotten worse. My breathing is labored and shallow. My neck and back are conspiring to seize. My hands and feet are so swollen that I need to squeeze into my shoes and gloves need. However, the real problem is my legs. All strength has left them. They have swollen up, are holding water and they are heavy like lead. The pace we are forced to beat is 25 miles per hour. After three hours of close racing through the Appalachian Mountains with a few lead changes, we are pushed back to second place.

Innovation Africa is just up ahead of us. We can see them and are trying desperately to catch and pass them, but instead it feels like we're losing ground.

Five days straight, no stops, no breaks. This race is by itself a killer, an unworldly endurance contest of 3,000 miles. It is truly just hard to believe a race of this size and length exists. We have been racing wheel-to-wheel with Team Innovation Africa as if we were competing in just a short 30-mile road race. The fact that our team is neck and neck with Team Innovation Africa after 2700 miles of racing is unprecedented in this event. We're now, within minutes of each other after days of non-stop racing. There was no way coming into this monumental adventure/race that I could imagine it would come to this. There have been no easy moments, no relaxing segments, and no warm-up shifts and no looking around to take in a coast to coast crossing of America. It has only been a series of flat out time trial efforts, day and night, nonstop. We are in a battle to the finish, to the death of us all. Win or die has become our cause.

Riding in the transition vehicle with Stephen and Will, Ben is on the road taking his pull. The two crewmen are arguing about directions. They're undecided where our next the transition point is. Stephen makes a left turn at an intersection before pulling over onto the shoulder as the two of them continue to argue. I get out and get ready to change with Ben. We have parked on a slight uphill after making a left at a four-way intersection. The Innovation Africa rider will be coming through just before Ben. As I get clipped into the right pedal and line up for the tradeoff, I see the Innovation team car's flashers coming up the road and I see their rider. They race straight through the traffic signal staring at us with confusion---and could that be amusement? Did they just make a direction mistake or are we about to make the mistake? Stephen and Will are in a panic and say it is our mistake and we will need to turn around. Ben is now coming into the intersection and it is too late. He looks over at us, shakes his head in disgust and keeps chasing. We jump back into the transition vehicle and race after them and up the road to find the next suitable transition point.

Into my next shift I am really physically suffering. I cannot make any good speed or find momentum on the rolling hills no matter what I do. I am crushed mentally and so afraid that I am letting the team down that I am having tremors throughout my body.

[HEARING BANJO MUSIC: Chasing team Innovation Africa through the Appalachian Mountains.]

The loneliness I am feeling is so great within me that I see my movements in slow motion. I feel paralyzed. Innovation Africa is pulling out ahead. I cannot see them or their cars anymore. At this very moment my exhaustion and emotions are tearing me apart. I am putting everything into my effort while I am angry and frustrated, torn up and crying at the same time. I can't believe that I've done this to myself; that I've put myself here in this miserable place. I heard once upon a time that if your dreams don't scare you they're not big enough. Well, "this is pretty damn big,"

I say to myself out loud. Answering my thoughts sarcastically, "WTF was I thinking?" "God please help me," I scream out loud, desperately pleading with all my heart. Three thousand miles of racing on a bicycle from California to Maryland. How did I get myself into this? Why did I get myself into this? I'm not even a true bicycle racer

[12 STATES AND 3,000 MILES: Course map of the Race across America]

Where should I start?

First, I will be racing a road bicycle in the toughest and the longest ultra-endurance cycling race in the world, the

Race across America (RAAM). This is the biggest, most unbelievable ultra-endurance cycling event. Starting in Oceanside, California, RAAM crosses 12 states, passes through 88 counties and 350 communities before finishing in Annapolis, Maryland. From the Pacific to the Atlantic. RAAM is the most respected and longest-running ultra-endurance sports event in the world. It is feared as the toughest race in the world. This year's RAAM is 3,020 miles long. The route has 170,000 feet of vertical climbing, (that is the equivalent of climbing Mt. Everest almost 6 times) Runs through the deserts of California, Arizona and Utah, over the Rocky Mountains, across the Great Plains, over the Mississippi River, across the Appalachian Mountains and finally to the finish in Annapolis. RAAM is not a stage race like Tour de France, a series of daily races. RAAM is one nonstop race. After the officials start the clock, it doesn't stop until you cross the finish line. The Legends of the Road will be racing without stopping day and night in an attempt to be the fastest four-rider team to pedal across America.

THE LEGENDS OF THE ROAD

Dave Zabriskie   Dave Mirra   Micky Dymond   Ben Bostrom

WWW.THELEGENDSOFTHEROAD.COM

[FEARLESS FOUR: The four-man team of Legends]

I am a member of a four-racer team. The other three team members are very special guys. I have joined these three to compete in RAAM's four man team division. They are a few of the best athletic specimens you will ever meet. We are four unique personalities who have survived extreme highs and lows in our lives and in our individual two-wheeled sports. Now we all live sort of quiet second lives, far from the once over-stimulated, high-profile lives we once lived. Our stories are all very different and somehow they are also the same. Although we come from different places we share a common love for cycling and competition. We are all ex-champions from different two-wheel sports and we all still itch to get into the mix and race. There is no other challenge in cycling quite like RAAM and nothing even near as big. Nor is there any such race in any other sport like this; an unfathomable endurance challenge that will surely show us all what we are made of, or more to the point, what we have become. Who are we?

Ben Bostrom: Ben is 40 years old and is a former Dirt track, Supersport, Superbike and Supermoto champion and X Games gold medalist. Ben has an extensive motorcycle racing background. Ben has raced and won on Harley Davidson, Yamaha, Honda and Ducati factory teams. He's the kind of racer that can pull together the moment on his will and win if he feels rightly motivated. Not many people are out there that can decide in the moment that they want it bad enough and then go out and take it just because. He is that good. After retirement from motorcycle racing he picked up cycling and has excelled as a pro mountain bike racer. He has a genetic gift from God for endurance sports with a tolerance for suffering. I say this because he can deal with pain with a grace that seems it's almost godly. So yeah, he just went to the pro class in mountain biking right off the bat. Ben is also a super cool guy with a positive attitude with a capitol P. He has the perfect personality for a road trip into this hellish journey.

Dave Mirra: Dave is also 40 years old. He's the most decorated BMX X Games medalist of all time in BMX Vert and in BMX Park. Only Bob Burnquist has more X Games medals than Mirra. Dave has also medaled in rally car competition and now he's competing in triathlon. I met Dave while working on the Tony Hawk Boom Huck Jam in 2002. Intensity is an understatement when describing Dave's demeanor. He has a natural intensity oozing off of him. Mirra's recent infatuation with triathlon has rekindled his old youthful intensity and drive that made him an extreme sports super star. Now, the transformation to endurance athlete will be put to the test in RAAM. Dave also has a great sense of humor and loves to laugh. He has a light switch fire that can switch on for both positive and negative reactions. But there is also a filter that favors the positive. He's a great guy that you would be happy to travel across the country with, especially in a small RV full of sleep-deprived and desperate strangers.

Dave Zabriskie: Dave is 35 years old. He's a road cycling super-hero. As a 7-time USA Cycling time trial champion he one of the best time-trialist ever. He's the only American to win stages in all three Grand Tours. Tour de France, The Vuelta (tour of Spain) and the Giro (tour of Italy). Zabriskie is like a unicorn to me. I have watched in awe as he competed in the Tour De France over the years. His talents as a cyclist are both natural and earned through years of hard work. As a friend and riding partner of

Bostrom we began to see his interest in RAAM. The fact that he was even interested gave me lots of hope that we were doing something right. I am still amazed that we have him joining us as a teammate and he gives us all more confidence going into RAAM. Dave's unconventional sense of humor also may be helpful to motivate and lift up the group. He's the only person here who may really know what lies ahead for us. But he's so quiet that he might not want to tell us how far over our heads this might be.

Micky Dymond: That's me. I'm 49 years old. I'm a 2 time AMA 125cc Motocross champion and have also won championships in, Supermoto Unlimited, at Pikes Peak and at the Baja 1000. I raced a career in motocross then had a second motorcycle career in Supermoto, off-road and road events. I have worked on the bike and off the bike in motorsports. I've created theatrical motorcycle shows, built X Games and freestyle courses and even trained a blind man to jump for a motorcycle world record. There has never been a project too strange for me to try, but, cycling has just been a hobby prior to this project to compete in RAAM. I am new to the ultra-endurance world. Truth is that I have never been known as a hard-training kind of athlete. At my age this makes me either a late bloomer or a very stubborn dreamer. Regardless, this opportunity was born from an endless expanse of crazy ideas. This one really turned me on though.

Altogether we call ourselves "The Legends of the Road." Under that team name we'll race 24 hours a day over a five and a half day period. We will start from the back of the pack of the four-rider teams and race up to the lead before the sun rises on day two. We will get lost and desperate as we give that lead away. We will lose and recapture that lead again and again. We will have personal moments of triumph and moments of loss and of extreme highs and extreme lows. We will bond together as brothers and feel a part of something bigger than ourselves and we will share our feelings with each other and we will share it with our crew. We will know without a doubt what we as men are made out of.

As if that is not enough too physically and mentally challenge any human being, immediately after RAAM I'll travel to Colorado Springs, Colorado to race a 1200cc Ducati motorcycle in the Pikes Peak International Hill Climb. Yes, I would trade the bicycle for a motorcycle. This race is awe-inspiring, extremely fast and one of the most dangerous motorcycle races in the world. This year I will be experiencing the race from a whole new perspective, both physically and mentally. Coming off of

RAAM I will be extremely fragile and emotional. I will be skinny from weight loss, totally exhausted and sleep deprived. Starting the week at Pikes Peak in this condition is a little bit crazy. I will attempt to be brave and fearless and although the motorcycle is where I come from and I feel it is an extension of me, it is not that easy in this case. A racer cannot approach this event as if competing on a standard racetrack. Imagine climbing a winding mountain road with a 35-mph speed limit; a tourist road to visit the peak for every other day of the year except on race day, when there is no speed limit. I will be touching speeds of over 130 miles per hour, passing guard rails, sheer cliffs, huge rocks, trees and other obstacles the entire length of the run. I have my sights set on the overall motorcycle record of 9 minutes and 52 seconds. I have had the record time before and would like to have it once again.

PIKES PEAK.

June 23rd 2014

Three days from the bicycle at 12,000 vertical feet on a mountain road.

Colorado Springs, Co. It has been three days since the battle in West Virginia's Appalachian Mountains. My bicycle has been exchanged for a motorcycle--a 1200cc Ducati motorcycle. The Legends of the road team and crew have gone home. I'm with a new crew now; the Ducati/Faulkner and Livingston Crew, or race team. The fatigue and the stress are still ever-present. In fact I'm even more tired and more fragile. Right now I am parked roadside waiting to ride. I am sitting in a cargo van trying to get motivated and trying to stay warm. It's 4:30 am and it's still dark and very cold. I have traded my spandex bicycling clothes for a full leather suit. I am awaiting the start of my first day of practice on the motorcycle and it's at 12,000 feet above sea level. It's a narrow and winding mountain road ascending out of Colorado Springs. Its 12 miles from the actual start line at just over 9,000 ft. to the top of Pikes Peak at 14,400 feet The12 miles and 156 turns of that ascent will be the scene of my next race.

I have taken over the driver's seat of the van. I'm trying to stay warm. I watch the action out the windshield as race trucks and trailers, emergency vehicles, race bikes, mechanics and all other personnel are revealed at first light. The rushed and haphazard parking positions and all other non-conformities are coming into view. The fire-drill intense movements of the racing community hide all the imperfections with urgency and purpose. There is a deadly serious tone in the air around here and it is almost impossible to not get wrapped up in it. Generators buzz, a few motors rev out into the distance and the smell of racing fuel mixes with my coffee spiking my vertigo just a little bit. I'm awake, stiffly, instinctually awake though I still close my eyes and try to drift off just a little more. I wish I had time to get a little bit more rest before doing this.

To see the sun rise from this place is an emotional experience. I think I need to be distracted with beauty and awe just now and it has my mind off of things. I get out of the van and stand facing east on this giant rock and I wait for it. But today, sadly, is too cloudy to see the sun rise, so I return to my tasks. When there is enough light to see somewhat clearly we will start practicing. The top section of the Pikes Peak race course sits well above the tree line. There is not much to see except rocks and dirt. This section of the course is fairly fast and circles mostly left or counter clockwise around the upper mountain peaks. It's fast and narrow. Most of the turn in points are blind, meaning that most of the apexes are well out of sight from the turn entrances. You cannot see any real markings, no obvious signs. You ride with feel that comes with practice. And by the way, there is no run-off, no safety barriers or air fences. Just off the road there are boulders, jagged hillsides or cliffs. You may not survive a high speed off-track excursion and you'll certainly be injured taking one. Just one look off the roadside and you know this to be true. So, the horn blows to call the riders to the starting point. I go to where the bike sits on its stands while the tire warmers heat up the tires. There are two aluminum stands that lift the front and rear wheels off the ground by a few inches so the wheels can turn freely so they can be covered with electric tire warmer

I sit on the bike visualizing my movements in the safety of my mind as the crew busy all around me. They let me do my thing without interrupting me. My body feels slow and tight but, this is more home to me than the 14 pound carbon Cervelo bicycles I have felt recently I truly love the feeling of straddling a motorcycle. The motorcycle ....She is like the most beautiful and

FROM 1 PEOPLE POWER TO 175+ HORSEPOWER: Devils Playground, Practice day #1, welcome to Pike Peak]

responsive machine ever. You may have thought I would have said she was like a woman. Not likely as a woman in this reality is way too unpredictable. On any other day, in any other place and in any other condition it is my passion to be on a motorcycle. Here and now it might not be and I would love to be with a woman instead of here. But, I know once I start to ride that will change and I will be on the bike riding hard and feeling that lovely feeling.

After removing the warmers and stands from the motorcycle I start the bike for a brief warm-up, rolling the throttle in my hand, like a drum roll a dozen or so times. Focus and concentration are extremely important and this is my mechanism. The bike sounds and feels powerful and healthy. I can feel this through my body. Finally, I take off, riding at an easy pace in a fairly low RPM and nothing over 80 MPH. The air is ice cold; the track surface is almost frozen. Moving around the bike my body feels a little stiff and still sluggish like I am asleep, like I'm still in bed almost. I test the motor a few times bringing up the revs with a few accelerations and then I test the lean angle to feel the tires grip. I drag my knee to the ground hanging off the inside of the bike in a few of the sweeping corners. The grip feels ok but the motor does not. Something is wrong. I am not sure what it is but, I know that it is an electrical problem. The motor revs to about 4,000 RPM's then cuts off on higher revs. I try it a few more times and it is the same result, then, near the top of the mountain with about half of a mile to the finish line there is another surprise, the road surface is white. There is a thin white layer of ice on the road. I do not know how slick it is but I am suddenly on it at about 50 mph. I slow without touching the brakes and coast to slow down. Riding very easy through the rest of the run, I make no sudden moves until I have come to a stop and sit atop the 14,000 foot Peak. As I sit there cold, stunned and pretty much freezing I notice the face of another rider who is next to me. Jeremy Toye. He stares into my eyes and says, "What the fuck?"

I cannot believe what I am doing right now. In a way it feels like déjà vu or feelings more like car sickness. I must like to feel so helplessly uncomfortable or why would I be here in this spot? I feel trapped in a bad place, trapped to the point of being almost paralyzed by the stress. WTF? I keep visiting these feelings again and again. Seems like every day now I'm in this intense place of both physical and mental stress. First was RAAM and now it's Pikes Peak. There is no way to get out of it. I get a twisted feeling in my gut being here at this moment. Moments like this make it hard to understand why I want to do this so much when it feels like a sort of punishment to do it. How much torture must I endure? It's like being thrown into a pit with a lion. By myself. The challenge here is just to survive without getting hurt. Win or die. Well, that type of thinking is pretty fucking distant in my mind right now. All I want to do is get off this mountain and back to bed-- right now. Why do I love these crazy things so very much? It is more likely that I will crash and be injured or worse in these conditions than ride safely, to race for the win, to run a record time.

WHAT DRIVES A MAN?

The Race across America and the Pikes Peak International hill climb are two of the most amazing races in the world. Seeing them at the pinnacle is like a sweet unattainable dream. The thrill of victory is so awesome. Drenched in a golden warm glow, sweaty brow, smiles a mile wide and draped with medals of gold. The achievement is one in millions. I dreamed of that to keep me motivated, to put in the work, to suffer on in as much misery as I could to be prepared, to be ready. I asked for this. I worked my ass off for this. No confusion about that. It's like I am challenging myself, or interrogating myself to be honest right now. I question my own promises. Did I lie to myself? This is not anything like what I have been telling myself it would be like. So, yea, now I'm just a little pissed off, like where did this endless stream of not so great moments like the one I'm having right now come from? The truth is, I imagined it and dreamed of it very differently. The high times are so amazing that the struggles seem acceptable or they seem a simple pittance, but there are more of them. Jeremy is absolutely right in the moment; it's like "What the Fuck"

Rarely, do I want recognize it in the moment. But these terrible and horribly uncomfortable moments are the good moments that I will cherish in a few weeks when I have had time to appreciate what I have done and what I have accomplished. These memories will stay with me to the end of my days. These are the good times, the gems. There will be more appreciation, more intense fond memories made from these absolutely absurd conditions and challenges than all of the other moments combined. I cannot see it right now but, this will be what I will cherish most.

Pikes Peak International Hill Climb, the race is on Sunday, but this event is a weeklong event. The schedule of training sessions and qualifying is long and full of complicated and sleep deprived time schedules. There are many press events and sponsor engagements, sleepless nights with daily practice sessions

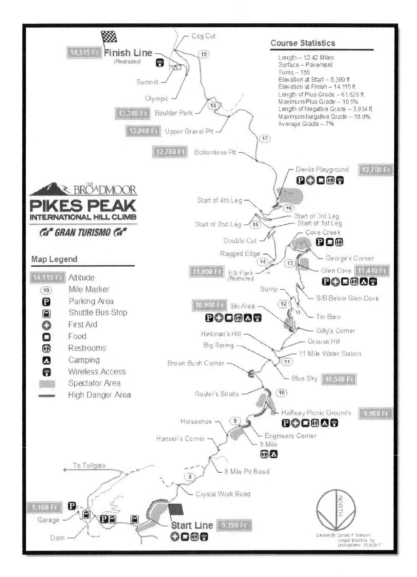

[PIKES PEAK COURSE MAP]

starting Monday going on each day till Sunday which is the race day at the end of the week. Next to the Indianapolis

500 Pikes Peak is the longest running motor race in the United States. It is extremely special to me and I have had the outright motorcycle record before and would love to have it once again. It is a 12.4 mile paved road with 156 turns up the 14.400 thousand ft. high mountain to the finish line at the peak. It is also one of the most dangerous and unforgiving motorcycle events on the planet. This year I will be experiencing the race from a whole new perspective both physically and mentally. I will be fragile and emotional trying to be brave and fearless? Although the motorcycle is where I come from and I feel it is an extension of myself it is not that easy. You cannot just ride up there as if you're on a standard race track. Imagine climbing a winding mountain road with a 35 mph speed limit while touching speeds of over 130 mph, passing guardrails, sheer cliffs, huge rocks, trees and other obstacles the entire run.

Imagine this. You are singing the national anthem at the Super bowl with a hundred thousand people in the stadium and millions of people watching on TV. You stand all alone, you hold the mike in your hand and your body trembles, reacting to the nervous stress, your body shakes and feels heavy and the fear has your throat in a chokehold. You try to clear your throat and it seems impossible. You must be perfect and hit every note flawlessly. Will your voice crack? Will you remember the words? Will you, get everything right? And what if the microphone cuts out? This is like Pikes Peak. I am alone with the motorcycle in my hands. No one can help me when I do my run. I must be perfect, I must hit all the right lines, the right gears, brake at all the right moments I must be fearless and flawless. If you mess up a note or your voice cracks for a second during the anthem you will just continue and finish and walk away. If I mess up on my run at Pikes Peak, I might be killed.

The Ducati racing team complete with sponsors and supporters had already been organized by Faulkner and Livingston. The team and crew were professionals not volunteers. There was nothing to worry about except to train and practice and be well-rested and super-fast. We did spend some time refining the Ducati race bikes during some scheduled track-testing days during the last few months. Truth is all the fitness I am gaining in preparations for the RAAM was complimenting my motorcycle training. Being on the motorcycle was always more of a safety concern. An injury could stop my training for RAAM. A bad injury could end my RAAM race completely I had been out to do a few motorcycle training days and a few races with caution that is a hard

[GO TIME AND SHOW TIME 2013. The starting line at Pikes Peak International Hill Climb. Possibly the most intense feelings you can ever have before a race are here. Ready to go from zero to wide open. Risking it all, racing the clock.]

thing to do. Go and race a motorcycle cautiously and to stay healthy and not get injured period. I felt that was not all the practice that I needed to be ready for Pikes Peak, but it was all I could get. I could rest assured that with this awesome team that all the other details were taken care of and we would be ready. To prepare for RAAM was a whole other thing.

YOU GOTTA HAVE FAITH

I am a person who gets the most excited about big projects or challenges. Who doesn't? I can really get excited about a project like this. It's a huge challenge, a seemingly impossible challenge. I didn't know if I was up to it or if I should even think I could do it. The two events together might be too much back-to-back and could end very bad as the most dangerous one is at the end. After I had taken some time and thought it through I began to believe I could do it. I had faith it was meant to be and I could prepare for it. And yes, I could do it. I have also accepted that all things will somehow always become Gods will. This is what I believe now is our will. I had Faith that I had found my way to this particular project for all the right reasons. I had faith that it/we/God would draw the right people and it would then find the support and the funding it needed. Surely, it would. I thought for sure it would. After a little while, I realized it was not easily coming together. Whatever does? Even if I could be physically ready there is a ton of work to be done to make it happen and the preparations are endless and quite a bit stifling; the sponsorship and funding part most of all.

I had a lot of help from Brian Bishop from Cycling Soul who I had partnered with. We had been working together on a RAAM project already. Bishop and I had worked side-by-side the previous year. Now we and a few other people began to seek out help and seek out sponsorship and funding in September 2013. There was little I could actually stir up alone in an industry where I was such a foreigner. All together we did as much as we could and that was just not getting what we needed. We were falling short. Like really short of what we needed. Ask God. How else was this going to work out? It's a sort of sad and completely human thing to do, to call out to be saved by God. This would not be the first time that I had asked or sort of begged God for help. And please, just know that I do love God, Jesus and the Holy Spirit. I would not be asking out of desperation but out of my growing faith and trust. I would put all my faith in him and let him do the work and I, would keep the momentum moving forward and trust in him that he was going to help it all come together. I had to just yield the control to him and keep right on going forward with or without confirmation of support, without a signed deal or even a verbal contract or without enough of my own money to backstop it. This would be my walk of faith. At least it would be the first one that I knew from the onset and this was the first step.

Did I have doubts that it would come together? Of course, I did. But, when I doubted, I prayed or read or talked about it with other people who had learned this way of faith or more to the point live this way. I was not so sure of how to live like this; how to just trust and relax. To think this way seems crazy to most people. I am used to fighting for things to happen. It is a lot of work to shut down so many habits I had lived for so long. I am not a super patient guy so yielding control and side stepping my normal urgency to jump at any challenges was very hard. After a while my heart was calmer and my mind was at ease. As I continued to work on trusting in him then everything would be ok. This strengthened my faith and saved my sanity. It is an ongoing challenging way of living. Sometimes nothing seems harder.

Every day I must want to be better and do better than the previous day. Was I and would I be able to keep moving forward, to keep growing? I have my good days and bad ones now. I can still be caught reacting like a little punk time and time again. I am only human, most of the time. This the "work in progress" part. An additional challenge is that I am fully aware of when I am messing up and doing a bad job. There is more to think about and more decisions to be made on the inside. I can tell you that when I get lost in a long and hard ride where fatigue breaks me down into a deep and quiet place, I can meditate with all three (God, Jesus and the Holy Spirit) and it is a good place to be. It is a special place for me. Anyway, I'm a work in progress.

BAGS ARE PACKED

I live in Santa Rosa, California with my girlfriend Brenda Lyons. She convinced me to move here from a lifetime in Southern California. Santa Rosa is just a bit north of San Francisco in Sonoma County's wine country. It's bicycle heaven, a place with amazing roads to train on in any direction I want to go; Sonoma or Napa, the Russian River, Alexander Valley to the coast or to the mountains. I moved here to prepare for RAAM. Brenda had sold me on it and I know she's always right. The original project was to race solo RAAM in 2014. That would have been impossible for me to accomplish. I moved here last year with Brenda (She is much more than my girlfriend and has a big part in this project and we will get into that a bit later) to help prepare myself for RAAM. Did I mention, that

RAAM is known as the "The World's Toughest Bicycle Race? By the way it is not a closed course. There are detours, road construction, trucks, trains, busses, cars, varmints and even livestock. You are on public roads, even interstate highways.

I will be driving my truck down to Southern California for the start of these 21 days of amazing and intense stimulation. So I fuel up the old Dodge 1500 and being careful not to forget anything, I pack up all the gear, the bikes, the food, the clothing and cycling related parts and pieces, then I do the same for the motorcycle gear. I had already shipped some things and had pre-organized quite a bit of the travel logistics. But still, it would just suck to show up with two left shoes or no shoes at all. Better check again. As I drive along toward Southern California on my way to the start line of RAAM, I'm wondering if I'm really ready for all this. Am I going to be strong enough to match up with my amazing team mates? Will I be too tired to ride well at Pikes Peak or more importantly, will I be too physically trashed to ride safely?

I have only competed in one ultra-cycling event, ever. Last September I did a 230-mile RAAM Challenge event held in Sacramento. It was one of a series of events that the organizers of RAAM put on each year as qualifiers for

RAAM. Even though I had been training for the event and had planned for the event it turned out that my other job-related obligations got in the way. I got little to no rest prior to the race. I spent the entire day before the race and most of the night filming "Riding the Line's" current episode (I will get Into Riding the Line in a minute). I ended up finishing the 230-mile road race in first. It was a tough race with temperatures over 100F degrees and there was a shit-ton of climbs. I had a tough time out there and learned a bunch. It was a true awakening. I think somewhere around the 120-mile mark I was really feeling stressed. It was about mid-day, the temperature had risen to around 90F degrees and that part of the course was in the mountains and had steepened up. I had not ridden that many 100 plus mile rides and this was getting tougher by the mile. After around 140 miles I was seriously hurting. Do you know the kind of pain that can slow down time? When a minute feels like an hour? When the top of the climb seems to keep getting higher and farther?.

The remainder of the race was spent trying to catch up to the lead rider who had been out front for nearly 8 hours and dealing with the pains of being in a lonely, quiet, inner place. I was learning how to eat and ride and had many ups and downs with my body. I'd have some energy then, no energy. I was feeling good and then was just dying. I'd have dry mouth and was spitting cotton balls and then have water sloshing in my gut when I had over compensated rehydrating and got all bloated up. All kinds of things going on during this 12-hour day. Most of all was the realization of this dream to do solo---I began to ask myself if I really could to it.

I was very glad to have won the race. But, the truth kind of hurt. Now I knew I would need much more time to train and develop as a cyclist to be ready for solo RAAM. After this race I knew that I may never be ready for the solo RAAM. At this moment I was thinking that maybe there was no way that anyone could ever truly be ready for solo RAAM. With less than one full year to train and prepare at that time I had my gauge and needed to adjust the plan.

TRAINING

For the last 10 months I had been training under the direction of Dean Golich, a world-renowned trainer working out of the Carmichael Training Systems in Colorado Springs, Colorado.

[RAAM CHALLENGE: Sacramento RAAM qualifier. 230 miles was an eye opener; I will need more training for sure.]

Dean has coached over 70 of the best athletes in the world including the Maple Leafs and the Edmonton Oilers, cyclist Mara Abbot, NASCAR driver Carl Edwards and motorcycle racers Nicky Hayden, Trey Canard and Tim Ferry. Dean was a perfect fit for me. He designed my programs on a three-week rotation. The workouts were all cycling. All of them were hard. It was hard just to complete the workout let alone hit the heart-rate zones or time and effort zones. There were intervals of many different durations, climbing and more climbing, endurance workouts, pyramids, and of course travel and rest days. I was so lucky to have his expertise and support to take on the challenge ahead. But, he hurt me regularly and it was major work on my part. Whether I wanted it or not, it was tough. He would give me all that I needed but I had to make all the necessary arrangements to make it happen. Imagine putting in an average of 25 plus hours of cycle training a week while travelling from San Francisco on Wednesdays to the East coast weekly to work 12-hour days Thursday through Sunday and fly home Monday. When I was at home for a few days I would ride day and night. On the road in the hotels and gyms; the same.

Staying healthy was no easy feat either. It was actually really hard to not get sick with my schedule and with a crew of people who just always seemed to be sick. But with Dean's help and guidance, we made it work.

Would the training throughout the year be enough? What improvements or gains could I expect when I was juggling so much between work and training? I work on a travelling theatrical freestyle motorcycle show called the "Nuclear Cowboyz." My title is "stunt coordinator," but to be honest I do a lot more than just coordinate stunts. I have spent five plus years with the Nuclear Cowboyz. I wrote the original show script and designed the set/ramp layout for the first season. I worked closely with All Access Staging (a company I continue to work with) to coordinate the building of the freestyle motocross (FMX) ramps and trials sets. The scope of my role with Nuclear Cowboyz included, created show theme, orchestrated load in for the ramp and prop set up in each venue to ensure rider safety and show flow, worked closely with crew to ensure the show ran properly and I directed live show.

This would continue to be my day job from November 2013 to May 2014. I tour with the show each year and have yet to miss one single show. There is a lot of work to be done during the creative process in the off-season as well as during the live show season starting in January and running consecutive weekends through May. I travel for 17 weeks straight. Every weekend I am in a different city and different state. Training is really tough. Maintaining a healthy diet, getting in my workouts, recovery, rest, staying healthy and staying on my training schedule is extremely difficult. And even if I got it all done, was my training going to be good enough? Could I expect to go out and be as good as the other guys? Not really!! They are all already amazing cyclists. They can just ride, train and race. For me, my job is sort of "necessary." I need the money. I do feel that the progress I had made since Sacramento is pretty amazing. But, I could only hope that I would be able to pull my share out there with these guys. We wanted to win. We wanted to break the record. We wanted an average speed of over 23 mph. We knew it would be hard. But, we believed we could do it. Why not? Really? I had, at that time never ridden a solo ride at 23 mph average speed for more than a few minutes and we were expecting to ride shifts at 25 mph for 20 minutes.

LOGISTICS

The Legends would need a crew of 13 people looking out for us four racers. They'd be an all-volunteer crew. It's crazy to think that people would go to this level of selfless service for the shared goal just for the love of the adventure. Most of the crew members were strangers to me when we started this journey. Some are friends and associates. Brian Bishop (Cycling Soul) and Michael Robson would be part of this project from the start. Bishop was running the Riding the Line production program and brought Robson over as a photographer during RAAM 2013. Robson would then become our crew chief. I had asked Wayne Dowd (a previous winner of RAAM to consult with Robson and guide him a bit. Wayne is a member of the most successful RAAM team ever, the eight-man "Allied Forces" team and a figurehead and strategist for that team. These three men would work together to guide us and the crew to a safe and fast RAAM.

We dealt with flights, hotels, transportation and food for California and Maryland including the special food needs for all the riders, Ben is a vegan and Zabriskie is fairly specialized with his diet. Both guys had brought a package of their own food but needed the hot meals that would be provided by our chef. The riders had a list of foods to be prepared just for us. The crew was to be fed from a different menu and snack foods like bars and gels would be separated for riders and crew. We had to have parts and tools, tires and wheels, lights and radios, rain gear and safety gear, etc. etc.

We would need two active vehicles (mini vans) on the road at all times and one RV with a kitchen and sleep quarters. These three vehicles would all need radios, GPS units bike racks, reflectors, flashers, additional safety equipment and gear, coolers for drinks, water bottles and food. Each vehicle also needed its own credit card for fueling. Riders would need 2 bikes each per shift, a regular road bike and an aerodynamic time-trial (TT) bike, spare wheels, personal food and drinks, spare shoes, helmet, glasses, rain gear etc. etc. Now consider the choreography of working sleep shifts and work shifts together while racing along 24 hours a day with only 5 sleeping areas.

Meanwhile out on Interstate 5 thoughts run through me like chills as I make the long drive south to Oceanside. I am nostalgic and I am sincerely scared of the future. Lucky for me I will have some distractions. I will have one stop to make along the way, Anaheim, California. There I'll visit my mom and dad, my kids. Most of my family lives in Southern California. I'll also grab a few more things there for my adventure. After an 8-hour drive I arrived at my father Ray's construction shop. I picked up a few packages from our sponsors that had been shipped late or just left behind by the Legends crew chief. I spent the evening with Mom and Dad and two of my three kids; my son Trevor and my daughter Ronni. My mom and dad have been supportive all my life no matter what it is that I am up to, whether that be racing motorcycles or directing a live show or racing Pikes Peak or RAAM. In high times or low times they have always been interested in what I am doing and have encouraged me to pursue my passions. We do dinner at Esther's Taco House in Placentia (a great little Mexican place) I take the kids there whenever I'm in town to visit. I do not live with my kids. In 2009 I had separated from my wife of 17 years. We married after a two week courtship in

1991. As a married couple we had our share of good times and bad times. The end of the relationship was a long and painful one with strings of regrets. We were young without a true understanding of what damage we were doing to each other. Some things will not be fixable; though we do have three awesome kids.

Anyway, I was ready for one last normal dinner out in a familiar place, at Esther's Taco house, chicken tacos with beans and rice and the best 24-ounce Dos Equis amber on draft. One more beer before RAAM. We have great conversation and do not talk too much about the race. We talk more about other things; funny things to make us smile and laugh, like the time me and the kids went Christmas shopping when they were young. We, or more accurately, I, got into a dispute with a big guy in a Cadillac while trying to enter a parking lot of the shopping center near our bank. The kids really love to relive the stupid things we do as parents. The guy in the Cadillac, I assure you, does not find any humor in this memory and it seems funny to think about what his side of the story must be like. That keeps this evening relaxing and fun. Seems like our time together has gone by too quickly and we are saying goodbye and calling it a night. After I drop the two kids off I see Hunter, my oldest son, and I am reminded of the bond I have with him and the other kids. Driving back to my dad's house where I will sleep for the night, I am instantly sad, missing all of them and thinking about the past.

In the morning I wake with a stirring excitement. I'm getting so close to the start now I can feel it. I take a ride on the Cervelo S5, carbon Road bike one last time. It is a super light and agile 11-speed with Shimano components and electric shifting. The bike is very new to me. I just got the bikes last week. The geometry of this bike is a bit aggressive and twitchy for a super long haul, but for the type of time trial efforts we'll be doing it may be perfect. In addition to the S5, Cervelo has given me a P5 Time Trial Bike for RAAM. The TT bike is so streamlined and aerodynamic like the triathlon bikes you see during the Ironman. I got fitted for this one at a shop near my home, Nor Cal bikes. Jeff and Wade set me up and did the bike fitting. A bicycle fitting is a scientific matching of all your physical measurements and physical attributes to the position you assume on the bicycle. Comfort being a key point to this is equally as important as power output. Having a proper bike fit is worth more than I could ever have imagined.

On a TT bike you are tucked into the most effective, wind resistant power position possible; an aggressive low drag attack like crouch, like a bullet. It must be calculated for your specific body shape and muscles flexibility or hello bad back and many other problems. The more flexible and fit you are the better and faster position you can assume. Imagine five days (with short breaks of course) in the fetal position pushing 300 plus watts with your legs. If your body is fit for that it will be awesome. If Not it will suck. A lot. I am such a first-timer that I can only hope for the best knowing only that I have the best bike-fit.

After coffee I ride back to my dad's house and prepare to continue my drive. I load up all my gear and begin the 90 minute drive farther south to the Oceanside guest house where all of the Legends of the Road will be staying until the race starts. It is Wednesday, June 11. The drive down the coast is surprisingly relaxing and it's a beautiful day. I like to drive sometimes. I will not have much more alone time to think and I have a lot a lot to think about during these last few quiet moments. I know that once I am there it will be nonstop action and reaction. The last few moments of calm before the storm.

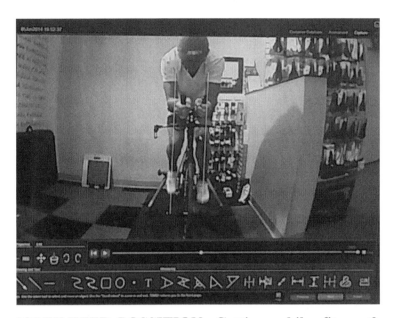

[OPTIMIZED POSSITION: Getting a bike fit on the Cervelo P5 at the Nor Cal bicycle shop in Santa Rosa, California]

LEGENDS OF THE ROAD

PART ONE, RAAM.
1 ROBSON, BRIAN, WAYNE AND CREW
Wednesday 6/14

After arriving at the guest house I quickly pick my room and start to organize my gear and bikes. The house is huge, plenty of room for the crew and riders. It is just south of Oceanside and is located very near the ocean. At any other time it would be a vacation rental property, a beach house for the summertime. The place was almost distracting because it was so nice; sitting just above the ocean in San Diego County, California. I had been slow to pick a room at the guest house during the training camp and ended up on the couch and I was not going to let that happen again. I picked a room downstairs close to a bathroom and the garage. I have tons of gear and needed the space.

Our cycling clothes or "cycling kits" as they are called, had arrived from our sponsor, Pearl Izumi. They are red white and blue with a number and name scheme on the back like a motocross jersey. Well, sort of. The jerseys had each of our names and numbers on the back. Ben had 23, Mirra was 40 I was 43. Zabriskie had slyly decided on 69. Pearl Izumi has an amazing group of designers that work off their computer software that can make your ideas come to life in real time as you talk in conference. I think the colors and the design are F-ing cool. After knowing the ease of creation process I would really dig into it next time; if there ever is a next time. These specially designed garments are designed to protect against chafing of our crotches. The fabric is specially made to keep us cool and dry by allowing our perspiration to evaporate through it and the close-fitting cut helps cut down on wind resistance. After I stopped honoring the finished product I finished unloading the rest of my cycling gear and personal belongings and headed outside to see what was going on. I am the first rider here and now I will connect with the crew.

Michael Robson is our crew chief. He wanted this job. Really, he did. The job of crew chief is an endless battle in the trenches. Last year Robson was with me and Brian Bishop covering RAAM as a photographer on the Riding the Line project. We connected and really had a good vibe going. We rode in the same car most of the time and became pretty close. We had a hell of a time last year covering the race from a tiny little Subaru. We had some great times and loved the adventure of it. Robson is the name we all call him and it seems to be sort of his first name now. I mean ROBSON is at least ½ of a first name or the reverse where it would be "son of Rob" or something. You could ask him about the origin of the word "fuck" if you like as it was used to its full capacity during the 2013 RAAM. He is an amazing photographer and I am sure he will be awesome at this crazy job.

Robson looks a lot like Wolverine from the Marvel comics X Men and he has an Australian accent which makes it even better. It's like being on camera with Hugh Jackman. I am not sure of his age but he is younger than I am. He's showing a little wear and tear now and he's going to grow a few years older by the time we reach the East coast and as I said, he wanted this job. He has a great sense of humor and he's going to need it. Robson is the kind of guy that starts all impressions super positive. First impressions they say!!! We have been preparing for this for quite a few months now on our spare time. Now that we have arrived here for the race it's surreal. We have been pushing hard and straight on toward the start on our word and on our faith.

Robson had recently taken hold of the reins of this adventure and I had been left a bit out of the details so I could focus on training and preparing. Robson and Bishop worked on schedules with RAAM organizers such as technical meetings and safety gear and the rules and requirements for the race. Together they also would gather up the sponsor parts and pieces from each company and organize the gear we did not have sponsors to provide all the cash we needed for outright purchases and that was adding to the workload. We had balanced the money and sponsored items as well as we could, but it was still going to be close. We may run out of money somewhere east. Robson had a list of items that we needed to purchase that were coming out of our very limited budget. I had started a company around the Legends of the Road and a bank account was set up. We would try to run all the purchases and costs through it. The Legends account would stay in my name and I would be in the know of what was being spent. This was both good and bad and a constant reminder to keep the faith and keep moving forward.

Bishop assisted Robson with most of the logistical matters and was managing our progress and focusing on media for the Legends. Brian produced and managed the Riding the Line videos that had focused on promoting RAAM in 2013. He had tried extremely hard to make the Legends of the Road the new focus. Our original plan, our goal, was to keep the videos coming and wrangle a sponsor to do more than just internet with the coverage. It seemed likely that someone would be interested in following us in a documentary style/reality type show for TV or for a documentary film. Brian had been searching relentlessly to find that partner/sponsor. Bishop tried very hard to make it happen, but nothing came together. Unable to secure a network or media partner the video element that started this whole project had been slid to the back burner. In the meantime Brian will continue to handle our media and sponsorships as well as manage and assist with our logistical plans. Brian has been wearing many hats and handling many jobs to see this project through. It had been Brian and I from the start of this project and I still want it to continue that way.

About a month prior to RAAM we organized a training camp. We needed this training camp. I had found a financial sponsor to pay for the camp. Stephen Cassar a friend and business associate was forming a new company, Race Interactive that would handle all the logistics of online registration for big events and it funded our camp in West Lake, California near Dave Zabriskie's home. It was during this time that Brian and I had our first fight or "disagreement." The strain spread and Robson got pulled in too.

[GETTING READY TO BE READY Bishop and Robson and the rest of us working on details at the guesthouse.]

It was pretty tough. The ups and downs of this project were always putting a heavy load on each of us. When you look at it from the outside it makes little sense to be working as hard as we were. We had so much invested in it, time wise and emotionally. Unfortunately at this very moment as I write this the three of us are not talking too much. This part of RAAM is like a marriage. Give and take is not always even or fair between us. I think I may be such a single-focused person that it wears them out or bums them out.

Training Camp

The training camp was a very good indicator for all of us about how much work it was going to take. DZ's friend Greg Anzalone had housed us and we went sparingly on all the rest of the related costs. When camp is in West Lake, Los Angeles, well, you know it's not cheap there. Thanks to Greg we managed very well in this prime location. We all needed this camp to learn if not a lot a lot, just enough about each other. It was our first official meeting. Robson, Bishop and I would still be working on sponsorships and funding for RAAM all the while. We would film it and document it in hope that we could get a last-minute sponsor who would be enticed by the footage we would quickly post on the internet.

The first meeting of the Legends of the Road was a good one. We went on training rides through Malibu and Santa Monica, up and down the coast line, in and out of the mountains. It was a perfect time and place to finally meet up. This would be the first time we had all come together. We rode; we hung out and worked together for three days. We went out to eat together, talked and shared ideas and thoughts. It was super fun to get to ride together and just to get together period. DZ picked the routes we rode and we had some good rides. It was really nice to see DZ, Ben, Dave Mirra and Wayne Dowd (our back-up rider and technical advisor) ride. I watched everything that DZ did on his bike. I learned a lot from watching everyone ride. We even had some additional riders join us. Eric Bostrom (Ben's younger brother), Jack Nosco another friend of DZ and founder of the Mike Nosco Memorial ride came along for a few of our rides.

Mirra was on fire and relentlessly competitive. We had a big climbing day that turned into a quest to break Mirra. Dave and Ben were looking for as much altitude as they could to break him down. Ten thousand or so vertical feet later and Mirra was still fighting. We had one last moment of truth when we rolled into a winery for a glass of red for Mirra but that backfired when we couldn't get past the entrance because of a wedding. The ride ended and then Mirra threw on his running shoes and said, "Let's go guys" It became a 5-mile run led by Mirra and that turned into a race at an under 5-minute mile pace for he and Ben. Robson even joined in as Wayne and I looked on, shaking our heads in tandem, glad that we were out of this one. DZ ended up with blisters on his feet and Ben and Dave Mirra were talking about adding a triathlon competition to their already too busy schedules for the following year. It was fun, but more importantly; it was a stamp of approval that we were good together as people. We could make this awesome journeywork together no matter what.

You would think from the outside that all four of us riders would just have a bunch of money lying around or it would be easy to find a sponsor to give us the whole pile that we needed but that is not the case. Even with the money from our very gracious sponsors we were still going to be short the funds needed to do RAAM. So in an effort to raise more funds Bishop started a Go Fund Me program. We also started The Legends of the Road website to direct people to donate. The Legends needed money. There were flights, hotels, fuel, food, drinks, snacks, travel charges, consumables and even personal items. We would need to raise more money to make it to finish. When we left Oceanside we would need to come up with more money to pay for fuel to return home with the RV and for hotels in Maryland. Personally I had already invested quite a bit of my own money and was feeling the stress of becoming the fallback for this thing. I knew we would get it done, but at what personal cost? More on that later.

[FOUR AMIGOS IN THE MAKING: The Legends at their first training camp.

Meanwhile back at the guest house Robson and Wayne Dowd are already hard at work on a schedule that has grown to gigantic. As Wayne puts it, there is a metric shit-ton of stuff to do here. Together the two of them must schedule the 3020 miles as a whole and as two separate sections divided by 4 to 5-hour rider shifts.

The riders will be separated into two groups of two riders. Food and water stops, fuel stops for the vehicles and water and sewage dump for the RV. The where and when must be planned out now and put into the Legends' RAAM schedule. These "rider shifts" will vary in time by the terrain and location as well as the potential weather, (a climb is slower than a descent; a head wind is slower than a tail wind etc.) As a four-rider team broken into two groups consisting of two riders and crews, each team will have 5-ish hour shifts. One team is on the road and the other team is resting in the RV. Transitioning from one team to the other is a matter of leap frogging up the road with the RV and finding a safe location in a legal location based on the timing of the active team on the road if all goes well they will reach the RV for the change out in 5-ish hours.

How did we come up with this plan? Wayne Dowd. Wayne was a member of team 4 Mil. A four-man team and the Allied Forces 8- man team that won the outright record for fastest time ever in RAAM. He is a wealth of knowledge of all things RAAM and also our back-up rider. He rode with us at the training camp a month back and is quite capable of jumping right into the role of rider if one of the four riders were to get injured or sick before RAAM. To have a guy like Wayne giving us his all was pretty damn lucky. During the final weeks were a few times that we were close to activating the backup rider. Even the day before the race there was a slight possibility that he would suit up, but we managed to start the original four.

Wayne is a pretty good-sized guy. No Jarhead at all but, full military style with a John Wayne persona that demands respect. He has a big voice and a slight twitch in his eye that makes me think that his reflexes are much faster than mine. He's a big teddy bear although he is also a retired Green Beret. So you'd better not piss him off. In addition to Wayno (a stolen team Allied Forces nick name) we will also have the expertise of the Allied Forces Crew chief of 2013, Jimmy Durough. Jimmy was not here with us, but he and Wayne were communicating leading up to and throughout RAAM. When Wayne needed help he called Jimmy. Robson had also been able to work together with Jimmy D during the weeks leading up to RAAM while planning and preparing. It is hard to explain the value of these individuals, but trust me; the overall chance of success in our race grew immensely with their help.

As I said earlier, the crew members are all volunteers. They're mostly strangers to me that were assembled by Robson, Brian and Wayne. These amazing people would give up one full week of their lives to work tirelessly and without much sleep or comfort or space to sit, let alone lie down. They would not be able to complain or protest, or fight. Well, that was the plan at least going into this deal. When you are stuck with ten very tired, hungry, dirty and over-worked strangers you learn to deal the best you can. At times there was no other way to release the tensions but to rip somebody a new one just because they were there. It was still very hard for me to imagine they were here to willingly give 100% purely as volunteers. The work going on at the house was pretty intense and there was no one sitting idle for more than a few seconds. Everyone had a list of items they were working on to get things ready. Even when they were not working, they ran in place to stay sharp and ready to get in there.

Wayne and Robson had brought a military style communication method to this crew and together they would get us safely across the United States, on course, without breaking any of the rules. And they were going to do it better than any other team. They were going to help us win this race and possibly break the existing record. Damn that sounded good, huh? Well, honestly there was a hell of a lot a lot more work involved to make that happen. With that being a main focus, to stay on course, to stay clean from penalties we were set. I can remember talking about penalties and being off course calmly at the house or even during the camp. It is not anything but a simple chat. On the road when you are off course it is a major catastrophe. Imagine the stress of all the team and the poor guy pedaling extra miles while losing the lead or losing the race. It would be very important to stay on course and stay clear of any penalties.

THE CREW

Crewing for RAAM is no easy ride across the country. It is a sleep-deprived grind of shameless servitude oozing with saintly purpose. All equal, all giving their all. The crew member's roles were specific to start and then growing into more of a one for all, all for one team. Will Swan would be our team mechanic. He was a perfectionist with a pinch of sarcasm. He has a lot a lot of experience as a cycling mechanic and is a hard worker. He can and will be able to roll with the punches and keep our bicycles in good shape. At the guest house Will worked on all of our bikes, changing out some parts with parts from our sponsors that we needed to run. He also organized the gear that would be most likely used and the staged all this gear and then the extra parts and where it might all be placed into the motorhome or transition vehicles. Will would have to be working inside a crowded motorhome when it was moving or in a roadside parking lot or field. He also took up the driver or navigator role on occasion. Will had an obsessive attitude that could be confused with sarcasm but in a humorous way.

Meghan Sims, our chef, web designer and sweet heart. Meg has been a sponsor and contributor as well as the best cook ever and is always up-beat without ever complaining one single time. Meg had also developed the web site for the Legends and created the Logo. She has invested both money and time to the Legends. Meg would need to be up when we were and cooking and prepping food for all of us riders. She was well-organized before we left the guest house, but she may need to be awake and working with only small breaks. She had pre-made many snacks for us riders; like sweet potato and rice burritos, rice, peanut butter and jelly wraps and she always sent us out with something hot and fresh as well as greeted us with a hot meal when we came in to rest. Meg would have to keep things going for the crew too—feeding a moving pack of 17 people. She would work together with our lovely soigneur, Paige, to keep tabs with riders' needs.

Paige DeVilbiss, Our soigneur, or the one who does what our mother would do if we were kids. She's the youngest and prettiest of our crew members and very knowledgeable about cyclists' needs, more than I would know about for sure. Paige was responsible for keeping us riders ready to ride and our gear and foods where we could get to them. All of our ride foods and snacks were packed for each of our shifts into little lunch coolers. Ben and I took ours in to the transition vehicle as the Daves took theirs out. Paige would make sure we had all of our consumables as well as our riding gear and weather gear etc. She managed the cooler inside the RV for us and for the crew driving and navigating the mini-vans. She would eventually be thinking for us as we became extremely fatigued. She was sort of the mother bear; tough on everyone else in a protective way about us riders. Lights and Garmin charging, cell and other things like laundry and RV transitions were also hers to deal with. She tried to revive my legs a few times even though it was a lost cause. She would keep us going out strong and coming in to rest she would assist Meg with additions like recovery drinks and my personal probiotic to combat the antibiotics I needed to take. Hers was yet another restless job that only had small breaks.

Drivers/Navigators. First was Rick Tillery, the "Man of Mystery." I had not met Rick in person until the guest house. We had a few phone meetings prior to meeting here. Rick would be covering many details together with Robson and Bishop prior to RAAM. But during the race he would mostly drive or navigate. Maybe the main role was for him to be in the follow vehicle. He was as solid and consistent as they come. His patience and demeanor where kind of perfect for RAAM. He loves cycling and that was really evident. I am not sure of his past in cycling, but he seems to have a wealth of knowledge about it in general. I knew I could count on Rick for directions and support, I knew he would be there for me if I needed him. He was one of those guys; the kind that could sort out any issues and makes the most sensible plan and executes it. He was the g-to guy in a pinch, the designated driver. If Rick had a partner it would be Dave Lemay.

David would also become Cardo man by default. David was very quiet and soft spoken. Cardo, a Bluetooth radio type of system was going to be one of our communication devices between riders, crew chief and navigators and needed to be sorted out on the fly. David got mine up and running and was on his way to setting up one for each rider until we, or rather me and Wayne, were struggling with it so much that in an instant we scrapped it and went to radios for all. Dave was immediately released from being Cardo man. David would drive and navigate as well as assist as sort of a jack-of-all-trades. Dave also has roots in cycling, is a hard core enthusiast who loves to ride and works in the cycling industry.

Brian Manley, the "Manly Man," is one of my longtime best friends. He would mostly be responsible for driving the RV. Manley is a hard worker and an optimistic and up-beat guy. It was not always this way for him. A newly bearded Manley showed up to the guest house to my surprise. I have known Brian since the early 80's. Brian and I have survived long careers in motorcycle racing. Brian was paralyzed in a motorcycle crash while we were riding together about 14 years ago. It was a dramatic and unpleasant life-altering event that I wish we never had to experience. I can remember it like it was yesterday. Brian is in a wheel chair and also uses a walker. But nothing is ever too big of a challenge and he has no problem getting shit done. Brian and I have done a lot of crazy things together; some fun and some not so fun and some just plain ridiculous. This one ranks right up there at the top of the list. It is really cool for me to have him here. We have had ups and downs in our relationship over the years and have been in and out of touch at times. Brian will always be a part of me no matter what I am doing or where we are at in our lives. Brian would not only do RAAM start to finish, he would then turn around and drive the RV home to California.

John Rushton or Rush, best photographer ever and the RV guy. MacGyver. Sadly, he was pulled away from film duty to do all the jobs on this trip. We should have kept him filming. That was our plan going in. We were lucky to have a guy with his photography credentials onboard to film. John had so many skills related to this trip we needed he was pulled away from his real genius. John and I met on a Nuclear Cowboyz show. He is good friends with Mike Mason the Freestyle motocross superstar who donated his RV to the Legends. Without these two individuals we would be screwed. He was given the nickname "sideshow Bob" based on his likeness to the Simpsons character. John has grown on us all from the training camp where he just came along to film. He's a super mellow guy who now had the cycling bug too. John would also ride back with Manley to California after RAAM.

Danny Kindregan is a super sweet guy with a heart of pure gold. Danny was another hard worker that did not want to take a break. Driving the transition vehicle would be Danny's main thing. A very sensitive and caring guy that put all our needs first, Danny had come to us only a few weeks before the start. He and I had met during the

Interbike trade show and when he said he would like to help if we needed him, he was in. He's the ex-husband of Laura Kindregan who has been helping me from the start. Danny might have it in him to be on the bike for a future RAAM. He has that sort of potential as a cyclist. He could project the cyclist experience to us knowing what we were going through. Danny meshed well with all other crew and that is so important. How could it be worse than to have a personality dispute going on within a vehicle for six straight days?

Scott King is the quiet one that always looks way too fresh and together. I hardly got to know Scott during the race. He was a friend of DZ and was very educated in the cycling world. Scott would also perform many jobs for the Legends. Driver, navigator. He was an upbeat guy who would give subtle gestures of approval at just the right time—so subtle you might miss them if you weren't paying attention. He was also pretty much plugged into the cycling world. Why do I have no idea of all these cycling people?

And then there was Stephen Glidden. This guy was a walk on. We met him through Dave Mirra at Oceanside. He just was there and we needed another guy and Stephen said, "Sure, sounds fun." He is sort of an ex-cage fighter turned honey bear type of dude. He had a tough ass appearance and a bit of an attitude. He would be incredibly focused on winning this race and that would carry over to us. I think he was ready to fight for us if we needed too. He was our muscle if we needed a champion. He would drive, navigate, and occasionally drive someone into a frenzy. I had no time to have more than a handshake with most of the crew. With Stephen, I barely had that. I think Stephen would be changed in the duration of our trip. He would be the final piece to our crew.

[THE CHAOS BEFORE THE STORM: Robson keeps the team up and happy as we get close to the race start. This is Saturday morning as the last bit of packing gets finished up]

In the meantime, the Legends crew would be kept busy prepping and organizing, cooking and cleaning, turning our vehicles and our bikes into "The Legends of the Road" Race Team.

With only two days to get ready for the start, it is pretty damn busy around here. If you are not busy doing something yourself you better get out of the way and let them work. If they are not working, they are meeting and thinking through or talking about the plans. They are discussing the rules and the safety gear. There are quite a few protocols that are in place for the safety of all the team. RAAM rules are many and if you do not follow the rules, we get time penalties. If the crew are not wearing the right reflective vests and lighting strips it will be a time penalty. There is even a rule in the rule book in which RAAM asks for a donation to the local homeless shelter in the form of canned foods. That is kind of a clever way for the organizers to see who read the rules or not—that crew looking sheepish while everyone else brings food to the stage—they didn't.

2 THE START OF RAAM

Saturday, June 14th. RAAM race day is finally here. Coffee is a must. No matter how nervous you are, coffee is no problem and natural. At least that's how I feel about it. Eating food is not as easy and I must force feed this morning. I am trying to think of food but it is hard work. I cannot remember what I had for breakfast but it was probably eggs and toast as I took a little time to sit and look around. Then it's a mad rush to pull together what exactly I am bringing and what I will leave in SoCal for my dad to take home with him. Last minute changes make me light and clean. There are a few group plans to be made for space on the RV as it is over packed with gear and parts. What we cannot carry would be sent back to Anaheim to my dad's shop to store until I return from Pikes Peak. After stuffing every last thing into the RV or a vehicle that would return to the shop were finally organized.

As a full team, riders and crew, the legends of the road gathered one last time before heading to the start line. First Robson laid out the plan for the morning and then let me say the prayer. I thanked God for these beautiful people, thanked him for loving us and asked him to help us through this next week, to love each other and to take care of each other, keep us safe, send us angels to care for us and to make us fast. I then returned it back to Robson. He stated a few serious words for us to remember. "We are all burying ourselves out here and we will not forget that. There will be no fighting, no issues. We will keep positive and keep going. When things go wrong we will just keep on it, fix it and move on. There is no going back to dispute it. We need each other helping each other, supporting each other. Everyone is important here." The prayer and the speech was just the right thing to launch this adventure. I could tell that everyone was buzzing with electric energy and ready to go. And then we headed to the RAAM start line at the Oceanside pier.

It is a banner type of a moment at the pier. The energy was building and building. Lots of official vehicles and banners all over the start line. So much going on and so many crazy last minute movements. Many of the teams were from other countries and were so stressed out they were ready to burst. All kinds of teams dressed into their colors, some were more like world cup style. The Brazilian team was waving flags, blowing horns. My dad met me in a parking lot to take over the two vehicles we were leaving behind. Last minute details were being settled and we had a few minutes to watch Mirra explain the proper running form in his socks on a hot pavement parking lot near where we parked the RV. DZ had a few interviews with TV and I had finished up all my last minute managerial responsibilities and handed over the reins completely to Wayne, Robson and Bishop.

In recent weeks, we had discussed that we would break the 4-man team into two groups of two. Wayne and Robson made the final call on who would be paired with whom and also who would take the first shift of the race. The Daves.... The Dave team was a good call and I was happy that DZ and Mirra would go out together for the neutral zone (a no assisted segment that required the riders to navigate approx. 15 miles with no vehicle assistance.). The Dave team would be stronger for the start. I think Ben and I together were grittier, tougher, but this was for the start and on a nice warm sunny day, the Daves might be the fastest twosome ever. Anyway, it shall be written as this and so it shall be done; the Daves shall ride first. There would be no looking back. Just so, I said it. I mean, Dave Mirra, Ben Bostrom, Dave Zabriskie.... Are you shitting me? These guys are true Legends. I am still in awe of these guys being my teammates and damn me if I do not need to become a super hero to be on the team.

The Daves had their plan to try 30-minute shifts. But first they must take the designated starting segment as follows: The opening six-mile section is on a bike trail at a 20 mph speed limit with a pace rider. You must stay with this rider all the way to the exit. At the end of the trail, the race is on and there are a few side streets that have a lot of car traffic. The bike lane usually has debris like broken glass and such that could be a real problem if you are not careful and get a flat. There would be major time loss if our rider were changing a flat here. As a precaution, we would have both Daves run the section together. Both Daves would cruise through the bike trail segment and hit the road hard and fast with the first rider working as rider two drafted and paced off rider one. Rider 2 would then take the first real solo shift while rider 1 rested and moved up the road in the transition vehicle. This was a good safe plan. If one rider flatted, he could stop and fix it as the other rider went ahead without losing any time. The rider who had fixed the flat would then ride to the transition area to join the transition vehicle, head up the road to the next transition area, and relieve the other. Soon both riders would be taking shifts and getting used to it. After they worked through the early sections of the course, they would be able to sort out the duration of the rider shifts.

The actual start would be from the Oceanside Pier with an assigned lead out rider to pace you. It is both an official send-off to riders and teams as it is a short parade zone out approximately 6 miles to the end of the bike trail. At the end of the bike trail you are then on your own. We would take off as a full team from the start line at the pier. Despite the more sensible plan from Robson and Wayne to just move Ben and me directly to the first team exchange location in the desert us riders wanted to be there to make the start together. It might be our only RAAM ever and we wanted to start the race together and finish it together. Anyway, it shall be written as this and so it shall be done; The Legends roll out together and then we would finish together in Maryland.

It was sunny, about 80F degrees and kind of busy at the start, but not too hectic. Many beach goers were on hand for the start even though many really had no idea about the race, they mulled around the start line asking us what was really going on here. After you would tell them, what was going and what the race was you could imagine the looks on their faces. For most of them, it was just too hard to understand. They had come to the beach to relax and we were here to start. What was in their minds? An endurance nightmare?. We had some surprise visits from family and friends that had come to see us take off. The most welcome sight of my beautiful daughter Ronni, my mom and dad, my sister Donna, with her daughters Meagan and Hailey. Good friends, Carl Harris, Joe Lawwill and many more were all I needed to fuel my desire to race and win RAAM. The only one missing was the beautiful Brenda Lyons. I was missing her a ton. She is always my rock, my strength and I wished that she were here.

Ben had some supporters too. A few very established riders from both cycling and from motorcycling including Josh Hayes, multi-time USA Superbike champion, Jimmy Button ex- motocross racer, and quite a few others had ridden in on their bicycles to see us start. Sometimes it can be stressful to have so many people around you when you are in the middle of your own stress. However, for this it is a needed and welcome send-off. A gift. We had worked long and hard for many months and we are finally here ready to get pedals turning. Dave Mirra had a few friends that were on hand to wish him well as he started. DZ had his family there too and his kids got to see their dad take off with this new group of total strangers.

The solo racers and the Race across the West riders started on Tuesday June. We would be behind them and would slowly reel them in and pass most of them before we made the finish in Maryland. For the teams start today the order was 2-rider teams first, then the 4-rider teams and finally the 8-rider teams. There were like 20 4-rider teams ahead of us. There were the men, woman, mixed and age divisions but there were a lot many 4-rider teams. There were teams from all over the world, Germany, Austria, Australia, Italy, England, Finland, Japan, Slovakia, Russia and Brazil. There were very serious racers here to win and there were teams raising money for a cause. There was a team of amputees, a father daughter team. The Duchess of Cambridge's sister, Pippa Middleton was riding on an 8-person team. RAAM has so many interesting stories, so many interesting and inspiring people. It is really something to be around a single person doing a huge life altering challenge like this and there are hundreds of them here at one place getting ready to go to the limit of their physical and psychological abilities.

We were the last 4-rider team to take off. Although Dave Mirra was technically the starting rider on paper for RAAM, All four of us Legends rode out together. It was a long time coming and a hell of a lot a lot of work putting this together and I wasn't going to have anyone miss the official start.

[NO TURNING BACK: Finally the moment of truth had come. We were racing now.]

This had all started over a year ago and I have been relentlessly committed, mentally, physically and financially. We had all dressed in our Legends kits or speed suits and prepared to ride out on our TT bikes. The four of us went off together and got a very impressive applause. I remember Dave Mirra sprinting out into a lead with a grin on his face, we all had a good laugh, and it really felt good to get under way. All the nervousness and stress went away in an instant. There was a buzz deep in my heart as we rolled out.

After our team start moment Ben and I would quickly jump into the motorhome just around the corner from the pier and head up and over Palomar Mountain to the lower desert to the first team transition point 80 or so miles out. On the first leg of RAAM you are alone and fairly isolated. It is 15 or so miles with no support vehicles. Having Mirra and Zabriskie together in this section to make sure we did not lose any time turned out to be a good idea. Mirra got a flat and he had a tubular tire. A tubular is a tire that is sewn around a tube and glued to the wheel; you cannot change out a tube and get back going with this set up without a backup whole wheel assembly. He had no back up with him. Zabriskie went on without losing any time, hell; he passed all but two riders/teams. Meanwhile, the plan to retrieve a rider who was stranded was not very fast and we had to leave Zabriskie on the bike for close to 50 miles. Dave put on a charge through the two and 4-rider teams and up and over Palomar Mountain. He got water from Wayne who was navigating from the follow car and pushed on until Mirra would get back in there and get a rest for DZ. The two would chip away at the lead from the remaining three teams that were ahead of them. They had passed all but three of the 4-rider teams before they would descend the Glass Elevator (The famed "Glass Elevator" descent begins 69.6 miles from Oceanside. Over the next 10 miles the riders drop about 3,600 feet and along the way are several vistas that overlook the Borrego Springs desert floor below.) And come in to team transition #1 where Ben and I would take over. We were now in about fourth position over all the four man teams. At the Christmas Circle roundabout in Borrego Springs between TS 1 (Time station #1) and TS2, we had positioned the RV right to the inside of the roundabout (a major team transition point)

It was about 100F degrees, at least 15 degrees hotter in the desert than it was in Oceanside. I would take the first shift for Ben and me. I got on the P5 Cervelo, my TT bike and took a few easy pedals around Christmas Circle to loosen up. As I waited for Dave the other teams began to come through, I watched the leading teams do rider exchanges. Each of them looked to be strong and the riders looked much more seasoned than I saw myself. I was feeling nervous, insecure and a little afraid that I was out of my league. There was a German team who had won RAAM for the last three years (I actually did not know that until after the race). These Germans looked like body builders; extremely muscled out and powerful. Then there was a team called Innovation Africa, They were a mix of very strong masters riders (age 40-49) and racers, some local California racers but, all Americans. One notable rider on the team was Chris Demarchi. He was a friend of a friend and I had learned that he was an incredible athlete and cyclist. Team Innovation Africa would become our opponent in a head-to-head fight for the next 5 days. First impression was a slap to my face. Anyway, my first ride was approximately 25 minutes long and I hit the wall hard. After about 5 minutes on the bike, I had maxed out my heart rate and had to back off and try to recover. I rode the TT bike as if it was the first time I had been on it. Feeling strange and guessing what to do, I pushed too hard. I went after and passed one of the Germans and then had to slow down and he just rode back by me as I was trying to recover. Embarrassing! I would do my first rider exchange with Ben and it went well. Ben was amped up and I really had to accelerate just to cross wheels with him. The guy gets so excited. You need to cross wheels when making a rider change. You can do it at speed to make it an official and legal. All good for now.

We had a plan so the riders never went backward on the course during a transition. We had the navigator or driver of the transition vehicle come get the bike of the non-active rider and place it on the trailer while the rider got into the back seat of the transition vehicle. Then we were off down the road to catch back up to the active rider, pass the active rider and go up the road approximately 5 miles to where the next transition was. Again, the navigator or driver would prepare the non-active rider's bike in a roadside position where that rider would walk to and mount the bicycle and wait for the rider coming in. This was repeated every 15 or so minutes. A few seconds each transition adds up over the course of 5 days to minutes and hours. After my first shift, I remember coming into the van gasping for air, "The pull is too long. I'm going to need it to be shorter." I said. So much for the 25-minute shift plan. It was going to be better for me to do 15 to 20-minute shifts to manage the speed we needed. After a while we went to 5-ish mile shifts and to the closest steep section, so our transitions were good. We started to build up a rhythm. We, mostly Ben, started to pick off the other teams and improve our position. This started to feel pretty good. I was really feeling the need to go faster—to lift my pace to match my teammates. Dave and Dave, or the Daves were awesome and I wanted Ben and Micky to be just as strong. It is still just hard to believe that I am here with these guys. It is even harder to perform as one of these guys.

3 THE DAVES, BEN AND I

Two days ago as I mulled over the many thoughts I have of the race and the team. I was sort of stunned with nervous excitement. I can feel in my body the extreme suffering to come as if it knows more than I am willing to mentally concede. I sort of feel like the man being led down to the gallows. As I looked through all the packages of various items in the garage area of the guesthouse, I daydreamed and tried to conjure a prettier picture. Lost in all the bike parts and food, safety gear and wheels, tools, spares of everything, I head outside into the side yard, I see bikes on bike stands, and Will is getting into packages of bike parts. I was the first rider here but the others will soon start to arrive. These guys I am riding with are amazing athletes. No doubt that we will be riding extremely fast out there on the road. I will need to be riding harder than I ever have. First Dave Zabriskie with his wife Randi and their two kids. Arriving in a minivan, it is like a family vacation for a couple days before for we start on Saturday. Dave is looking happy and so are the kids. Dave has an anxious tension that is oozing off a new haircut and a clean shave. Dressed in partials (Part your own clothes and part sponsor clothes) he surveys the layout here at the guesthouse. Most athletes wear a mix of things that are required team wear and other things that are more comfortable. Dave is the most accomplished and outright cyclist on our team. He is the real deal. I am still blown away that we have him on the team. He walks up and just says, "Legends" with a gleam in his eye. I think to myself that he is ready to be awesome.

Dave Zabriskie is a super star of cycling. He is one of the best cyclists of the latest generation or any other. He was a star when the world of cycling was caught in between ambition and science. Some people took what was a simple advantage of physical performance and really ran with it until Dr. Frankenstein could have started a successful training facility. Dave was one of many or almost all pro cyclist who belonged to the world's greatest cycling peloton during a very strange normal. What was normal? I do not believe any of us outsiders have any idea what was the norm inside their world. This was perhaps the craziest times the sport of cycling has ever seen. What was normal? For lack of a better term, I will call them the "chemically challenged" years. What does not kill you will make you super-fast and climb mountains like a superhero, even if it might cause you to die young. I don't know, again I will say I do not have a clue what really was going on for these guys but it was not pretty in the end. That is history and we are in this moment now.

In my past, I have been connected or compared to the Pink Floyd song "Shine On You Crazy Diamond" I can also see Dave Z in the lyrics. Dave has a little sadness about him. I can only guess why. I believe that he really loves to ride first and foremost. He really seems happy when he's riding. Maybe he no longer cares to be out there in the pro peloton. Who could challenge his feelings about that? However, I think he truly misses it. Not all the recent bullshit, but I think it is very hard for him to be so completely away from racing and an un-prejudiced future in cycling. It is obvious to anyone who ever has the opportunity to ride with him that he was meant to be a great cyclist--so naturally positioned on a bicycle and talented and powerful and genetically gifted. Riding next to him it's easy to he has an exceptional engine. It is easy to see the strength. He just has tons of it. In addition, where that may be more than enough he also has that fierce will when he summons it. I find it very strange to see someone that has been, somewhat exiled from all their life's passions and all their life's work. It is a sad reality, with puzzles of penalties. "Remember when you were young, you shone like the sun."

Dave retired in 2013. I have only spoken with him briefly, regarding his racing, just casually, not in any depth. I believe he has dealt with a somewhat forced retirement the best he could. Considering it is still very raw leads me to believe that he should be riding with us. I think that he needs us as much as we need him. We are all happy he is here. He is our beast to unleash on America. DZ has made us all feel confident in ourselves and as a team. We are all stronger knowing he is our anchorman.

[LEGENDARY: DZ takes a ride from the guesthouse a few days before the start of RAAM. Note the Captain America sticker on the water bottle.]

DZ sort of talks like a gunfighter, slow and stealthy. He often answers questions with additional questions. Upon his arrival, Dave wastes no time at all in finding his room for the next few days. It just so happens the room he chose is the room that Wayne was in. Wayne had just announced that we riders can pick our rooms first and so Dave takes the room and Wayne regrets his own words. I want to know more about this guy as I have watched him in numerous tours on the TV. I am intrigued by him and his savvy! He is a puzzle, he is a survivor, and I believe he is genuine. Nevertheless, he is still a puzzle.

During our camp Dave helped plan the rides and the locations. I am a moto guy and had no idea how to plan a camp. He must have had some laughs in the beginning at the proposed schedules that I sent him for approval. Dave was so relaxed about the whole thing and would just tell me, "Don't worry about it. We can just go out and ride." He was right and, that is just what we did. He had arranged a great house for Mirra, Wayne, Robson, Bishop and I. Dave had organized rides for us from his local training rides. They are Dave Zabriskie rides so they were very worthy to say the least. Look up the Mike Nosco Memorial Ride and you will see. Jack Nosco even guided us during one ride. Anyway, Dave was so fluid to watch ride and I watched everything he did. I was amazed at how smooth and effortless his pedal stroke was. He moved purely and without any wasted energy. He looked comfortable and natural in the aero position, kind of like he was in slow motion. He never seemed to be above his normal resting heartbeat and I don't think he ever got sweaty and it was like 90F degrees and sunny. I took as many notes from him as I could during camp and put them into my training rides.

Ben Bostrom is next to arrive with Rush (John Rushton) our camera/crew man. They have driven in from Vegas in Mike Mason's RV, our home on wheels for the next week or so. Ben is always upbeat and tends to lift up everyone around him. Ben is already hard at work infecting all the crew. There is no protocol, it is just who is next in line. He moves without prejudice through everyone along his path to the house while passing contagiously positive energy along the way. It is hard to believe that this guy with so much going on for himself can be so humble and gracious. He is interested in everyone and has time for everyone. Ben checks in with a smile getting the last room that has two single beds in it. He and Dave Mirra will have to share and he does not care. Ben could have been a hippie, but in a more physically motivated spiritual setting. He actually is sort of a hippie. More modest than any other Superbike

Champion ever. He is one of the most gifted motorcycle riders to have lived and that is fact with a capitol F. At the Supermoto X Games, he showed that he has a ton of fight in him as well by taking the gold medal after a race long duel with Europe's top Supermoto champion Eddy Seel.

Ben is also a spaz with a capitol "WTF." He is in so many places at once both mentally and physically that it is hard to reach him at any time. When Ben says I will be there you can count on it, but on time is whole other thing.

Micky to Ben - Ben, can you give me your sizes for the new riding kits from Pearl Izumi. I need them now so they can get them finished in time for RAAM.

6 days later.

Ben to Micky - Hey bud I'm in Africa, thanks for the message, and the hard work on the team. Talk soon, BBOZ. ????

I'm like what size?? Eventually I called his brother Eric to get sizes for Ben.

This is sort of standard communication with Ben. He is great to get on the phone and has endless ideas and enthusiasm but it seems to more a matter of luck to get him. He cannot be fully gauged or understood because he seldom has a single focus. I mean he has many irons in the fire and never sits still for too long. I'm not sure if he really sleeps or just takes small breaks. I know he needs sleep aids or tranquilizers just to slow down his overactive mind and let him rest. We are talking the kind of sleeping pills that Michael Jackson was using.

I think Ben and I are alike in many ways and very different in others. I love the way we can share the same thoughts at times and it feels good to know I am not alone in these thoughts. Whether it is a motorcycle bicycle related doesn't really matter. I am going to say that he may be a little bit more superstitious than I am. He inspires and motivates all of us Legends. And Ben will be a constant reminder to all of us to give 100% at all times on the bike. You know that he is going to go hard every time. There will be no excuses, get on and go 100%, every time. There is no other way and there will be no exceptions. Just do it. I know that without a shadow of a doubt that he is going to push himself to the edge every time and there is absolutely no way he will ever give up on me or the other Legends. Ben would sooner die than give less than all he has.

Ben's diet is not like a normal human's diet. He is a scientist regarding his vegan diet. Like Einstein his knowledge is gifted to anyone that will take time to listen to him and share ideas and knowledge about foods. This is a blessing for me as long as I can keep up. Ben was very forthcoming with suggestions for my diet. In a quest to bring my performance up I asked him for his help in designing a diet plan for me. Ben responded in his usual way, slowly but surely. When he finally got back to me, he came back with a long list of items that have now become my daily routine supplements, mostly vitamins to help me with energy, performance and recovery. I am, as Ben had promised me, "1% better for it."

[CAPTAIN BOSTRUM: Ben or "Team Captain," as I always like to call him, regardless what we are racing or who might be on the team. Here at team camp he realizes the moment he got soul.]

Ben, his wife Nikki and his daughter Ella look like they just got through a catalog shoot for Bloomingdale's or Calvin Klein. But don't let that fool you; they are amazingly generous and down to earth people. It is rare when they are not busy traveling or on amazing errands. The Bostroms are really super nice people and have good vibes oozing off them at all times.

Dave Mirra arrives later by plane from North Carolina, while, DZ, Ben and I are making a very important visit to NiteRider, our lighting sponsor. When we return to the guesthouse Mirra, "the miracle boy," is building his bikes and organizing his gear and so on. We had heard that Dave was not feeling too good after the long day of travel but that seems to not be the case now. Dave is a sweet but very intense guy. He has a great sense of humor and the ability to laugh at anything or anyone, including himself. He too has an energy that is contagious and unstoppable. There will be no nonsense with Dave Mirra and after our training camp none of us are going to give him anything but positive feedback. Dave once boxed the entire Metal Mulisha into submission during a fundraiser, but contractual obligations and good sportsmanship required it be reported publically as a draw. More to the point, it was Metal Mulisha's (a clothing company that caters to the

Freestyle crowd) very own Brian Deegan. I cannot imaging boxing Dave Mirra and I believe that Brian Deegan feels fortunate it's over now and that he only had to do it for three rounds. I know that both Mirra and Deegan sincerely have deep respect for each other.

Evel Knievel once said that if a man has no gamble in him then he isn't worth a shit. Mirra had lived a life of gambling; taking big risks in BMX Vert and Park was the standard. Mirra became the first rider to do a double backflip in a contest. By chance and coincidence, I was there when he pulled it off during his run at the San Francisco X Games in 2000. Mirra would win 24 X Game medals, numerous Gravity games and Dew tour medals before he retired. "The Miracle Boy" Dave had developed a work ethic during this time that would rival Bruce Lee. I worked with him on the Tony Hawk's big extravagant early 2000's tour "Boom Boom Huck Jam. was a little gamble and a shit ton of practice and skill. He would only stay on the Huck Jam for a short period before he became the host of the MTV reality show "Real World" and we would not see each other again until now.

Dave came out early for our training camp and stayed at my house for a couple days. We trained a bit and took a few rides throughout Sonoma County, one ride was a 60-

miler on which we took a recon of the Vine Man Triathlon course he was planning to attend and compete on later this year. We had taken my friend Chris Fillmore along for the ride. Chris is a pro motorcycle road racer that has also competed with Bostrom. The three of us took a speedy loop around the rolling hills through Nor Cal in the Sonoma wine country. I think he liked the place a lot and I quickly learned that Dave was strong and committed to RAAM. Moreover, Dave was cool. We had a few nice dinners and lots of good conversation. The guy is so funny, Filmore, Brenda and I were lucky to have Dave out for a couple different occasions that were all good times for sure. If you ever want to make an impression with Mirra bring a bottle or two of good red wine. He loves his wine.

Dave Mirra doesn't really sleep much either. In fact, I believe that Legends do not need as much sleep as normal people. Is this sleeplessness training related or an emotional penalty to the selfish focus? We all seem to have it. It is a Legends thing. I used to be able to sleep just about anywhere at any time when I was younger. Maybe it's age?, Regret? I don't know. I think the exercise and the meals, certainly alcohol and an over active metabolism. I guess all four of us seem to have the same problem. During Mirra's stay at my house, we kept running into each other in our only bathroom at 2:00 am or 4:00 am. I know the house and can navigate through the dark in an autopilot cat-like mode. Dave had to hit the lights to find me on the can or roaming. I could have said, "Hey!!" And scared the shit out of him, but I didn't. I just waited for him to hit the lights. "Sorry dude," I would say and he would sort of pause and laugh at the same time. Then at around 5 am I would hear Dave leave the house to go for a run. The dude is intense.

As for myself, I am blessed with great family, beautiful kids and good friends. I am unprejudiced and I can dream big or bigger when most human people will not. I love real, cool people and I am lucky to know a lot of them. I have inspiration and I love beautiful things like Brenda Lyons who makes me a better man than I used to be. I am a work in progress, but who cares? I was given huge amounts of faith from God. I love God and Jesus and believe they love me too. I am retired from motorcycle racing, though I race on occasion and still can go for the win here and there in the special races in which I choose to compete. I really can ride just about any kind of bike or machine in any kind of racing. To be totally honest I can quickly learn to operate any kind of machine like an extension of my own body.

[BREATHING LIFE INTO IT: Dave Mirra builds his own bike as we look on somewhat dumbfounded by all the parts. Dave is so funny to be around and has this explosive intensity that keeps you on your toes.]

I have three AMA National Championships, two in motocross in 1986 and in 1987 and one in Supermoto Unlimited in 2005. That is a 21 year gap between my second and third. I believe that is some kind of a record. I have won the Pikes Peak International Hill Climb, have held the record for the fastest motorcycle, and would love to recapture a record time again. I have a Baja 1000 victory from 2007 in class 21 and the amazing experience and endless stories. I have won a freestyle event (MTV Sports and Music 1999) and am in many freestyle videos like Organ Donors, Crusty Demons of Dirt 2, 3 and 4. I have also designed and built Freestyle courses like X Games San Francisco, MTV sports and music festival as well as many others in the USA or abroad. I have help create events and theatrical shows. I have designed, consulted or produced many motorcycle related projects over the last 20 years. This sort of special niche has enabled me to live a fairly charmed life even though it has no real solid foundation. Motorcycle racing has made my life pretty amazing. I have always gone for the adventure first and now will most likely be financially challenged until my death.

Bicycling used to be just a fitness-based hobby for me. . Recently it has become serious. I used cycling to get into shape for motorcycle racing which was pretty serious. Even when I was injured, I was able to train the heart, the lungs and the legs on a bicycle or bicycle trainer. Over the years, it became inevitable that I would grow into a fairly decent cyclist. Thanks to people like Brenda Lyons, Joe Lawwill and Mike Bell (Mike "Too Tall" Bell, another amazing motorcycle racer who I was able to work with during the recent Supermoto racing years) I was able to create a mind for training and improving on a mountain bike, road bike or stationary trainer. Cycling became more interesting than motorcycle racing, (to a point that is) However, I will instinctually forever be tied to the motorized two-wheelers.

It always feels incredibly awkward describing myself. I know that I can really talk up a storm and I love to tell the stories of how it was done, not just that I did it but it's easier to talk about the other guys. It is an honor to know these three monstrous guys. They are Legends for sure. I love heroic people with freaky strength and huge hearts. These guys are like unicorns right before my eyes. I get to ride side-by-side with these amazing dudes into a dream world of human endurance. Suffering sounds so good, huh? I will be in the company of superheroes. How awesome is that? These guys are going to be unstoppable. Well, this sounds good, but I will be put to my limit just to keep up to their standards. Just to pull my own weight will be a journey into the red zone at every shift--maximum efforts or die. For sure, it was going to be hard to be the oldest guy on the team. But the slowest guy? I don't want that. I want to do my part. Suddenly it sounds a lot harder to be me in this deal. How high is that bar I just set for myself?

[DRESSED WELL, FEELING WELL: Just being a part of this is overwhelming in the very best way. At this moment anyway.]

4 THE PREP, THE PLAN AND THE TOOTH

Thursday morning, just two days before our RAAM start, when I woke up the guesthouse, it had become more of a mad house. All the crew members are busy with one thing or another. Meg is cooking and preparing meals to pack and store for the race and has some test meals for us to eat for breakfast. Will is working on bikes (Ben had an issue with a frame and the two of them are making a lot of last minute changes or exchanges with Bens TT bike, Mirra has jumped in and is helping too.) Robson and Wayne are getting things prepared for the Legends team technical inspections that will be on Friday. You must have your shit together for the inspections or lose your place in line. There are many details to work through and you must have all of your gear, safety equipment, vehicle details and proper paperwork in order or lose your place in line and have to come back later. If you are truly a mess, the RAAM officials can assess time penalties. Bishop is organizing media and has the distinguished honor of being chauffer for the riders. We have appearances for photos and one last onsite registration deal to complete before we are 100% cleared and ready to start.

All of us riders have taken small rides to spin out the legs and check the bikes one last time. The vehicles are all stickered up and the bike racks are on. The vehicles get flashers and race numbers as well as sponsors stickers. We outfit the support cars with race maps and radios, plug-ins for chargers and a plastic seat cover for the transition vehicle to protect the seat from the sweaty riders. We are also going through food plans for each rider and picking our snacks and drinks. There is also a need to minimize all the carry-on bags and extra stuff because there is little to no room in the RV. Plans are hatched to send all the gear we cannot carry along during the race. It will go back to my dad's office. Robson and the crew have masterminded a sleep station for the two riders on break to sleep. It is in the back area of the RV, the garage area, two small cots with foam pads. It came out pretty good, sort of like what you would see at a disaster shelter.

The proposed race strategy would be to break the 4-man team into two 2- rider teams. We were all sent an email about a week ago regarding the pairings of the teams. Ben and I would be paired together (the A team) and the Daves were paired (the other A team). The moto guys vs. the cyclists. Robson and Wayne had discussed this thoroughly and there was little to no resistance as far as I know. I was happy to not have any responsibility for this and thought that it was going to work out well. Ben would turn out to be my inspiration. He would be a perfect teammate. We both would be easy but assertive when we needed it. As for the race strategy, we all had our own thoughts. We needed to come together and work out the plan as to who would start the race and how long each would rider stay on the bike etc. Ben and I would be able to choose what we wanted to do and the Daves would choose their plan.. How long should our shifts be? Ben and I wanted to shoot for 25 minutes. Long enough to build good rhythm and short enough to be able to ride at maximum effort and speed. There would be fewer rider changes and that should make it faster as long as we could stay strong the whole time.

Out into the race we would learn quickly what would work best. After the first few shifts, we would know what to do and make the changes we needed. It was kind of easy to figure out and we could change it right then. We would be able to talk on the radio and tell each other what was working and what was not. We could make adjustments for climbs or descents, for headwinds or tailwinds. It would be easy to adjust and it could change at any moment. It might never be steady and consistently the same. Eventually the shifts would be shorter as we tired over the race.

The Daves had a more ambitious plan, starting at 30-minute shifts. They too would learn quickly where their happy place was. For the speed we wanted to carry throughout this race we all needed something manageable to keep it at a full throttle pace with equal rest. We would also need to handle the transitions well from one rider to the next. We should have had more planning and testing and practice because there would be more than 600 of these transitions during the race. Gaining 5 seconds at each of these would add up to a substantial chunk of time. It is like a full hour spread over 5 days. There were better places on the road to do rider changes. We would plan to do uphill sections that were slower and we could change out riders without losing any time. We had practiced rider changes at camp or more to the point; we had practiced a few changes at camp and discussed a few ideas about rider changes over a few beers. Regardless the rider changes were all good efforts and some were really good.

Robson and Wayne had come up with a plan to rotate through five and 6-hour team shifts for each team on a 48-hour rotation that gave a 6-hour rest through the night for each team every other day. On Saturday the 14th the start was at 1:00 pm (5 Hour shift). At 6:00 pm was team change #1 (5 Hour shift) and at 11:00 pm team change #2 (6 Hour shift) At 5:00 am team change #4 (5 hour shift) at 10:00 am team change #5 (5 hour shift) at 3:00 pm team change # 6 (5 hour shift) at 8:00 pm team change #7 (5 hour shift) at 1:00 am team change #8 (6 hour shift) at 7:00 am team change #9 (5 hour shift) And so. It was supposed to run about like that. This plan was looking good to all of us. Each team would get an extra hour rest every other day through the night. It sounded good, but I think it was going to be too long for the riders on the road and we would ditch it after the first night. However, the plan, for now, looked frigging solid.

As things began to feel organized after our pre-race meetings and a press obligations, we slowed down a bit. Tonight we have a team appearance at the Endurance House, a really nice cycle/triathlon shop in Oceanside. We will have a press conference and sign autographs. Our time there together is super relaxing and fun. Some of my friends have shown up to support the Legends and me and it is good to see them. During the press event, I started to have a throbbing toothache. I had lost the crown from one of my back teeth. It was a wisdom tooth. It had actually started bothering me last night, but now it was throbbing. My whole head was throbbing. Now I am thinking I need to get it fixed right away before it gets worse. During the afternoon, I had tried to visit a local dentist office in Oceanside to see if they could fix it. They would not be able to get to it until next Monday which by then, if everything went according to plan, I would be halfway across America. It was not looking good. If I could not get this fixed, there's no way I was going to be able to compete at my best. I might have to get some pliers and do it myself. As luck would have it, or my dear God had planned it, one of the people that came to the Endurance House to show their support for our team was an incredibly resourceful guy named Terry Clanton. He is an old friend of an old friend of mine who is also a dentist. Terry is an old motocross buddy from the 80's who quit competing and working in the motorcycle industry to became a dentist, but I had not talked to him in forever and last I heard, he was 80 miles away from where I was right now. After my friend Terry had assured me that it was my only hope. I was on the phone with my old friend and dentist, Steve Wiedler. "Engine tuner turned dentist". He would need to do a root canal on Friday the 13th (sweet! Friday the 13th) at his office in Canyon Lake, California, not too far from Oceanside.

My faith keeps me moving forward. It was so lucky. I cannot imagine what would have happened if I had tried to pull the tooth myself in a haste. That would have been very bad. So, on Friday the 13th I would go to see the dentist. At noon my driver/escort, John Rushton and I made the drive to Canyon Lake to see Dr. Wiedler. We arrived at the office where we met with Steve and he quickly got me prepped for the procedure. He had a regular schedule that was already full and had to slide me in between the other patients. Root canals suck. Is anything worse than having a root canal? I had broken my leg once so severely that I had compartment syndrome and that may be worse by a little bit. In your mouth, the nerves in your gums and your teeth hurt worse and are more sensitive. Rush (John Rushton) would film this completely miserable experience for the Legends, or as much as he could stomach.

Dr. Wiedler (Steve) has big hands like a basketball player so my jaw was getting its ass kicked. Rushton is filming and asking questions that I cannot answer with a fist in my mouth. Steve tried to answer for me and explain what he was doing to me. At one point, my jaw started to cramp and my mouth was stuck wide open as Steve was grinding and scraping and his pretty assistant was suctioning at my open mouth. During this white-knuckle melee, Dr. Wiedler was telling stories about racing motocross in the eighties; specific stories of my history in racing from the early 1980's. It was nice to lose myself in the stories and God knows I did not want to focus on the tooth and the exposed nerves.

I have been around the world racing motorcycles all my life. I have been a winner and a loser in so many places. However, there are no better memories than those from growing up racing in Southern California. Steve was there when many of the moments happened. I began to drift away a bit from the unpleasantness I was enduring in my mouth. Soon Rush had dropped away from the intense dentist office shit and went out to the vehicle to sleep for a while. Lucky for me Steve had inserted a vintage video from the motocross files or some, moto video to view on a TV monitor in the office. Steve Stackable, Jimmy Weinert, Bob Hannah, and then Warren Reid, Jim Tarantino, Doug Dubach and many other names filled my mind and refreshed my memory. Steve also had a few magazines from the great moments of the eighties for me to sign. And I did so happily.

After few hours of intense grinding and root plumbing, it was over. The procedure that is, the pain and discomfort would last throughout the remainder of the day and well into RAAM. The tooth would be sensitive for weeks to come. Nevertheless, the tooth was fixed. I could now rest assured that I would not have any emergency out in the race. At least I shouldn't. Steve was so awesome to pull strings and get me sorted out with the very best quick fix. Steve is proof of the awesome nature of true moto people. Rush and I had to hurry back so I would not miss the last mandatory meeting in Oceanside. I would need to take antibiotics that Steve promised would be ok to take (And legal by the race rules) the meds might make me feel like shit, but I would still be able to race. The big issue seemed to be the antibiotics. They would make me feel sick to my stomach. If I tried to go light on the prescribed dosage it could cause swelling in my jaw by an infection getting in there, so it was a full dose, a big ass handful of antibiotics, vitamins and minerals followed with a probiotic recovery drink and some pain killers. That was the plan anyway.

After the long and grueling trip to the dentist, John and I were back in the company of the team and attending the final group meeting with the event organizers. The auditorium near the pier was where all the teams had gathered for the big pre-RAAM meeting. It was completely packed with all the teams and crews. All the teams were announced one by one. Each team was called up to the front of the auditorium to be presented. There had been so many 4-man teams, looking fit and strong. We were almost the last team introduced. I think we got the biggest applause of all when we presented our lovely selves at the front of the hall. Finally, I was feeling some relief. Not the way I wanted to start a 3020-mile bicycle race, but it is what I had to do. It was the last night before RAAM. The Kings were winning the Stanley Cup playoffs. I love hockey, but I couldn't break away from this need for a good rest. I took a few phone calls from family, my daughter Ronni and finally from Brenda to strengthen me. Brenda's voice is like a long soft hug and a warm kiss to me. She lifts me up when I am alone and feeling insecure. I like to have intimate words with her to feel there is a place for me. I needed her here, but I had to do it alone since she couldn't be here. She sweet-talked me to a warm safe place and soon I was able to get some much-needed sleep.

My dreams are filled with familiar faces, mumbled words with music and a voice yelling and screaming something in French, I think. I wasted no time trying to figure it out and pretty much forgot it completely in a nanosecond. At my age, I tend to sleep less than I used too and I have to go to the bathroom a few times a night. Falling back to sleep is tough and takes far too long. I am anxious and ready for this race to get going. I am tired and all I want is to sleep deeply, but I can't. I truly despise these moments of waiting and guessing. What is this need I have to put myself into these places in my life? Why do I ask for so much pressure in my life? WTF am I doing this for? And to think my ultimate goal is to do RAAM solo. How fucking tough is that going to be? I should be writing this down. poet Charles Bukowski (AKA "Barfly") has nothing on me right now. Finally, I relax again and then I have to pee.

You can look at this as the moment of truth or the sudden awakening of the truth. On the other hand, is this the beginning of a mental breakdown? I am careful not to let that negative mindset come in here and fuck with me. Did I ask for more than I can handle? Maybe. Probably. Does it matter now? Not really. I am fully committed now and could not back out if I tried. Only death can bring this thing down for me. Now it seems even funny when I think about it. I am trapped now to ride this out no matter what happens and it feels like I am screwed no matter what. At this moment, I start to meditate and pray. Thank you God for giving me all this faith. Inside my heart, I know with God's help I am capable of much more than even I can imagine and that is where things begin to lighten up. It is true. There are times that I have been to the deepest parts of my being where I know I have nothing left, but still somehow I have come up with more. Now I believe this is meant to be. I mean, I better be able to rise up and take this on with everything I have regardless of how I got here.

5 THE MEETING, RIDING THE LINE

Let's go back a bit and let me explain how I came to be here in the first place. In about 2008, Brenda Lyons and I met through a friend and started to build a friendship around cycling. I was still with my wife at this time. I was working hard on my fitness. Cycling was a second hobby as well as just a means to train. I rode with a few different people weekly; friends like Mike Bell and Joe Lawwill. That led me to ride with Brenda. She worked in the cycling industry and was a retired pro cyclist. When I first met her I saw that she was an obviously fit cycling specimen; racing as a pro at the time, she was visually and physically refined for cycling. I would ride with her maybe once a month, usually meeting up on a group ride. She was so strong it was somewhat intimidating to ride with her. Brenda is 5 foot tall about 110 pounds and is extremely fit. She has legs like a sprinter that made me feel so envious. I knew if I had her awesome legs my career in motocross would have lasted much longer. Her body was like a fitness model. She was so beautiful to watch, always out front with me always chasing. She was small and very light. She is Italian and looks like it with dark hair and dark skin. She is very beautiful and feisty too. She could drop me whenever she wanted at that time. I always had so much motivation to improve after we rode together. I would work hard on my daily training so that next time we met up I could surprise her with improved strength and endurance. Actually, I was training for motorcycle racing, or, to be a tad bit more specific, Supermoto racing.

After a year or two things were changing for me. My marriage was coming to an end. It had been falling apart for a long while since the late 90's my wife and I had lost interest in each other or more to the point, she did not give a shit anymore. We were living it out for the kids and that was it. I finally moved out into a temporary place nearby. My racing success in Supermoto was steady and life was going on as usual. Cycling was a growing passion for me and I was spending a lot more time on my bicycle. Brenda and I were doing so much more cycling together our other interests became of interest. She attended a few motorcycle races and finally, it just happened that we were getting closer and closer. I started to think about her as more than just an awesome cyclist. She was becoming so attractive to me. The more I got to know her the more I was falling for her. I could not take it any longer and just decided to tell her I wanted to be with her. She thought she had won the lottery. Ha maybe not, but she was mutually revved up.

Anyway, she is a retired pro cyclist you know... divert here...

[BICYCLE BONDING: Brenda and I in 2008 on San Juan trial. We had just started to ride together on occasion back then. My friend Joe Lawwill took this picture and had organized the ride.]

I really loved to ride with her because she was always willing to share her knowledge about training. "You're just a hammerhead!" she would say and then tell me why and help me to be better. We rode these rides together called the RADS ride down in Laguna Beach, mountain bike rides with a mutual friend Joe Lawwill. You had to have an invite from one of the Rads just to know when and where the weekly ride was. These rides were somewhat tough for the both of us as they had a very tough physical element as well as a serious technical aspect. We both had a few crashes on these rides resulting in a few injuries. Anyway, the RADS rides were on Wednesday nights and ended with a survival style meal made in a fire pit and a few beers. It was a good place to share time with each other and in hindsight I truly liked to be with her as much as I could.

In 2013, Brenda was once again working in the cycling Industry representing a company called Cardo. They make Bluetooth radio headsets. We used them on our rides together as radios or alone I could make or take phone calls while out on rides. The system made great sense for riders that were into the ultra-endurance cycling world. It was mid-February. Brenda had a work dinner meeting with some of the folks from RAAM regarding the sponsorship from Cardo. She wanted me to come along. I thought that it was only regarding a sponsorship that Cardo was giving to RAAM. Ok, so I went. The meeting was with three gentlemen, Brian Bishop from Cycling Soul, Fred and Rick Boethling from RAAM. The Race Across America.

The four of them had thought it would be a good idea for me to host a web video series called "Riding the Line" to promote outside interest in RAAM. More to the point, Brian Bishop had made the efforts to take me into the role. The complete design of my hosting the videos would have me learning about and following the race through 3 amazing solo riders (Christoph Strasser, Reto Schoch and Chris Ragsdale) and a few teams such as the women's 4-rider team, Love Sweat and Gears and the men's 8-rider team Allied Forces. (Four US military and four British armed forces riders) The final component was for me to be learning what it takes so that in 2014 I would take on RAAM. What a surprise.

At this point we ordered a few beers and the guys began to talk about RAAM. They were very convincing and a lot of fun to talk with. Fred had actually held the solo record for the 60-year-old division. He was a nice guy that seemed confident that I could do it. Brenda had also given me props when talking about my fitness for this type of race. We continued to talk throughout the dinner about Rick and Fred's experiences on the race and other riders and teams. They explained that they could help me to get through the initial details and costs. I was almost feeling committed and had to step back for a moment. I went into the restroom, looked at myself in the mirror and began to sweat it a little bit. After a nice meeting and dinner, I said I would think about it. Brenda and I went home and I asked her if I could do it. She said if I work hard to prepare then I could.. But I wasn't feeling that she was convinced. I suspected she was not being 100% honest with me and was just trying to be nice.

I did truly love the idea, but I did have some serious reservations because of my life and work schedule. "There's no way this could be happening," I thought. How could I possibly be ready to do a 3,000-mile bicycle race by next year solo? And, how long does it take to train and be ready for such a thing as this? I have never actually done any type of an event like it. There was my work that had me busy as hell for the whole first half of the year, traveling every weekend, working for All Access staging company for the remaining months of the year in Torrance, California. The actual pay was not very good so I would be paying for the majority of my training and having to go get sponsors and support. It would not be easy and it would not be cheap.

I started to look up video and written stories of RAAM and the famous racers. There were many amazing stories about some truly amazing people. Then there were the actual accounts of the rider's teams. I had no idea so much work would have to be done to make this happen. A crew of people would have to be gathered. A set of vehicles, a coach and trainer, a medical person, a mechanic, a nutritionist, A MacGyver called the crew chief and a couple drivers/navigators and then a host of parts and supplies and bicycles too. I had plenty of reasons to just say, "No thanks." However, I couldn't walk away yet. I had said that I would think about it and get back to them and I went on dreaming about this amazing RAAM race.

I also started to read about RAAM. I had found a book called "Hell on Wheels" and fell in love with the event, mostly through one of the racers, Jure Robic. I loved learning about Robic and reading what he had to say, what he did during the races, the struggles he had, the pace he rode, the hours he went without sleep, and the victories. I had become buried in the book and had only RAAM on my mind for a week or so bringing it into our (Brenda and I) conversations, every conversation for a time. "Brenda," I would say, "Do you know that Jure Robic only slept for 9 hours in 8 days while racing the RAAM?", or, "Robic won RAAM 5 times!" Brenda began to request that we not talk about RAAM during dinner. Nevertheless, it was so much more exciting to me than anything else I had been working on in long time. really was hooked.

In Amy Snyder's book, Hell on Wheels that covered the 2009 RAAM, Robic was at the final time station when he dropped out to protest time penalties he had received. He could have just accepted the penalties and finished second. However, he did not. Robič swore never to enter RAAM again, but changed his mind and came back and won again in 2010. He had this beautiful tough face with an iron jaw. The pain was not masked by this face, so tough and hard, but so honest. His will could match or overcame any challenge with stubbornness. He had a look that was scary strong. His broken English was somewhat charming when he spoke and that was often in defiance during the video of the race. Robic would be my hero for the solo RAAM and the dream of my own experience of RAAM were born. Robic was tragically killed in a collision with a car later that same year while descending on a narrow mountain road near his home in Slovenia. Reading the book, I cried when I reached that part of the story. At that time, I truly loved the idea of doing this race solo, but never believed I would ever really have the chance to do it until now.

After only a few days of discussion with Brenda, figuring out how I would juggle my schedule, my job and all the rest of our lives and responsibilities together, it was decided that I do it. And Brenda would help me. I was not sure how it would work out as far as the training and the preparations to develop a crew. And I would need funding. I had only my strong faith that it would all come together. I just seemed to believe that God had laid this out for me to do. It has always been like that in my life. Some things you just know. I knew it would be extremely tough and nearly impossible to accomplish, but I was in.

Soon I was working with Brian Bishop and the photographer, Tage Plantell. Riding the Line got started in March 2013 and so I began my preparations to ride solo RAAM. I loved moonlighting as video host and training like a serious ultra-cyclist and I was falling deeper in love with RAAM. I began to schedule my life around training for RAAM. We shot in California for episode #1. It was pretty cool to get into it and we did shoot on the bicycle and on the motorcycle. I think Brian and Tage (pronounced Taga) had a good time too. We then shot for episode #2 and #3 during a three-day weekend starting on a Friday. I flew to Colorado to interview Anne and Julie from the Love Sweat and Gears team. Friday went well with a sit down interview. Saturday started early with a 5 am spin class with Anne and then a 10 am gym workout with Julie.

This was a hard morning for me at altitude. We then went over to Boulder to meet Billy Edwards of the Allied Forces team for a ride into Boulder, Colorado Mountains that nearly had me smoked. Luckily, we had an after-ride interview at the Boulder Brewery and I got a rest and some beer.

We then flew to Seattle for an interview and ride with Chris Ragsdale, the American hopeful in the men's solo division. We cruised around Seattle and did some B- roll shots (extra filler shots that may or may not be used in the final edit) after we arrived then met with Chris at his home. Chris and his very young family were very generous and accommodating. It was very clear that he was an incredibly fit athlete. In the morning, we met Chris and a few of his training partners for a 160-mile ride through the greater Seattle area. We even passed the home of Kurt Cobain. It was a long haul after the last few days, but I pulled it together and barely finished the ride. I was completely trashed but invigorated after the three days; Chris had told me that he had training blocks that were like this:

Day #1 – 100 mile ride

Day #2 – 100 mile ride

Day #3 - 200 mile ride

Day #4 – 200 mile ride

(Chris Ragsdale Training block)

Are you kidding me Chris? That is fricking crazy. After the tiring and eye-opening weekend, I had a new outlook on preparing for RAAM. I would need to bust my ass all year long and then some. I could not skip a workout. I could not get sick and miss workouts. I had to change my diet. I had to change my lifestyle. I was going to need more money. Realistically there was not enough time. I needed a few more years to be truly prepared to do solo RAAM. Holy shit. I think I am having issues here. In the documentary movie Bicycle Dreams, Jure Robic said, "You must train all your life for the RAAM," and he wasn't joking.

As soon as I could accept the challenges and what I was going to be dealing with, I was committed to taking on RAAM. Right away, I was in full training mode. Not a single day passed that I would not train. It was all cycling all the time, indoors or out, rain or shine. I began to increase mileage and time on the bike. Workouts became marathons. It was not unusual for me to leave the house in the early morning at like 6:00 am and not stop pedaling until dark. I trained in the gym, in hotel gyms, on my own trainer when the weather was bad or at night.

[REALITY CHECK: Top, Billy Edwards and I get a ride and chat in Boulder, Colorado. Below, Chris Ragsdale and friends out for a 160 mile ride through Seattle, WA. I was completely wiped out after the weekend.]

Wherever I was, I was getting the workouts done. I had to create ways to get through some of the harder days or longer days. Sometimes I would end my super hard days at the Brewery and just crash into food and beer.

Throughout the remainder of 2013 and into 2014, there would be some serious roadblocks to hurdle. By mid-August, nine months away from RAAM, we had to be realistic. Touring the Nuclear Cowboyz arena show from November to April I am travelling. First, creative meetings and then rehearsals and during the tour I am at each venue co-directing each live show. While at rehearsals, we had 12-hour days, often followed by lengthy production meetings. I remember putting in 14-hour days with the addition of three to four hour workouts on cycle trainers. Some days the gym closed and I have to do them at the hotel on a seated trainer. My back got calluses from the rubber foam seat and do not get me started about saddle sores. I would do just about anything to make sure I completed the workouts and usually went to work in the morning pretty trashed. Then there was Pikes Peak International Hill Climb, which I had committed to. That would follow RAAM by just 2 days. Anything less than a fully rested body and mind was deadly for Pikes Peak. Brian and I discussed the idea of a 4-man team for 2014 with the idea that I would be able to race RAAM solo in 2015 and Rick and Fred from RAAM agreed to support the adjustment and stay on schedule to assist it in any way they could.

So now, we just had to come up with three riders, all similar retired personalities and all capable athletes who would like to race a 3000-mile nonstop bike race, and, to do it for free or to even have to come out of pocket to do it. Yeah, "this should be no problem," I said aloud rolling my eyes to the back of my skull. No one is ever going to want to do this.

6 ASSEMBLING THE LEGENDS OF THE ROAD

Brian and I had made a list of guys that we would ask to join the team. Tim Johnson, Travis Pastrana, Ben and Eric Bostrom, Dave Mirra, Travis Brown, Patrick Dempsy, yes, that Patrick Dempsy aka "McDreamy." Hell, even Lance Armstrong was a thought; God knows he needed some good press as of late. Ben Bostrom and I were going to be racing at a Supermoto event called the Superbikers in Mettet, Belgium in October. Mettet is a super fun race in a little town in Belgium near Brussels. It is an annual event that we had both competed in a few other times. As American Supermoto riders, we are not racing full time or hardly at all these days and that brings us together as teammates. We have to stick together for the four or 5 days we are there on and off the track. It made for a good place to sell Ben on the idea of RAAM.

I think it was mid-September that I began texting and emailing Ben about RAAM. He was slow to respond, but when he did, he said that he liked the idea. He told me I would need to keep bugging him about it and that is what I did.

[AN EARLY LEGENDS TEAM MEETING: Ben, on the right, and I on the left at Mattet Superbikers race in Belgium.]

At Mettet we had a great time together as friends and teammates with a couple other American riders Jeff Ward and Chris Filmore (also potential RAAM riders) I sank the RAAM hook deeper. Ben also threw me additional names like Ben Spies and Dave Zabriskie. He seemed to think they would be interested. I could be totally excited to know those names but became quickly faced with the reality that I would have to call them and convince them to do it. So I took the possibilities in stride and stayed positive. I kept the faith that this would come together. Truly only God could carry me to the start line with any of these guys. After some time went by and I kept talking with them I felt a good connection with Ben and Dave Mirra.

I had developed a very impressive email with pictures and an exciting highlight video from various "Riding the Line" clips and a very well done video documentary of the Allied Forces from RAAM 2013and I kept sending it to each guy. Over time, Ben came on board. Then Mirra was in, then Mirra was out and then Mirra came back. Dave Mirra was so fun to talk with about it. I could tell he wanted to do it. He had become so locked into triathlon and endurance cycling. Each time we talked about RAAM, he seemed to want it a little more. He would ask many questions about the effects it would have on his current plans and schedule for triathlon. I really could not answer because I honestly did not know. Dave and I would get on the phone and I would have a list of details and questions to go over. We would get to talking and an hour would go by and we would be laughing and carrying on about all kinds of stuff then we would have to hang up and we had only covered like two of the 20 items.

The word from Brian was that Tim Johnson (US cyclocross champion) was in as well. I had never met Tim and was wondering what kind of a person he was. But, after a little while others told me that he opted out due to scheduling conflicts. I heard also that he had no interest in doing a series of time trial efforts across the country after having done a full race season. Sadly, I never actually talked to him and maybe that would have made some difference in his decision. Time was becoming an issue. The end of the year was on us already. For a few months there was little to no updates on confirmations. Time had begun to run out for us. I was trying to text back and forth with Ben and got the following message; "EB (Ben's younger brother and accomplished road racing champion) or DZ were both down to do it. Ben was in Africa competing in the Cape Epic, a huge mountain bike stage race and it was now up to me to hurry up and get the team finalized.

After cold calling both Eric and Dave Zabriskie I learned that Eric was a new dad and would not be ready to leave his new baby in time and that Dave was rather new to the Idea. Eric said no thanks, but maybe next year. Dave?

He was fun to talk to and had a curiosity about him. I could tell he was Intrigued by the idea. Dave said to give him a bit of time to think it over. He also is a dad with a couple of young kids and has a lot going on at home. I was trying not to sound desperate so I said, "sure, let me know after you think more about it." I think he called back in the next few days and said, "It sure sounds like an adventure. I am in." I had to take a walk around the house and down the street to feel it come all the way into my being. We were going to have Ben Bostrom, Dave Mirra and Dave Zabriskie on our Team. How could this get any better?

Now that all the guys were committed to the project, we needed to come up with a team name. We all threw out ideas and nothing would stick. 4x Athletes, Team 4x, OTH, 4 Suits like that in a deck of cards but nothing was sticking. Mirra sent me a list that had a few names on but one was "Legends of the Road". I liked this one and decided to put it to the real test and I showed it to Brenda. She had disapproved all previous names. She looked at it and said, "That's it. The Legends of the Road is perfect for you guys." Brenda has been my sounding board for all creative things I have done in the last 5 years and never turns out anything but gold. Now we would be alright. Complete. The Legends of the Road. I was so excited that I bought the domain name and started a company, acquired a tax ID and opened a bank account in a few days' time. Bob's your uncle, we were rolling.

7 THE RACE IS ON

Back in the California desert. It was approximately. 7 pm Pacific Standard Time, Saturday, June 14. Race time is Eastern Time so that would be 10pm race time. The sun was still out and the golden hour was at full effect. Sunset in the California desert is pretty amazing and just the right temperature to do all-out 100% efforts for five hours. Ben was so strong. He was flying, 25 plus miles per hour on the average. We were catching the top three teams now and closing fast on them. As we came into the night and it cooled down a good 10 or so degrees and we crossed the state line into Arizona. All the front-runners were just ahead of us. I could see the flashers up ahead marking the riders and follow cars. I could also see that we were gaining on the leaders. That had both of us amped up. At night, you have a direct follow car that sits approximately 50 feet behind you at all times. You have the vehicle headlights as well as a head light on the bike to light your way. We had lighting from our sponsor NiteRider (surfer Tom Carrol developed the lights for night surfing and he and his wife own the business.) and just the bike light was super bright. These lights makes the night riding awesome, especially out here in the desert this time of year.

Riding at night was somewhat new to me and strange at first. It was nice, cool and clean. The follow car lights against your back cast off shadows up the road and that constant flashing yellow added to the overactive shadow rider. There was a quiet solitude without the feeling of being totally alone. It started to feel good to ride at night. You knew there was always someone right there in the follow car just behind you. Radio communication with the crew was there too if you needed anything. Rider changes were slower. You could actually do a stop and go style exchange in the glow of the exchange cars headlights. We could see the other team's flashers up ahead of us like a big red and yellow carrot out there in the distance.

About 150 miles into the race we entered some rolling terrain that was like sand dunes, little rises and then equal descents. We were pounding out a good pace now and with the leaders just up ahead, maybe a little less than a mile or so. On the P5 in the rolling hills, I could manage close to 30 mph. It really was feeling good to be so fast. Then, we had some bad luck. I caught a train that crossed just in front of me and slowed to a stop. I could see it coming and I knew I would not make it by. It was slowing and sure enough, it came to a full stop. Now it sat motionless on the tracks. "WTF?!" I'm thinking. We sat there for   20 minutes without moving.

[HURRY UP AND WAIT: In RAAM you have to deal with whatever arises; rain, wind or in this case, a slow moving train.]

The teams we had just passed caught back up and the front-runners pulled out another 20 minutes on their lead. All these team vehicle with flashing lights and riders sitting together waiting for a train to move was like one of those movie moments, like a scene from Cannonball Run. The second the train started moving all the riders and teams got ready and as soon as the road was open, we took off. Again, I went too hard and quickly hit the wall and had to regroup. This time no one came by me and I reached the next transition with Ben. Ben and I finished our shift well and handed off to the Daves. I am not sure how close we were to the leading teams. It was late in the night, like 11:30 pm when we finished our first team shift. My throat and lungs burned from the very hot and dry air out in the desert. It felt like I had a blow torch in my throat. I could taste blood in my mouth from the efforts we were putting out. "Lots of water and make it cold." It was a race for sure at this point. I had no idea that it was going to be this hard. I thought it would have been moving much slower than this. It had been flat out the whole time, chasing the leading teams. Get on the bike; take the exchange and ride, ride flat out for 15 to 20 minutes. Ride at 25 mph or faster. That is what we were doing and it was hurting already.

Now I know how hard this race is going to be. I am thinking, no, I am hoping that we will pass the other teams and pull away eventually because we are closing in so fast. It might be that we are pushing ourselves too hard right now. I have no way to tell if this pace is too hard or if we'll burn out if we try to keep it up. Anyway, it will be tough to maintain that speed and intensity for five plus days straight. I have no real clue what else to think. Get on the bike and ride. When you finish your shift, you need to eat, to feed the legs for a good recovery. You force-feed yourself if you have to when it is this hot and dry you're not really hungry as much as thirsty. However, you need to eat. You also need to clean up your under carriage and try to lie down right away to sleep. It is a lot easier said than done. The RV is moving most of the time and it is hot in there. Each rider has his own cupboard to store his personal items. I kept all my goodies in there; food, drinks, clothes, riding gear plus saddle cream, vitamins and my meds. I also kept one pair of workout shorts that I wore when I was not riding.

Ben kept about three grocery bags full of food and supplements, as he is the most technical eater on the team, maybe the whole planet. He is a vegan, with the deepest diet knowledge of anyone I have ever met. Luckily, he was open to sharing his insight with me along with whatever he had and thought I needed. I am 1 % more "better" than I used to be now thanks to Ben. A usual feeding off the bike would consist of actual warm food such as rice, sweet potatoes, eggs, toast, beans and all cooked food was followed by a serious hand full of vitamins, minerals, oils, seeds and powders. I also had to take my antibiotics and pain meds before sleeping and not forget to wash that down with the probiotic/protein shake. At first, I am trying to go light on the antibiotics to try to keep my stomach working and so far, I feel fine. I have been taking 400 mg witch is short of the prescribed 1200 mg daily dose

From my experience following the race last year I knew just how long this race was and that, the only way to win was to be the fastest to the finish line. It didn't matter who won the race to Arizona or to Colorado or Pennsylvania. What mattered was who was leading the race in Maryland. This is a good rule to follow. But we are all racers and trying to cruise when there are still racers ahead of you is hardly possible. It would be risky to sit back in second or third waiting on the other teams to fade or weaken. What if they didn't? That was a chance we didn't want to take. We wanted to be in the lead and pulling out a buffer and then be able to relax. Alternatively, we can balance our lead without the pressure of chasing with an all-out effort just to catch the leaders.

For us Legends it was feeling like we were managing the race damn well. Yes, this was early in the race. But, we had been pretty solid. Once we had our wheels turning we settled into a grove with no real problems at all so far. We had the little issue with Mirra's flat, but had recovered well and it seemed like we had not lost any time thanks to DZ pushing on for an extended shift. In RAAM 2013, the Allied Forces 8-man team was so fast and well-choreographed that it was hard to keep up with them in a standard vehicle running at the speed limit. For us Robson and Wayne were in control and the Legends' pace was even close to the 2013 record pace of the Allied Forces and well above the 4-man team record. Rider changes and team exchanges were clearly running smooth and all of us riders seemed to be in good shape. This was just as we had planned it to run. All things were good.

Meanwhile out on the road the Daves were hammering out a strong pace somewhere near Salome Arizona, about 350 miles into the race. That pace had brought them all the way up to second place, just behind Team Innovation Africa. Team Innovation Africa was made up of four strong American riders. Innovation Africa is a non-profit organization that brings Israeli innovation to African villages. It is a cool thing that they do, raising money and really changing peoples' lives. For now, all we want to do is beat them up. Riders, Chris De Marchi, Kurt Broadhag, Andre Gonzales and Tony Restuccia made up the foursome. These guys were going to be our strongest competition. Other teams included a German Team called four Athletes Powered by Stinger Bikes; Peter Sheets, Frederic Fust, Frank Vertical and Robert Dicks. They too were incredibly strong and an amazing team. We would battle with these two teams throughout the race. Throughout the night, the Daves were awesome, duking it out with the Germans and inching up to Team Innovation Africa. They had made up a ton of ground. I think it was like 4:30 am when Ben and I had been woken up to take our second shift. I would take the handoff from DZ.

The next moments are about waking up and getting dressed quickly, eating some breakfast and having coffee to make it all feel normal. Outside it was still dark and a little chilly. My body did not feel like being awake yet. My legs felt heavy and sluggish, but my mind was still excited. I could tell my pulse had already climbed a bit and now I could feel my muscles buzz. The crew had been up all night and they looked like it—tired and ready for a break. Mirra came in with the transition vehicle about five minutes ahead of DZ. Mirra was still amped up. He said they were right on the leaders now and we could take over the lead if we go hard. Our overall feeling was still super high about being in the race. This was the first race morning. Wake up and race, like an emergency that forces you to rise and react. No pressure, just go out and fight for the lead right now at the crack of dawn.

In the distance, I could see the shadows coming from the cars' headlights; a little freaky looking, like monsters coming at you from the darkness. When the two teams are this close, you cannot be sure who it is until they are literally right on top of you. It is an eerie sight actually. The rider is just a silhouette against the headlights and looks like a big insect churning back and forth. I was straddling my bike in front of the transition vehicle's headlights, waiting with one foot clipped in, ready to go, waiting for Dave Z to come in for the tag. Then as the first rider came in, I saw that it was Team Innovation Africa. And as they whizzed by I could see DZ and our car just behind them. As Dave screeched into a stop he said, "Ok, there they are MD. Go get em." And, I took off. I was sure that we were making it happen now and saw that we must be stronger because we had caught them. I pedaled out and into the shift again a bit too hard and quickly into the red where my heart rate maxed out. I tried not to show it and just started to maintain at a slightly slower speed.

I actually thought that this probably would not last too long. This was only the beginning of the race. We were surely going to pull out a gap on the other teams. After we had a lead, we would be able to focus on the clock and that would be it. It was still dark. After I let off the gas a little I recovered and then just tried to stay steady and I followed close behind the Team Innovation Africa rider and follow car. I did not fight for the lead but stayed steady and soon I was able to pass I did. There was a brief exchange of words as I came alongside the other rider. "It's about time" I think I heard him say? "Time for what?" I thought to myself. It felt strange to put out a big effort to make a pass then to slow down once I had passed. I just tried to recover and maintained my pace. DZ must have been sitting on them and letting the pressure get to them. Just a little while later they had increased their pace and went back by me, but there were no words exchanged this time. This was going to last until the sun came up. We went back and forth in the lead, staying close all the whole way to time station #6 in Congress, Arizona.. Ben would usually make the passes and I was usually being passed. The road had started to straighten out. I could see the silhouette of a mountain ahead in the distance as the sun began to rise. I cannot be sure but on this night or morning, Ben and I would be paired up against De Marchi and another rider. Maybe Andre? That was what it seemed like so far. I think they were doing the same 2-man shifts that we were. We were not sure of their strategy and the way they shifted in and out.

Just before we got to Congress, De Marchi passed me. When he came by me, he slapped me on the ass, smiled back and pedaled up the road. Damn, I was trying to maintain a 23 mph average speed for much of the shift and now we had a steady stretch of road that had a slight incline. I was riding the TT bike and actually starting to feel good on it. The seat is a little strange for me and my ass was feeling it. My sit bones had developed a sore spot from the front edge of the seat, like a little marble full of nerve endings. I remember the speed I was pedaling was 20 mph. Not quite 23 and I was putting out a lot of effort at the time. As the sun began to light up the distant mountains, the crisp cool air of an early morning in the desert, felt good against our all-out effort. De Marchi is damn strong. On the flat roads these guys we going to walk away from me if I did not get my ass in gear. I knew I needed to lift my pace somehow.

De Marchi is an amazing athlete. He is a long time racer and triathlete. He lives in Southern California, right by my old hometown. I do not know him personally but we have some mutual friends. I know more of him than him personally and his legend is growing. He has a reputation for being super strong no matter what it is he is doing. Damn, I cannot believe he slapped me and smiled like that. He and all of his teammates were going to be our battle. It was going to be a regular occurrence to be standing with my bike roadside while waiting for exchanges and seeing these people pass. We would often be offering encouragement and support to these guys and they would do the same for us. Other than the time stations on the race route out there on the RAAM you had only each other. You had your own team and your competition. It felt natural to be in it together and we saw it as a good reason to support each other.

The Congress, Arizona Time Station belongs to and is supported by the "Bull Shifters" bicycle club a group of some real RAAM supporters with incredible hospitality. They put out a buffet of food and snacks, multiple rooms to shower and rest, a pool with cool water and a few amenities that are more special. They have been an important stop for RAAM over the years and they are a fun and festive group of people who treat everyone as a hero. This is where I would transition with Ben. As Ben took the road, I stopped at this famous "oasis in the desert," as it is so often called. Right away the people remembered me from last year and were super happy to see me. It was uplifting and it was nice to receive such a greeting after the night's long hard battle. From Congress we had a serious climb leading out of town, the daunting Yarnell Grade. Ben wanted to do the whole climb by himself. The climb was maybe three or so miles and would take close to 20 minutes. Ben took off after De Marchi hauling ass until he broke a chain. The follow car guys changed him out with his TT bike after he had lost close to 5 minutes. All I could do was wait up the road and listen over the radio. We had only TT bikes for the remainder of the shift and we lost a little ground but not too much. We would descend into time station 7 in Prescott, Arizona and make a team change. I think it was like 11:00 am race time on Sunday the 15th. I can always tell when I am in Arizona by the red chalk color in the asphalt.

At this team exchange, we started to get it right. It felt more organized and comfortable and it was easier to read each other too. We were also getting tired and looking it. The crew was beginning to look haggard and spent. Bodies were not moving as fast as the day before and there was an easy feeling to the madness of it. The brain starts to get a little sloppy, fuzzy and slow. Wayne in particular was looking like he needed a sleep break. I'm sure that he had not gone down since the start. When I came in, I was going to eat quickly, clean my crotch and go to sleep. The last shift on my bike was racing for the bunk on the RV. We handed off and quickly dropped for rest. "See ya Daves."

[THE MORNING SHIFT: DZ prepares to take over at the team transition point while Mirra, Robson and Stephen stand by. Rush was filming throughout the first few days before he too became a true crewmember and the RV MacGyver.]

As the Daves went to work on Team Innovation Africa, Ben and I would get some needed rest. I was not feeling so great and my stomach was in a twist over the meds and nerves. I had gone way too light on the meds, my tooth was now aching, and I was now dealing with a shitty stomach. Ben seemed to be in a bit of pain and discomfort too. This showed me that I was doing ok because I knew if he was hurting too. It sounds strange to put it that way but it was true. I just wanted to know that I was not alone here and that we all were feeling fucking wiped out. The Daves managed to put us into the lead while we were resting. There was so much going on out there on the road where the drama played out and it felt somewhat strange to be trying to sleep when I wanted to ride along and watch the Daves race. It was hard to get to sleep and then became hard to wake up too. I had started to wheeze from congestion and it got worse when I lay down. This would play out every time I slept and it would get worse all the way across the country.

"What day is it, damn you?" That would be the feeling when we would wake up. Wake up, dress, eat then ride and we were going to be just in front of or behind Team Innovation Africa. It would be the same every time we rode. Full gas for 15 or 20 minutes and then Ben for his shift and we would do this nine to 12 times a shift. We would continue to repeat this again and again as the race travelled across the country. At times, we would be trashed and lethargic. We would be ruined. Moreover, at other times we were lifted up on a high that rolled us along like a freight train. Then we were just riding along like shadows or ghosts just dancing in with the wind without much feeling at all, just humming along to a song. "I'm just sitting here watching the wheels go round and round, I really love to watch them roll. No longer riding on the merry go round. - John Lennon – "I just had to let it go" It was all these things and then some as the scenery passed you by. I think this was the time that music began to be on my mind a lot. It kind of sucks if you have a song on your mind that you are unsure of all the lyrics and you just keep repeating the sections that you know again and again—for like 4 to 5 hours "Awake, Shake dreams from you hair   My pretty child, my sweet one,   Choose the day and choose the sign of your day, The day's divinity, first thing you see,", The Doors...Songs to meditate to and meditations to keep my rhythm. I would wake to songs that were stuck in my mind, echoes of my dreams, skipping repeatedly and over the same section of the song. Sometimes I sang aloud and others I might just hum. I also tapped and grinded my teeth to the rhythm and matched the pace of my cadence. It was a needed distraction at times and a healthy motivator. Next time I will surely have a music player on me.

Out on the road the Daves made the pass on Team Innovation Africa. The Legends were now into the lead. I think the high temperatures were getting to all the racers today. In the high 90F degree temperature the RV had become like a sauna. I heard that both teams were really motoring and changing the lead back and forth before the Daves were able to pull away a bit. Ben and I were up and ready for our shift with an excited and upbeat attitude. This was the only time that we were both sharp and ready to attack the shift--maybe just a bit too excited. As we got ready, we had heard the good news that we had the lead. It was just over 24 hours after the race had started. Ben and I had a section ahead of us that looked like mostly descending. Add a tailwind to that too. Thank you God. We were in a good mood and ready to get rolling. Trouble was that the rider coming in was here faster than they were expecting and all the vehicles came to a stop together. Drivers and navigators had hopped out to change with fresh ones and mass confusion took over. Who was going in what car? Who was resting? Who was changing this and that? I had started to pedal when DZ and I crossed wheels and Wayne screamed, "Stop" So, I did and froze for a moment like a gun fighter with an itchy finger.

8 LOST, PAIN AND AWE

Flagstaff, Arizona. I had been ready and had started to take off directly and had not allowed for the change they had planned. The navigator had not been ready and for whatever reason we ended up getting off course pretty much right out into the shift. Perhaps a bit of mental exhaustion had begun to play a part in our race. We zigzagged through Flagstaff for nearly 40 minutes making no forward progress before finally getting back on course. I was on the bike; Wayne and Dave were in the follow car. I just kept rolling with the direction changes until I found myself off in some golf course community and just lost it. I just flat stopped and started screaming at the two. "I am not fucking moving until you know where we need to go to get back on course, this is bullshit!" Wayne may have made a mental error because he had not slept in the last 40 or so hours. Compounding the situation was my quick exit from the transition. By the way, we had dropped to third place overall now. This would be tough on both Wayne and me. We were both getting fired up. Even the German team had passed us. While I was traversing the local strip malls and a few residential districts, the other teams were pulling away. Ben was up the road parked, watching us on Tractalis (a transponder system that tracks each rider's location). WTF are these guys doing? I was tired and needed a change and just to be back on course. Finally, after a heap of extra mileage and a few return car rides we got back on track and pushed hard into the lower desert. Panic is not good on RAAM, period. Getting lost was just unacceptable. Truth is that it is very confusing at times and hard to stay perfect the whole 3,000 miles.

Before the start, back at the guesthouse, we had Garmin 1000 GPS's for each rider, with backups and we had units for the vehicles. The best GPS systems available and we had overlooked this one small detail and its importance. The manual, reading the manual and knowing the operations of these amazing devices. There was no go to guy with Garmin along and no one in the crew seemed to have read the manual thoroughly. I know I had not read it. I am a rider I thought, and a fairly lazy and stupid one, especially now. Without a figurehead, no one would manage or teach the system to the riders and or navigators. As for the riders, I never got my 1000 as it seemed to disappear almost instantly so I used a backup 800., DZ lost his during the first shift when it fell from the bike mount, Ben used his own and Dave Mirra managed his, but was unsure how much to trust it because he really didn't know it that well. We had planned to use the units on the bicycles as a backup and follow the directions given by the follow vehicle, or, navigator. They were guiding from the RAAM maps. First the RAAM maps and second it was the Garmins. It was tough out there and when you had made such huge efforts and built a lead only to lose it due to a navigational error, you were pretty pissed off. I had heard that Mirra was riding the crew a bit regarding some missed directions. Robson, our crew chief, had been blitzed a few times by Mirra. Clearly, Mirra was not here to lose this race for any reason, especially not a navigational reason. I have to laugh now about this, but in the moment, you really feel the stress racing through your body at maximum heart rate.

Finally, we are back on course and the ride is nice again. Leaving Flagstaff there is a huge steady descent into time station #10 in Tuba City. I still could not see the leading teams ahead of us but the view was amazing. As we came from off the mountain into the valley, I felt like I was in a post card. We had a tailwind and were cruising at around 40 mph for like 20 minutes. I was all tucked in and riding the wave when a red jeep pulled along next to the driver and me started to yell something I could not understand. I was thinking, "WTF, what an ass. Why is this guy messing with me like this in the middle of the desert?" I glanced over and realized that I actually knew the guy from the neighborhood where I grew up. It was weird seeing someone I knew out here in the middle of the desert. After my shift, he pulled into where we had parked and we talked briefly before moving on. His name is Jim Tolly and he had read my recent Facebook posts and knew we would be coming through. It was super cool he came to see me. Super good person, always has been.

This section was really fast. I can only guess the average speed. Most of the mileage was downhill with a tailwind. It was hot out and the sun was beating down on us. You could really get the feel of the dry desert air and the constant winds. The scenery was epic, just like a post card. The views were pure American Wild West, history book style. This is cowboy and Indian country here. The shift was fast because of the wind and the long steady descent. We were at the team transition point somewhat quick or maybe it just felt that way. I hoped that we closed up a bit of the lead we had lost so the Daves would not be too bummed at us. The Daves woke up to news that we had gotten lost and we were now like 10 minutes behind Team Innovation Africa. They were not pleased and let us know it when we came into transition

[ROLLING REUNION: Jim Tolly shot this picture of me through the window of his jeep. I'm smiling here but a few moments before this picture I was sort of annoyed at this red jeep pacing me and a guy yelling out the window at me. RAAM is a crazy race.]

"Go get 'em, Dave," is all we could say as the Daves took off into one of their best shifts of the entire race. They would regain the lead and had the beautiful backdrop of Monument Valley with tailwinds to do it. Mirra said that he actually powered by one of the Team Innovation Africa guys on a descent at about 40mph. The Daves were pleased with themselves as they came in. They had really put in a huge shift. I think both of them rode at their limit to get back into the lead. I could not help but wonder what it was like. Wayne, Robson, and the crew must be getting to see some awesome racing and riding. I mean, Dave Mirra and Dave Zabriskie on TT bikes with a 20 mph tail wind... It was late in the day and the sun was starting to go down. We were on the eastern side of Monument Valley on Highway 163. Ben and I would take over. We were entering Utah. The Sun was setting as The Daves came in. Ben would take the first shift. Zabriskie came in and said, "We're out front AGAIN. Don't mess it up." Ben and I were equally motivated because of how the last shift went and were ready for this one. Ben went out hard and set the bar high for us. Ben really is a beast of an athlete and he was really pushing.

There was a good feeling in the transition vehicle as I got out and ready to change out with Ben. The first shift I took turned out to be a real killer. I couldn't breathe deep or clean and shallow breathing is impossible at this pace. During the break or our sleep session, I developed some more congestion in my lungs. What was happening to me?

I was now spitting up big, bloody, phlegm cookies. I could not take a full breath. I was hyperventilating. To make things worse I looked down at the speedometer and it read only 17 mph. I tried to talk to Wayne over the radio and could barely speak. Then in the second shift with hope to improve, I was hardly any better. I was struggling the same. When I got on the bike, I was in complete agony, just gasping for breath. I could not understand it. What was happening to me? I needed to check out mentally, I was in such a state of confusion. I just quietly went inward and tried to think of something else, anything else, until it would pass and I could ride. There was a silence on the radio and I could just imagine what they were thinking, "What is going on?" The dread of feeling no strength at all was scary. I was scared I would let the guys and the whole team down. I just kept pedaling and detaching until I could feel like I was somewhere else. Feel like I am dreaming without the physical pain. I began to repeat God's Prayer over and over in time with my cadence I breathed out the words over and over again. Tucked in and aerodynamic. And eventually I was gone, or the suffering was gone.

There were some magical moments out there as well. The moon would become so big in the evening sky to light our way along this death march to the east. Sunsets pouring golden fire over the desert floor through the fading light. And a sense of warmth that can ease the pain of extreme efforts and calm the soul. Wind and tailwind, beautiful. We were moving through Utah and into Colorado. Monument Valley was so beautiful and we were there at sunset. Everything was lit up in the golden hour and we were so fast, 30-ish mph for what seemed like hours. Eventually we went into the night and the winds finally died so we were cruising at around 25- plus mph. Each shift seemed short and the 5-plus hours went by so fast. Ben and I were caught in a moment that would last for the remainder of the race. At least this feeling would stay with us, lifting our spirits.

Back into reality, I was still having a bitch of a time breathing. I had just told Wayne on my radio. I was actually gasping a lot. I could taste blood in my mouth from the efforts. What else is new? The terrain heading towards time station 12 in Mexican Hat, Utah (approximately 730 miles into the race) was rolling hills and desert shelves.

[MONUMENTAL MOMENT: Awe inspiring views on a warm June Monument Valley sunset to start Monday night's shift and another slugfest with Team Innovation Africa.

We had just gotten a smoking fast, cross/tail wind and we were starting a long but rolling descent. TT bikes are very new to me. I have absolutely no clue what to expect from the bike or of riding one in cross winds. The Cervelo P5 is such an amazing bike. Nevertheless, at 50 mph with a cross/tail wind it was sketchy as hell. When the wind hits from the side it feels like you are in a shopping cart. I am just trying to get some weight on the front wheel. The front end feels so light, like it could just slide right from under me. In this kind of wind, you can go with the wind or turn into the wind to manage good traction, but you only have a little wiggle room for any surprises. I went with the wind to get more speed. Trying to force it is risky, shit. It is all risky riding in this kind of wind, but I didn't want to lose the speed. I needed to make up time for what I had lost in the flats.

After I had suffered so badly and slowed over the recent rollers, there was no way I was going to hit the brakes or sit up into the wind and kill this momentum now. I stayed tucked and went with it. There was a moment that I could hear Wayne on the headset telling me to take it easy and then a few ooohs and awes based on my body language and then a moment of silence as I was shoved out towards the centerline by a huge gust of wind. I was trying not to hit the center reflectors or go into the oncoming lane. If you hit the reflectors, the front wheel was sure to deflect like a stone and skip sideways. When you hit a reflector at that speed, it feels like hitting a hand grenade. All the energy goes right through your hands and into your body. The oncoming lane is, well, let's just not go there because there is a truck over there coming up the road at us. All this risk seemed necessary to make up the time I lost and worth it. Really? The road veered left in the same direction as the wind and started to flatten out. "You ok buddy?" Wayne asked. "Yeah, I think so," I said. Then, as the sun went down and it cooled off a bit, I started to feel a little better. My body regained some strength and my prayers were answered.

And suddenly it seemed like it was pitch black everywhere outside the straight shooting beam of our lights. There was a bridge, a river crossing at the bottom of the hill and then a sharp right. I was breathing better, feeling better. This was going to be a long pull for Ben and me. A long and hard night. Ben was riding strong, as usual. I was thinking to myself, "He just keeps getting stronger. Is that possible?" It is a bit freaky really. Ben is a specimen. Watching him hammer inspired me to put in a similar effort, at least the best one that I could.

[NIGHT MOVES: This is what a RAAM follow car crew sees for hours...and hours...and hours.]

We were both suffering, but we kept feeding off each other and, we became stronger as a team. Fifteen-minute intervals are not really that long when you think about it. Fifteen on. Fifteen off. We got equal the rest to balance out the effort. I would look forward to that chance to regroup; I could trust that my skyrocketing heart rate would get an opportunity to settle down to normal, for a little bit anyway. I knew that the pain would last no longer than that 15 minutes and that is all. Leading up to RAAM I had been doing interval training under the guidance of my coach, that masterful man Dean Golich. All that practice gave me acute awareness of my ability to recover. Awareness gave me confidence. Confidence that could make or break me.

The remainder of the shift was extremely tough. My very slow start had given Team Innovation Africa a chance to close in on us. They were right behind us again. I could see their headlights and flashers behind us and soon their transition vehicle passed us. It was really getting tight. While Ben was on the bike, we positioned for the next rider change at a section of road that was also a road change from highway 162 to Ismay Trading Post road. This is in the middle of nowhere. As we parked the transition vehicle, the Team Innovation Africa vehicle pulled just in front of us for their exchange. We got out and got ready for Ben to come in and they also had a rider on the road waiting.

I guess this is RAAM, you are not just seeing and racing another cyclist, you are seeing a follow vehicle, a transition vehicle and occasionally a motorhome. There are two or three crew and a second and sometimes a third cyclist. All the vehicles with flashing lights and busy crews, jockeying for positions for rider changes in the best roadside locations that are all first come first serve. Vehicles racing past, stopping abruptly, riders and crew jumping out getting ready for a rider change as you pass, and this is going on throughout the shift tonight. After approximately 33 hours and 820 miles into the race this is happening at 11 pm-ish in the middle of nowhere USA and all this crazy stuff is going on and it is as intense as Indy 500 pit stops.

Looking back down the road for Ben I am feeling a bit bad that we (or I) have let them catch us and I want to make a good ride to the next team transition. I do not want to let the guys down. I see Ben is coming in first. As Ben comes my way, the Team Innovation Africa rider readies for his incoming rider. I take off right in front of the other rider and his follow car coming in. I take off with my follow car in tow with the Innovation rider and his car just behind. They are right behind me so I stay steady for now, making sure not to overdo it and cook myself. The road is rolling up and down; it runs next to a dry riverbed so there will be some rolling terrain for a while. It is pitch black except for the lights of our bikes and cars. After a few miles I can tell by the shadows cast from the cars' lights that I have pulled out just a bit and see that this is my chance to get ahead. I'm feeling better now and breathing almost clearly. Not gasping anymore. I start to pick up the pace. I am watching only the speed on my Garmin. It is not easy to accelerate without a price though. I begin to hit the wall and start to fade a bit. But they must have had the same problem because we kept pulling ahead. Soon I transition to Ben. Ben is actually surprised that it is just me coming in with a lead and jumps to the occasion with his full effort and we continue to surge ahead. We both have risen to the occasion on this tough night. There was no way I could have seen this improvement in my body during this shift. I cannot explain it. When we come into time station #13 in Cortez, Colorado we are all smiles, but totally wiped out. I am happy for now but I also have to say I am fearful of the next shift, as my body will surely feel tonight's effort. The cost of efforts like this is unknown to me right now, but there really is no other way. I must be at this pace or I will let the team down and I know this. I have no choice, maintain the pace or die trying.

maintain the pace or die trying.

9 THE TRAINING

For the last year, I had been training hard with the guidance of Dean Golich. Dean had designed my workouts very well and I did exactly what he had laid out for me to do. Dean was my trainer/coach for the whole year in preparation for RAAM. He is a highly respected trainer for "real" world-class athletes with Carmichael Training Systems. Honestly, I am not sure of the details that brought us together. I believe it was Brian, Rick and Fred who had arranged it. Regardless, I was very lucky to have Dean's help. Dean and I hit it off pretty quickly and did have associations with a few motorcycle riders that he worked with. To be ready for this RAAM we did a ton of mileage training for endurance, interval training; climbing too with quite a few alternative types of workouts. This year I had ridden over 10,000 miles of road training and countless hours on the cycle trainer in my home or on the road at hotels and gyms around the country. Still, I wish I'd had more time to train. I wanted to be faster than I was and certainly more fit.

When the plan to do solo RAAM had changed and became a 4- man team, Dean was able to change up the program to a more intense schedule of intervals and TT style workouts. We already had some base fitness to work from. In a sense, it was a blessing to have trained for the endurance first and then started to build speed. I just needed a few more years of it to do solo to be totally honest.

Remember that Jure Robic said that you are training all of your life for RAAM. It is true. This race is so long and tough that you can only prepare by doing it all the time. If you are to run a marathon, you must be capable of running for 26.2 miles straight. To train you can run repeatedly half that distance and even 16 or 18 mile distances etc. That method doesn't apply to RAAM; training ride simulations for half the distance of RAAM would be like 4 or 5 days straight. It is like riding from LA to Kansas just for training. I am officially training for the solo RAAM now and forever because I want to be ready in 2018 or 2019 or whenever I can make it happen. Anyway, there is so much to do still to be ready for it. It is all the training in all your life that you will need and more.

I have never been so fit for an endurance race in my life, yet there is no substitute for youth and I do not have that anymore. Dean has been the only way for me to get it together. The perfect guide. Any fool could take a young athlete in his or her prime and make it happen physically.

Shit, nowadays you can just Google it. But for me, I am nearly 50 with a huge list of old injuries and a long list of, shall I say, issues. I used to smoke a pack of cigarettes a day, drink like a fish and I had a habit of destroying myself chemically on the weekends. It has only been a handful of years that I have started to treat myself with the love and respect as we all should. It has made me a better listener as well and one that wants to find a better way. Brenda always shares what she can about diet and rest. Her knowledge about the body is deeper than anyone else I know and thank God, she is on my team.

I had also gotten help from Jennifer McDaniel from CTS on my diet and to see if there were problems or room for improvement. I had to jump through a few hoops to get to the bottom of three days of complete detailed and itemized accounts of all my foods and drinks. Apparently and unbelievably I was close with the diet thanks to my Brenda. I had been losing weight from all the long endurance workouts already but there was still a need for more power. Power to weight ratio is no bull. That is constant work for me. I love to eat even when I do not need it and I love beer. Anyway, with the new team and plan I am really focused to get my diet right. I would also get some help from Ben with vitamins and Brenda would keep me honest by reminding me about what I was consuming and suggesting meat or vegetarian and so on. And she would give me a verbal beating when I had too many beers.

Dean would typically give me a three-week program to work from. This consisted of endurance workouts, speed workouts and intervals. Most of the workouts would work on either the road or a stationary trainer but the climbing workouts needed to be done on climbs. You can simulate a climb on a trainer, but it is just nowhere near the same. Once I got the TT bike, I had an addition to the intervals that was cool. I had a place near my home where I did intervals on the TT bike. It was flat with a few roller style climbs and had only stop signs; no traffic lights. Depending on the scheduled intervals of the workouts, whether they were 3minute, 6-minute, 9 minute, 12-minute, 15-minute or 18-minute intervals, I could do them there. It was a retirement community called Oakmont in Santa Rosa by my home. It was a circular loop of 8-ish miles through neighborhoods and around a golf course. When I started doing 20-minute intervals, it worked out perfect. There was a bench seat at my start point and it was just over twenty minutes a lap at threshold (full effort). I would do 20 minutes on and 20 minutes off, resting on the bench. I would do as many intervals as Dean had designed for me before returning home. During RAAM, I would be doing a lot of these. Like 5 hours every other 5 hours.

I also added a few simulation of the race. During a slower travel week in March, while Brenda was gone I tried a new work out. A three-day 4 hours on and four off. I rode four hours of 20-minute intervals and four hours of rest for three full days. During the night I would wake up every four hours and get right on my trainer to do 20-minute intervals for four hours then return to bed or just lay down on the couch. I was able to simulate the actual race feeling and testing the sleep deprivation too. On the trainer, it is hard to simulate the loads on your legs but there are not any stops or coasting either so it works out to be hard work. Four hours on a trainer is like 8 hours on the road. One plus or minus is that you sweat like a pig indoors. You can lose some weight and you can get saddle sores. The house smelled like a gymnasium for a while after I was done. I watched a lot of videos. Bicycle Dreams (a RAAM documentary film) and The Bible series, both were well worn from these workouts.

At times my life schedule was making it, not just challenging to have time to train, but just way too hard to stay healthy. Occasionally Dean would say he didn't know how I could be balancing work travel and still keep the training going without getting sick. I had over trained back in 1987 when I was a pro motocross racer and as a result I got Epstein-Barr virus. The virus could reappear if I get too tired and worn down and that could spell defeat or end this program completely. If I were to get sick again like that it would be over for sure. Dean took all of it into account. He was supportive and thoughtful of what to do. He made sense of it and he had worked out a perfect plan. I would go to the start line with the confidence that I had put in the work, that I would be better. I knew that I had the very best guy preparing me for RAAM. Dean was there with me to the end.

10 THE ROCKY MOUNTAINS

Through the early morning hours of Monday, June 16, the Daves really charged the Durango, Colorado. climb. The temperatures had dropped to near freezing. DZ had prepared for the cold from his experience as a cyclist and knew what to expect. Even he would later say that he was not ready for this type of cold. Mirra, on the other hand, was more worried about other things than cold. "Just give me my bike and let me ride," he would say. He was the hammerhead out there ready to get on and ride and not worry about extra layers of clothing. Mirra would find out just how cold it could get in the Rockies on a summer night.

Regardless of the cold, they were able to pick up a little more time and stretch out our lead. The Daves were deep into the climb when it really got cold. DZ had started to share his jacket with Mirra and they managed to get through it. Zabriskie would recall his younger days racing in these mountains in the Iron Horse Classic. It was daylight the last time he was there riding through the night and the cold was something new. It would be Zabriskie who would take the descent into the team change at time station #16 in Pagosa Springs, Colorado, 920-ish miles into the race. It was approximately 7:00 am Race time Monday, June16.

At dawn Ben and I woke up to take on Wolf Creek Pass, which at 10,857 feet, is the highest point on RAAM. It was cold out and I dressed for the occasion with under gear plus, arm and leg warmers. I got out into the air and started to hack up chest cookies. I would take the first shift from DZ at the team transition point at a 24-hour gas station. I got onto the bike and just got into it. The first shift was a rolling sort of a warm up for the actual climb. This would be the only time I felt like I could ride slowly into my shift and actually get a warm up. It was still dark, cold and quiet. I rode out of my sleepiness through the beautiful mountain scenery. The air was surprisingly thin and I could feel it. It was so quiet. A stream ran next to the road and I could hear the water running over the rocks. It would be a good time to fish I thought and could imagine my boys Hunter and Trevor fishing. I began to meditate on my pains. My lungs were wheezing and I was hacking out some ugly mucus. My legs were like lead. I needed to check out again and began to meditate, "May the words in my mouth and the meditations in my heart be pleasing to the Lord, my strength and my redeemer." David used this meditation and he went up against Goliath alone as a kid. I would repeat this until I got over the looming monster silhouetted by the rising sun, Wolf Creek Pass.

At the steepest part of the climb, Ben and I would take 1-mile shifts to manage a decent pace and to save strength. If you had not already guessed that I would say it, Ben is an awesome climber. He was pushing 12 to 14 mph on his turns and I was closer to 10 mph on mine. I had hoped for 14 mph and the actual grade would permit it, but the altitude was killing me. I could taste blood in my mouth from trying to keep 14 mph. The actual grade is easy and never gets too steep, but there is no oxygen. The cool crisp air felt great and it was a great time to get to this climb done but it had an effect on my lungs as if I had swallowed a torch. At around 7:00 am the sun was rising and there was a very peaceful, easy feeling that was completely humbling. Looking around gave you an immediate realization of how humble we all should be in this amazingly beautiful world but at the same time I am grinding the pedals and gasping for air.

There was hardly any traffic so rider exchanges were easy. Robson and Bishop were in the transition vehicle and seemed fresh. As we chipped away at this alpine climb, I noticed a guy standing on the side of the road up ahead. As I got closer, I could hear him yelling at me to suck it up and push harder. Are you kidding me? At first, I was thinking who would be out here at this time of the day just to bust my balls like this. As I got closer, I recognized that voice. It was Billy Edwards form last year's winning 8-man team, the Allied Forces. Billy is one amazing athlete and a good friend to me during the last year's coverage of RAAM he was probably the most covered and highlighted rider we followed on "Riding The Line."

[IN TRANSITION: Ben Bostrom pulls in as I pull out for another 10-20 minutes of "fun."]

Billy Edwards had made the drive from Boulder some three hours away. He had come all the way here at this time of the very early morning to cheer us on. Only someone that has done RAAM before would do such a thing. He was so inspiring to me at this moment. I remembered watching his team last year on this same climb. They were putting such huge efforts out to make good time. I had to show Billy I could be tough too and so I did suck it up. So thanks Billy for being there. I really needed the boost.

After multiple rider changes and a collision with our own transition vehicle, we reached the top in good time. Yup, on one of the rider changes I actually ran into Ben trying to come around the transition vehicle. I bounced off Ben and ran into the minivan and bounced off with my hip and shoulder. I didn't crash, but it did not feel too good either. We would later hear that the Team Innovation Africa guys had accused us of holding on to our own vehicles during the climb. Seems silly now, the thought of holding onto a parked vehicle to gain an advantage. It would make sense if the vehicle were actually moving. It is still a close competition between us and sometimes that can bring out the very worst of some people. There would be more attempts made to assess the Legends time penalties. Love that early desperation with only 2,000 miles to the finish line. Back at the climb it is just, "Ahh the relief of seeing the top of the pass." What does not kill you makes you stronger, or maybe weaker because there are so many more climbs to come.

The descent would be Ben's. And just as Ben took off on his TT bike and I sat into the transition vehicle to rest there would be a battery issue with his bike. The battery that powered his Shimano Di2 shifting was dead and he was stuck in the small chain ring, the one used for climbing. The batteries need charging every so often and all of Ben's were new and may not have gotten full charges before the install a few days prior. So, I jumped out with the P5 and got to take the descent. I was not expecting it but this is RAAM, and things change every moment and you must be ready. That is kind of a RAAM motto, "Shit happens. You deal with it, and move on." Gee, take the descent? Why not? It's all downhill. This was one hell of a morning. The road was still quiet without many cars. It was perfect for a while holding onto a good steady pace. After a while, the roads really flattened out and we met some head winds. It is demoralizing when it looks as if you are descending and you are working like a bitch and cannot make any good speed. Once Will, our mechanic was able to sort out Ben's mechanical issues, Ben and I would be on the road for about another hour and we would be changing out a few more times before we came in to make another team transition at a little service station at time station #18 in Alamosa, Colorado.

185

We were now 1,027 miles into the race. It had been almost 43 hours since we left Oceanside. Ben and I would drop fast for our rest. In fact, I cannot even remember any of the details here so we must have been tired. The Daves were back out there and they were banging it out once again on the TT bikes for a few hours until they reached Rough Mountain and Mt Mestas where they would switch to their Cervelo R5 road bikes and handle the climbing. It was getting windy and it was getting hot.. I heard it was like 90 degrees and it had the feel of Southern California's Santa Ana winds. There would be a good descent into time station #19 in La Veta, Colorado. Mirra took the descent and was doing his BMX thing bunny hopping and jumping stuff on the way down. Dave Mirra used to be a big flatland street guy back in the day., "Mr. Double Backflip or "the miracle boy" said it was super killer descent. From La Veta there was flat and rolling section before more climbing to our next team transition near Boyd Mountain where Ben and I waited. I believe that this is where the race is the toughest. The Rockies are the biggest hurdle in RAAM. There are many tough sections all the way through the race, but the Rockies are the toughest of all. They may not stop you here but the effects from all the thin air and massive climbing may get you later. I mean that if you are strong you will get over them and keep moving but, the damage you do to yourself here could end the race for you later. For me, it would leave my lungs in worse shape than they already were and they would get worse as the race went on.

After the last shift of climbing at altitude, I thought that we would wake up and be out of the Colorado Rocky Mountains. I wanted to breathe in some dense oxygen. But no. Robson woke Ben and me up in a place called (wait for it) Colorado Mountains! Shit, it was windy, and we were at a ski resort, or a camp. "I'm screwed," I thought and actually said the words out loud. I got dressed and went to Meg, our cook, and got some eggs and coffee. Dean Golich, my coach, had ridden his motorcycle to connect with us. Dean had been watching us on Tractalis. We had 15 or so minutes before the Daves would arrive and Dean and I got to visit. I told Dean how I was really doing. He was so excited that this was coming out so well. I was suddenly aware of what we were actually doing out here— what we were accomplishing. I was learning that people, many people were watching us race and following us. In the beginning a lot of people were sure we would not even finish the race. Well, Dean, the super smart guy that he is, gave me some suggestions to pace myself and to get some rest and healing. He understood how close this race had become and offered some suggestions about what I could do to save my strength and take care of my bronchial issues. He also told me that I should not get caught up in a race now. He said, "Wait till you are in like, Indiana to start racing." For now I should just ride the pace and speed that will leave me with some strength to finish strong, Let the race start with 800 miles or so to go. I know that he saw how spent I was and he could tell that I was going too hard and wanted me to keep some in the tank. That sounded good to me. Ben took the first shift out of the team exchange. He powered through the winds and the climb straight away. He started banging out the Ben Bostrom pace. Ben was up for the climb. I got my first shift in and the winds were actually swirling, so it felt good to have a breeze while climbing in this heat. I had to try to match Ben and show Dean that I was good. I wanted him to see that I was for real—a real fucking athlete. I needed to make him proud of me. I love that guy. The scenery was amazing, it could suddenly be a distraction from the pain of the steep, and oxygen deprived mountains. We pushed hard through a few shorter shifts to the top of the climb. After an hour or so, we started a steady descent that was going to last for the next 20 miles

[ROCKY MOUNTAIN HIGH: Ben powers over the top of La Veta in the Colorado Rockies.]

The afternoon heat felt good now at 30 plus mph. The wind had kicked up and turned an easy downhill cruise into a gusty and sketchy swerve fest. It had become hard to stay in the right lane. On one steep downward pitch a gust of wind pushed me across the centerline and the front wheel stepped over about a foot and it threw me into a swap that could have crashed me out. Dean would see the whole thing and I am sure he would later have laughs about it. A bike that weighs around 15 pounds goes flying when a big gust hits you sideways. Whenever you have a descent, you want to take advantage of it and make gravity work to your advantage. However, in this particular situation we needed to ease up and be safe rather than sorry.

Crashing in spandex at 50 mph on hot asphalt would be so hard to handle the winds were tricky but were also helping our pace. I passed a beautiful lake on top of this ridge called North Lake. It was not very big. It totally reminded me of Forrest Gump when Forrest said, "I just felt like running," and looked across this lake and pondered where the Earth ended and heaven began. As I looked across the lake, I could see two landscapes and two skies. The mental picture was taken and filed away with all the others that I experienced on RAAM. Every instant is another opportunity to capture a piece of Americana. About this time, we started a very long, gradual descent to time station #20 in Trinidad, Colorado. The wind had shifted and we got tailwinds all the way. As we descended, we keep looking back, realizing that t Team Innovation Africa was always close and there was no time to relax—ever, thanks to these people. Bastards! Why won't they just give up the battle?

Julie Lyons or Lori as I sometimes call her (I don't know why) was at the team transition point when I came in. Ben was riding the last leg and I came in the transition vehicle a few minutes before Ben would get there. I would hustle all the gear of Ben and I out and one of the Daves would throw their gear into the transition vehicle before heading out on their shift. Julie is a past RAAM champion from the 4-woman team Love, Sweat and Gears. I had the pleasure to meet her and Anne (her teammate and also amazing RAAM champion) from LSG last year. She came by to see us and brought me some presents, shirts and socks. When you are surprised like this, it brings a new sense of motivation and it brings a sense of fun again. I feel that "happy to be alive" and blessed feeling. This was a welcome reminder that this is an adventure I am living and not just about feeling broken down into this miserable suffer fest.

The Love Sweat and Gears team were taking the year off. Both Julie and Anne had been sending messages of encouragement to me for the whole year since we followed their race in 2013. I had thought that I might see a couple people that were around by coincidence and that might be it. For someone to come out and be there to show support still blows me away. Julie lives in Denver. That is like 200 miles from Trinidad! She drove all the way here to chance a quick meeting to support us. "What do I ever do for people I care for?" Is what I keep thinking. Julie, Billy,

Jim and that is just for me, Ben and the Daves also had support from friends and family. What a race this is! I could be at a race and see a friend out there on the track 30 feet from where I was standing and I would wait to see them until after the race. Maybe from now on a little effort to show support is what I will do. I will go to the fence and shout for them. I will wave and holler my support to them

11 THE CREW AND THE RV

The crew are really the tough ones out here. I may be suffering through shifts riding my bike but I get to lie down and sleep every five or so hours. These poor souls stick it out for 24-plus and they are not in comfort. They are stacked up in this RV like sardines, trying to keep motivated and manage roles in and out of the RV. Meg, our cook, is trying to keep the riders fed and handled as well as the crew and herself. Will, our mechanic, trying to keep equipment in top shape working in the hallway or anywhere in the RV. Once I saw him in the bathroom working. Robson and Wayne are working together to manage the race and the stops and the crew and the riders and themselves. Manley and Rush are keeping the motorhome and generator running so we have air conditioning, sometimes, well most of the time. This is sort of like the movies National Lampoons Vacation and the Great Race at the same time.

Our drivers were totally spent. Danny Kindregan was beat. Trashed. On at least one shift, he jumped out of the car during a riders change and forgot to put the car in park. The car drove itself out into a field but was not damaged. I heard that DZ was still in the back seat of the car when it drove off! I am sure there were was an interesting verbal exchange after that. Danny had been on a fast without sharing that information with us, which was surely contributing to his craziness. We had to stop for fuel while Ben was riding. A quick stop, right? Fuel up and go. We were at a gas stop and Danny was inside paying the bill. We were waiting a long time and I am in the transition vehicle at the pump with Rush, the navigator. "What is he doing in there?" I said to John. He said, "I don't know." Danny walked back super slowly and said the card was declined. I was getting a bit testy and said. "Well, say something man. Ben is out there on the road, let's get moving." Danny was then going to walk back in to use the bathroom and I yelled, "Hey Guy, we don't have fucking time for that." Danny is a great guy with skills up the ying-yang but, this type of fatigue wears anyone out and poor Danny was out of it. I could have just got pissed and left him there. Just drive away and got back into the race. However, we waited and Danny got it together.

Truth is that the crew role may just be more demanding than the rider's role. Maybe more work and a lot less fun. If you cannot get your rest, your condition deteriorates in a few days. There were some much testier crewmembers during the race because they were forced to step all over each other's toes. Or sleep on them. The RV was just not big enough to handle all these tired bodies. It kind of resembled a triage center during some kind of natural disaster or like a zombie movie where the survivors were held up in an RV. "Who was going to crack first?" I thought. And looking around the group you could only guess. Making things even more interesting was the way they had started to refuel themselves with gels, especially the double caffeine ones.

There were at least 10 people in the RV at all times. Brian Manley would become full time operator/driver and Rush would become our MacGyver, for the rest of the rig and troublesome things like the AC and electrical system. We had a few drivers to begin the race but after a few close calls (potentially bad close calls) including a near collision with a Team Innovation Africa cyclist (that was totally our fault) we insisted the Manley handle driving the RV permanently. Rush on the other hand had come on board to film. Then, he had taken the job as driver; navigator and then he would be the only one with the RV knowledge to keep the RV running and providing electricity and most importantly, air conditioning. This man was very important to our success and the safety of all persons here or on other teams we might meet. Rush, walked on water and we began to expect only perfection from him, which added to his stress.

[THE MOTHER SHIP: The RV had 10 people in it at most times during RAAM.]

The RV had two bunks in the rear area where the two riders off shift could sleep. This was off limits to the crew and for the riders only…If a regular crewmember were to be caught in a bunk, it would be a death sentence or a bus ticket at the next truck stop. It was set up with two cots that were bolted to the floor against the side walls. Two make shift clothes racks made of string or rope hung across the back and were full of rider's kits, jerseys and socks. The laundry hung to dry over piles of suitcases and boxes of stuff against the back wall. On the driver's side was the cot for Mirra and I. There were bottles of beet juice and other bottles of drinks under and around our cot. On the passenger side, DZ and Ben would share that cot. Their goodies would fill that side of the rig. It was stuffy and hot when the AC was off, which was often as the generator was on the fritz. There was a nice small kitchen and a shower (cold showers, low water or no water after Colorado. It was a crapshoot that usually ended with wet wipes) there was a couch on driver's side and across from that table was bench seats. These were occupied with bodies and gear. Above the driver and navigator was the only place for crewmembers to fully lie down for rest. With only room for two at a time, it was sacred ground for them. All other storage was located in belly boxes of the RV.

As we got deeper into the race humidity made things steamy, hot and the need for air conditioning grew. When we had no AC our attitudes went first to bad and then to plain ugly. We got very edgy. At those times, we were happier to be out on a shift. It was cooler when you were out on the road busting your ass. After a few miserable hours, sweating in the RV the only real noticeable resting place was in the transition vehicle between shifts. You knew you were resting in there and it was cool with the air conditioning or the windows down and the breeze flowing. Even for the short 15-minute break, you could feel the body release. A few times, I came in and actually slept for a 5-minute period. With food in my mouth and a bottle in my hand, I was out cold for a moment. We had a silver plastic cover over the back seat of the transition vehicle and a giant white cooler living where the middle seat used to be. It was filled with bottles of water, bottles of juice, Coke and a few lingering bottles of beet juice that Mirra had stationed there rolling about the ice and water that sloshed back and forth each time the van changed directions. It was strangely comforting to climb in and lay back while catching your breath.

The two vehicles and the RV started to have a frat house or beach house feel with food wrappers, pizza boxes, dirty socks, towels and shirts, empty bottles, unfinished cycling foods and extra gear strewn about the floor. In all the vehicles there were massive, overfull trash bags tied to cabinet handles in the RV or the seat headrest posts in the mini vans. The smells were getting awful. There was little time to do anything but keep moving and watch the mess grow big enough that it started to get in the way. At one point, there was a bag of trash hanging on the passenger seat headrest of the transition vehicle that was completely full, all 55 gallons of it. You had to hold it inside when you slammed the rolling side door or it would get caught.

At the start, we (riders and crew) were mostly strangers or only knew each briefly. Not to toot my own horn, but I travel in style most everywhere I go and I know that most of the other crew and all the riders do too. This was like travelling in an RV with Cousin Eddy, "Now that's an RV Clark." Regardless of the situations, the crew kept rising above personal challenges and making things happen. Just 30 or so hours after coming together as a team in Oceanside and we had been thrust into the intensely intimate setting of RAAM. After 40 hours on the road, there was no room for privacy or time to create it. There was only necessity. Anything else was added hassle that no one could give time to. Frankly, there was no time to give a fuck about vanity, personal hygiene or grooming. Race then food and rest were all we worried about.

We always had food to eat thanks to Meg. She was always ahead of us with preparations and seemed to know exactly what we needed. She is so caring and made us all feel like she was worried about each of us.. If anyone on this crew had ever given her a hard time the rest of us might have killed the culprit and left him out on the road somewhere. She was that important to us. Paige, our soigneur, managed us riders with the care of a single mother in a combat zone. She would prepare each outgoing team with all the necessities in our very own lunch boxes. They even had our names on them. She would also keep on top of our riding gear; helmets, gloves, glasses etc. She would then handle the incoming team's messes and reorganize. She managed both of these simultaneously. She would also provide care for any other ailments we riders might have. She took each of our issues into account and work on them with us to keep us strong. Ben had a broken rib just prior to the race and he would need to have care for this with some taping, icing and stretching. She also made sure that Ben had his Melatonin to help sleep. I had my root canal and needed meds and probiotics. We all had a list of items that she would need to prepare for us like recovery shakes and our preferred snack foods for each shift and finally one emergency stash of gear in case of any adverse weather.

Rick Tillery, the man of mystery, was growing on all of the riders with his solid, unbreakable optimism. I had a flush of calm come over me every time he was with Ben and me in the follow vehicle during our shifts. Usually at his side was Dave as his navigator or the roles were reversed, it made no difference. Many adjustments with crew were

[WASH DAY: Danny and Rush help Paige with the laundry. During roadside stops, the crew had to adapt to any and all conditions.]

happening all the time but there was just an added sense of comfort when Rick was there. It is very hard to stay confident and keep pushing your limits without a supportive crew. I can tell you that it was becoming very hard to not give 100% because our whole crew was giving at least that, 24 hours a day. Will, our mechanic had been busy maintaining all eight bicycles and now that we were a couple days into the race he was jumping into navigate to give other crewmembers some rest. In addition, we had Stephen Glidden.

Stephen Glidden may have been in the wrong place at the right time. He was our walk-on, a guy that just dropped by to wish Dave Mirra good luck at the start. Stephen lives in San Diego, close enough to drive over to the Oceanside Pier to see Dave start. He would be hurled into the RAAM on a day's notice. Mirra told him we were a man down and Stephen said, "Not anymore." I was putting the hurt on my body and soul every shift because they were too. We were all in this together. Did I mention that the crew was all volunteers? Yeah, I know I have. But damn, they were awesome! I cannot be more thankful for the job that they all did. Robson, Brian, Wayne and the rest of the crew were amazing. They were human too though and that made for some very interesting moments out there.

I am sure that there was a ton of stories playing out all over the place with the crew on board the RV, in the follow car and in the transition vehicle. With no privacy, no personal space, no sleep and no consistent meal schedule these were some irritable and testy people. I probably missed all the good stuff, but I saw plenty. Did I mention that Danny had been secretly fasting? He had a plan to cleanse and lose a few pounds I guess and did not find it relevant to share that with Robson Wayne or me. His behavior became a tell-tale sign as we lost the car off the road then when we stopped for gas and he seemed totally too relaxed to get moving, no urgency. I witnessed Paige and Robson having a meltdown about the laundry one morning and Stephen and will had a 5-hour dispute over control of the transition vehicle while highly charged on caffeinated cycling gel snacks. I had to jump in and throw a couple of cents in there too claiming I had had enough and that we would pull over at the next rest stop and get them a bus ticket home if there was not some calm restored to this vehicle.

12 KANSAS, MISSOURI AND DELIRIUM?

Ben and I would take over the road somewhere in Kansas. We knew the Daves had been pushing a fast pace and we wanted to match it if we could. We wanted to pull away and stretch our lead. Anyway, all four of us wanted to win and set a record. Oh yeah, there was the 4-rider record time of, 5 days, 8 hours and 17 minutes for an average speed of 23.06 mph. Now we were ahead of that time. I am not sure how many times we had gone off course, but it was starting to add up. If we were going to have a chance at the record, we had to pull things together on our navigation and stop getting off course or lost. We could not afford to lose any more time. That was going to be hard to do. The sun was setting behind us as we raced hard into long, straight stretches of roads in between endless cornfields. As the light fades, the fireflies start to clock in. The late evening light fades and you can see all their little sparkles of light Streaking about.

After 1,400 or so miles into the race, we were well into Kansas. It was late night; Ben was on the bike when we passed through Mullinville, home of acentric artist M.T. Liggit. We visited him last year and to he's an interesting guy is an understatement. He was downright scary and intimidating. He was also very protective of his territory. He had chased us around while we were trying to photograph his art. He had a crazy look in his eyes as he charged at us in his beat-up old truck. It was a good thing that it was late and he wasn't around. As we passed Leggit's property, I told Ben over the radio to look to his left. Ben was a bit shocked at the images of these giant statues of Leggit's lining the road. Some have political references of historic nature. There are swastikas, presidential goofs, cartoons of real characters and a woman with pointy breasts with a sign that read "Rapunzel." They are one of the eight wonders of Kansas you know. The artist's steel statues line the road standing at nearly 10 feet tall. They are mostly designed with moving parts that spin or rock in the wind and they move and creak like they are alive. The art has much symbolism and could not be more ironic and menacing staring down on the weary travelers of the road here in this Middle America farming community.

Kansas is pretty, ah, flat. Ben and I continued the night shift. It was warm with an eastern breeze. Many of the roads have what looks like white asphalt. Their roads have no bends in them. There are roads going east and west, north and south But, other than that it's kind of boring, like the movie Groundhog's day. You feel as if you are not going anywhere. I kept an eye out for Molokai and the children of the corn but nothing ever came out of those quiet, swaying cornfields but frogs, raccoons and armadillos. We stayed true to our pace. Ben did have a meeting with a raccoon the size of a small bear that demanded most of the roads shoulder beyond the fog line. I could hear him on the radio saying, "Holy shit! Was that a bear?"

Big rig trucks would come screaming by at 70 mph and scare the living shit out of us. I had heard that after you get tired out there during RAAM you start to like it when they pass because they pull you along with a vacuum-like suction. If you're struggling to maintain 25 mph and a truck blows by you, you will gain about 5 mph for at least 75 yards or so depending on how fast the truck was going. If you lean into them you really get sucked along. It was a sort of compromise with your safety in exchange for a few short-lived   miles per hour.   That night there was a crosswind that was both good and bad. It helped when I was going east and sucked when I was going south or southeast. I started to drift off into my thoughts, trying to divert my growing chest pain. Tonight I have the Bob Schneider song from Bicycle Dreams on my mind; I am singing it for most of my shifts.

"I have reason to believe the grass might be a little greener on the other side"

"I have reasons to believe that if I turned myself inside out I might get out alive"

"And I have reason to believe that if you get it right just once you would be…satisfied" Da, Da, Da

For a little while, I had pretty much forgotten that we were still in a close race with Team Innovation Africa. I had been so drawn into my own world that I had all but forgotten about them for most of this shift. The warm air and wind felt like summer time night pulling in memories of sensations my body had lost or forgot. The pain and the lack of power is what I could not forget. My body was having a hard time converting and delivering the oxygen to my muscles and every muscle in my body burned when I push hard. I just have to keep trying to think of other things. I started to think about Pikes Peak. I thought about how good it felt to ride well there. I recall the feeling of the horsepower of that bike, how hard it accelerated and how much fun it was to slide that big sucker into corners. The bike has like 165 hp. I was excited to go to Pikes Peak again. I had ridden there a couple weeks ago and it felt very good. I sure could use a little of that motor right now.

In 2013, I was the fastest qualifier at Pikes Peak. I was riding really, really well. The bike I rode was a 1200 cc Ducati Multistrada. It was a race version with special parts; it was 100lbs lighter than the production model found at your local Ducati dealer. It was very fast for this type of motorcycle. At Pikes Peak, the course is a twelve-mile winding mountain road ascending from 9,000 feet to over 14,000 feet. It has a 35 MPH maximum speed limit. There are like 156 corners and lots of bends and kinks too. The Multistrada is sort of an upright handlebar position road bike. So I can ride it like a Supermoto bike some times and a road racer other times. I love to slide that big bike into the corners and drag my knee through them. Top speed is somewhere near 165 mph on a fast straight. Riding this bike hard really feels good. Riding it hard at Pikes Peak, well, there is nothing quite like it in the world of racing that I have ever done that compares. It has such an effect on me that afterwards I have an emotional reaction that lingers for days. I can recall moments like these that carry me to a place that is far off from right now. I stay there as long as I can in my mind until Ben and I can be done with this shift.

I cannot recall the team exchange we had with the Daves or when it was. Damn, I cannot even recall when we got onto our next shift. This is the black hole called Kansas.

This is the place that we need to have a wormhole to fold time. There was a time while writing this story down that I actually thought that the team left me to sleep while the race kept going without me. I could not remember this section of the race for a few weeks and even now, my memory is vague at best. I remember being in the transition vehicle as Ben had crossed the official halfway point of the race in Pratt, Kansas. However, for the most part I have given up trying to remember it all. I used Google maps to get satellite photos of the course to see if I could remember it. But even then it doesn't all register. After RAAM, while I was at Pikes Peak I called Mirra after having a mental episode. I called Mirra when I needed a tune up sometimes. This time I accused him and the other riders of leaving me asleep in the RV while they raced, taking my shift. He just laughed at me and said that had never happened, that I had just imagined it. The problem was that I could not remember like 15 hours of the race. Mirra said it was all in my mind. He laughed at me for even coming up with the idea. I felt confused. But, he had talked me into laughing at myself and then we both just laughed at the idea. Our conversation turned into another talk about everything and nothing at all, just goofing on ourselves. Then it was his turn to go a bit crazy. Suddenly after I was calming down

Dave told me that he thought our crew chief Robson and Wayne had sabotaged our race so we would not break the 8-man overall team record. He seriously was convinced of it. I in turn laughed at him and told him that never happened either. After a while, we talked our way into some clarity about the mental fatigue we had experienced. I love the way a super tired mind gets all paranoid. The mind gets super mad and then super confused, even sad, and then it thinks everything is funny. I just love that.

It was not until we had reached the Missouri State Capital that my memory returns fully. I suddenly am awake and aware and I am on the bicycle. I had gotten on the highway and then got off then on then off again. We turned from the exit left then right onto a service road. It had to be early morning. I think it was., I don't know. But I know it was dark and there were hardly any people out, just partiers and a few vampires looking for a bite to eat. We were still managing to keep up the intense pace. Not long after I had raced at full speed around the Missouri State Capital building I passed time station #33 in Jefferson City, Missouri. We have now raced 1,900 miles. Even though I didn't stop, people at the time station were waving and yelling from the top of a grassy knoll to my left as I went down a road that flanked an interstate highway. I think they were wearing glowing lights or Christmas lights and costumes. I heard someone yell my name. Alternatively, maybe I was still a little goofy.

It is so uplifting to a rider's heart and soul to have the support and appreciation from the people at each one of the time stations, even if I am just imaging the costumes. I can only guess what it must be like to solo in this race, to be so alone and feel so tragic at times. Even for us as a 4-man team they can surprise you. When you are head down and pushing yourself to your physical limits you forget where you are and what is up ahead unless the follow car crew tells you over the radio to look. Time stations can be like a challenge or goal from one to the next. For us they are at times just transition points, mile markers or landmarks. However, they are always welcome stations for the RAAM racers and crews. We as a team must check in at all stations by phone as we pass. Each one is special in its own way. Each station has the standard equipment and amenities required by RAAM but it is the people staffing these outposts that add their personal touches that make each one special. They are all angels of mercy and of motivation and all of these people are volunteers. Is that a dying breed or what? I asked my son to volunteer for my RAAM crew and he asked, "How much does it pay?"

As for the end of the shift for Ben and I., I am without a single memory of the team exchange or where it happened. It was becoming very hard to focus on anything more than pedaling or sleeping. Eating and dressing were becoming chores. At this time, we were going off the directions and instructions from Wayne or Robson. They dictated when we rode and when we rested. Once I was on the bike or in the transition vehicle, I was into it. I was into the race mode. Did not matter where we were we would be riding hard and would fully feel a part of RAAM. However, when we were done and resting it felt like everything that we just did left us immediately. There is so little I can remember throughout this section of the race. I cannot recall if it was day or night that we transitioned with the Daves. Even months after the details are still missing. All through this day and night the memories are bleeding together. I can only go forward to the next clear team transition. Anything is possible out on the open road and with sleep deprivation; it was going to get hairy at times.

Ben and I awoke to our next shift. It was 5:00 am and still dark. We were waiting in what seemed to be a foggy marsh. Our RV was parked on a dirt road just off a small two-lane paved road. We had coffee and some eggs. It was a good start to the coming day. It would be a few minutes before the Daves would get to us. We actually got to be awake for a few minutes before the Daves came in for the team transition. The paved road reached back into the night and we would soon see the car headlights coming at us from over a mile away. I was taking the first shift and got out on the road with my Cervelo P5, all ready to go. They were close. I could see headlights in the distance. As they closed in, I could make out that it was our transition car. DZ was on board and hopped out with a smile and said, "What's up?" We talked briefly, everything seemed to be fun again, and we had some brief, but needed laughs. Then we could hear some shouting over the radio, Mirra screaming, "WTF?!" They were within a few miles and somehow got off course behind the transition vehicle. After a few minutes, Robson took off in the transition vehicle to go back and get them. Soon they were back on course and coming in. I would learn later when the sun started to light things up that this was not a wooded marsh at all. It was more farmland. This glorious early morning was nothing special but I can remember it clearly.

Into the dawn, Ben and I rode through farmland, on service roads and through the maze of cornfields. As the sun burned off the fog, corn was all that we could see. I was on the bike then and soon came out of the cornfields, around a couple rights and lefts and soon I would be crossing the Mississippi River. It was an early morning and the traffic was light on route 67 when I had the honor of crossing the bridge over the river. Cool, not just anybody can say they rode a bicycle over the mighty Mississippi River. The bridge was like going over a small climb, actually. There was a lane shut down for construction and our driver Rick Tillery was still at nighttime follow car distance of 50 feet. We backed up the traffic by a few cars but no big deal. We continued into our next transition area up the road at time station #36 in Greenville Illinois. Mile 2097. Less than one thousand miles left to go.

The motorhome sat in a McDonald's parking lot. I was starting to get excited to rest and here it was. The Daves were off and running and with a decent advantage over Team Innovation Africa. The sun felt good on my tired body as I took off my kit and took some air. Exhaustion plays out on everyone differently and it is funny how you act instinctually when you are so f-ing tired. As we sat there waiting to get moving I had been airing out my sore undercarriage. I remember that I asked Danny for a coffee and then just seemed to drift off as I stood there--alone, but not alone. The air was feeling good on my private parts. I was standing between the motorhome and a hedge as some time passed. Cars were driving by and suddenly Team Innovation Africa raced by on the road that paralleled us not far behind us, about ten or so miles. I knew that we must have a good 30-minute lead and the Daves would surely extend it. I waved as the team van went by and then their rider as I continued to air out. I would learn later that there was a potential protest against us for indecent exposure. Oops. I had been standing there naked.

After three days and a bunch of hours, we are truly in our own Missouri. This crew, they were now family. We accepted each other without vanity, without shame. To react to things from instinct without thought is clean and easy. Exotic or flat, with or without. The ego has left the equation. You start to peel away layers of yourself out there. You lose bits of your typical need for modesty; you just do not have the time or energy to care. The standard bullshit is gone and there is no worry about what anyone thinks.

We are ahead but not too far ahead of Team Innovation Africa. It was not a huge lead and even though a five-mile lead sounds huge, it is not when you consider that the race is 3,000 miles long. On a TT bike, you can cover five miles on average in about fifteen minutes. Fifteen minutes is nothing in a race that lasts over five days. Those mere five miles give or take seem sort of unthinkable now. Add fatigue, sleeplessness and stress to this and it was truly becoming intense. When we rode it was at maximum effort for us, and I am sure it was for Team Innovation Africa too. We couldn't get away from those guys. I thought for sure by then we would've been somewhat able to relax, even for a little bit. It was like a sprint to the finish every time we rode.

13 MANO A MANO IN ILLINOIS & INDIANA

We were over 2100 miles into the race and I was physically smoked. I had to mentally use my will to keep going hard and make my body do the pedaling. I was usually in some kind of meditative state where I spoke to God or pleaded to God. When I lay down to sleep I wasn't getting much rest anymore. It only took about an hour for the fluids in my chest to build up and for the wheezing and coughing to wake me. My legs started to retain water and swell while I rested. They weren't hurting or painful, just really heavy and dull. Sleeping became very difficult. Ben was taking Melatonin and slept pretty much right through the episodes, so at least he was getting some rest. Ben had been toughing through a broken rib that had him stiff and sore. We were quite a pair right at that moment. His sleeping aid looked to be working well and I wanted to try it, but was kind of scared I wouldn't wake up. At times it seemed he was slow to wake up and often looked pretty out it when we got up. He needed a Code Red style alarm clock like from the movie "A Few Good Men. Even when I was able to sleep through our rest shift and be woken up by a sweet, soft voice and a gentle shake it pissed me off because I wanted to stay asleep. The ice bucket alarm was a backup plan and had not been used to get anyone up…yet.

We were late into day three. Almost four days now of racing flat out and we could feel every effort in our bodies and minds. At that time, we are riding into Bloomington, Indiana, with only 720 miles to the finish line. On the bike, things felt good. Over the previous eight hours, The Legends crossed through Illinois and into Indiana. The story was the same though as far as our race with Innovation Africa—they were within 5 miles of us at all times. We had a couple of close moments and even lost the lead briefly. It was now a fight to stay up front. Mano A Mano. Their team seemed to have gotten stronger as the race progressed. We chose to do a split with 2-rider teams, to do equal shifts of 5 hours and it was working. But what had they done with their team's strategy? I heard that they were rotating three riders and letting one rider sleep for eight hours. Could that be a better strategy? That

It was interesting navigating through mostly major city streets and landmarks such as the sacred ground of the Hoosiers, Indiana University. It was late afternoon or early evening and it was kind of nice--hazy sunshine and a bit humid, but comfortable without a lot of traffic. I was on the TT bike racing through town with only one or two more shifts left for Ben and me that day. In cities, you can count on catching plenty of red lights, so we did get to rest a bit. It was a game of racing from the green to the next red light. We were soon coming in to a team change with the Daves. Over the headset Rick Tillery, the Man of mystery, tried to motivate me, I guess I was cruising a bit slow. He kept me informed of the landmarks and directions to remind me of the need for speed. The Man of Mystery is a pet name. I think I overheard DZ call him that back at the guesthouse, so that is what I started calling him. It felt good when he was there with us. I tried to pick up my pace from stoplight to stoplight while keeping an eye out for Ben and our next transition point. It suddenly seemed warm out, but it could have just been that my efforts had gotten harder. This place looked and felt like that eastern setting of the Golden Hour around a college campus. It turns out that it was actually around 1:00 pm and not evening at all.

Ben would take the final shift and I would ride in with the transition vehicle to the RV for the team change. At the RV, the team change was a bit messy. The crew coming in and the crew at the RV were not communicating well and the Daves were not ready. The exchange point was a strip mall parking lot. We lost some time as well as our cool. I could only look on without too much concern, as it would not benefit me to be involved in the frustration. My extreme fatigue and lack of interest could have been mistaken for Zen-like personal control, as I did not even bat an eye. After the mess, we quickly tried to get everyone moving and get back on the road. In our haste, we tried to pull out of the lot too quickly and almost ran over an Innovation Africa rider. They were much closer than we thought. Many words and flying finger gestures flew over the incident. F U. No one is hurt and everyone continued on. We were definitely in a close race. The time gap between them and us was maybe 5 minutes. As the Daves go to blows again with Innovation Africa we tried to rest. This time with no AC.

It was very hard to rest during the break. The roads we were driving to the next team transition were slow with many stops and direction changes, making sleep almost impossible, not to mention the extreme heat and humidity in the motorhome. It was hard to not lose it and just go on a wigger like a lunatic and start to scream at someone. I felt some wind through the small window and that is where I propped up my feet to try to pull it in toward me. The tensions built and soon my mind was full of stress. I could not believe that the Innovations riders were once again right on top of us. These guys are really fighters that just will not give up. Back at the start line, we had been hearing that many people thought that we were a joke. To think that there were many of the established ultra-endurance racers and teams that believed we would have quit the race by now. I wonder why there were so many people that did not believe in us. All of us have been successful in our other sports. We are all fit and extremely motivated. It seems that they had underestimated what kind of athletes that we are. They were wrong about us.

While Ben and I got some rest and I mean some, rest. The Daves got to work out on the road. I know that they are feeling pretty beat up as well, having spent the day in this sweat box with no air just to get out into a hot afternoon into sunset in humid old Indiana and Ohio. Mirra's patience was tested when he was sent off course again. I heard he had ripped Robson a new asshole again. Dave Mirra and his intensity just made me smile. I can just imagine that exchange with poor Robson trying to calm him down. Ohio would be somewhat flat you would think, but it really is not. There are all these little bumps that are steep little buggers. They are painfully steep when you consider that we were trying to keep a 25 mph average. As the Daves pulled into the team transition, we passed like ships in the night. No discussion that I can recall took place. Then again, it is hard to remember details other than "hurry up and get going."

Ben and I rode the late shift. Fireflies lined the country roads as we began. There were farms and marshes and rolling hills, and those nasty little steep pitches to blow up our legs and hearts. A thick blanket of fog covered the lower sections and we popped in and out of it as we rolled through. TT is the call for bikes tonight. We were making good time and were staying on course. A few turns were well hidden and tight. The headlights of the follow car can only travel so far and it was hard to see street signs to match the course map. The GPS is a key to staying on course. At night, there was no problem of heat or humidity. It was cool but not cold and felt refreshing in the wind as we rode. We passed a solo rider that had pulled over on the side of the road to sleep. It was an eerie sight to come around a bend and find vehicles and people moving about with flashing lights and reflectors. At first, I thought we might have come upon an accident. A serious snap to attention and respectfulness came over all of us riders and crew. We knew what they were going through and we all could respect that. We also passed another solo rider on the road and we took a moment to cheer him and his crew on with the feeling that we just saw a unicorn or a mythical being. I was reminded of the idea of solo. When I imagine myself riding solo for this whole race, I am emotional about it. It is so deeply stirring to my soul. I can almost feel it in me. I love imagining myself being in that hauntingly deep place on my own. I pray it will become a reality for me soon. I have faith that it is only a matter of when. After this long-ass year in preparation for RAAM Brenda had asked me to wait at least one year before I do my solo RAAM. It may be more a matter of time and money than anything else. I am crossing my fingers for that.

We knew, Innovation Africa was close that fourth night of RAAM. When I was in the vehicle, I was constantly looking behind us for cars with flashers. Whenever there were headlights coming behind us I would think it was them. They were so close that when we look at the Tractalis we had to zoom in so tight just to see the separation of our number and theirs. It seemed were separated by less than mile. I could not stand that we could not pull away. As I rode I wanted my legs to do more than they could. I took another Motrin to soften the pain in them, but my legs were just dead. My lungs continued to get worse too and that wasn't helping the situation. As I watched Ben tapping out a strong tempo, a very respectable pace, I felt as if I was the weak link. I wanted to be like him. He was a beast out there that night. I was praying, more like begging, God for the strength and courage to do the same pace as Ben. No matter what I said I couldn't seem to summon the power. There was no answer to that prayer, no miracles that night. I was so tired that I could sleep during my 15-minute breaks in the transition vehicle. Really. I could sleep for five or so minutes then ride and repeat. Thank God for Ben Bostrom to carry on so relentlessly and driven to take more time from those bastards. There was no giving up or even letting up for us. And the Daves too. No one ever let up. All these guys are warriors who went to the full limit again and again. I can also say with regards to Team Innovation Africa that I am equally impressed with them. They were worthy of the same respect as are all riders pushing hard to finish RAAM. I felt like we were dying a deep and painful death to beat them all and loving them for making us be our best.

That terrible night was super hard. My emotions were fragile and my temper was short. I was racing hard and trying even harder. I was at my limit of maximum effort, which at that point in the race was maybe half of my "normal" maximum effort. I was struggling to make speed and getting frustrated. Riding through a residential area and grinding over the small climbs and I was really losing it. It felt like I was coming undone and couldn't do a damn thing about it. Frustration and desperation were getting the best of me and I could hear myself screaming, "FUCK!" again and again. I wondered why I had the wind to scream words and not the strength in my legs to make power. Rick Tillery couldn't help but hear my screams and quickly pulled up alongside to see what was wrong. Rick asked, "What's wrong buddy?" I barked back at him to leave me alone, "I'm fucked." My legs never returned and all I could do was grit it out. I did the math in my head about how many more shifts I had that night but soon realized that I was crying; sobbing like a baby. I thought of turning into oncoming traffic to end it. But there was no one out here at that time of the morning to kill me. Then, as I continued to pound at the pedals with relentless desperation in my tearful eyes, through my dry throat I coughed out a chuckle of laughter. I was laughing! How desperate. Cracking like this is damn funny when you think about later, as in a month from now later. I can only guess if the man of mystery knew what I was going through that night, or what the poor residents might have been thinking. Can you imagine a cyclist and a follow car with flashers driving through your neighborhood at 3:00 am with someone screaming "FUCK, FUCK, FUCK?"

I can remember pushing myself to the limit during my career in motorcycle racing. Getting to that place where your physical limit meets your pride. They do not care a single bit for each other and there is no way that they can be friends. There will be no deals made with these two. You cannot keep them close to each other. When I was younger, my pride got beat a few times and it still haunts me, even today. I was just 18 years old and racing the 500cc United States Grand Prix in Carlsbad California in 1984 I was a factory Husqvarna rider racing against the world's best international riders. In the first 45-minute race, I rode very well and finished fifth. I gave it everything I had in the first race so the second race was going to be a real physical test. In race two I started around 10th place and was riding okay. However, I was so tired, so completely tired. The exhaust pipe had been burning my leg as I clung to the bike with my hips and legs. I was so tired that my hands were falling off the handlebars, so I had to cling with my legs. The burning got to me and I just gave up. Less than half way through the race, I pulled off the track and into the pits. After I had stopped for only a few minutes and I felt as if I could go back and finish the race but it was too late. I had quit. My team was so bummed. I had a chance to finish in the top five overall in the USGP.

And I quit. As I have grown older, I know that the physical limit must rise to the challenge. You must never just quit and why would you? Only you can demand these limits for yourself if your courage is strong enough you may do anything. So, I meditated on that for a while to get through that night.

I cannot remember how we finished our shift, but know that Innovation Africa was still so close when the Daves took over and I remember is that we were right together again. We were always right there with these guys. My fifteen minutes on the bike is played out like this; I would get out when the car stopped and got on my bike. I would get going when Ben stopped and ride as fast as I could for five or so miles and when I'd see Ben, the transition vehicle and their flashing lights, I'd stop and get in the car again. I did not think, I just rode. I'd just ride as fast as I could and I was still looking for more from my tired and sluggish body.

The Daves had some problems in their next shift with lots of missed directions and wrong turns. Mirra later told of riding side by side with Chris De Marchi from Innovation Africa and both of them and their team cars were lost; neither knew for sure where they were going. All they could do was follow Mirra's Garmin. Mirra also remembered an argument that ensued after being told over the radio to follow the Innovation Africa team who turned and despite being yelled at to follow the other rider Mirra went straight. He was right and had chosen well and the other rider had to return to the course after a short detour. When we would get a lead and would be slightly clear, we seemed to always get off track and then give it back.

Navigation errors were making everything super close. It seemed like whenever there was a gap building between our two teams an off-course detour would bring us back together again. After one last detour into the twilight zone the Daves were hard pressed to catch back up to Innovation Africa. Both teams, riders and crews came in together, side by side to time station #46 in Grafton, West Virginia where we stopped for our team transition. I was dressed, ready waiting for Mirra to come in, but not like this. I was blown away at what I saw. First, I and the Innovation rider and car pulled in to stop just across the traffic signal, then Mirra and our follow car came up behind him. Mirra rode right down the bike lane to be side-by-side with our rival. This would be the race. This shift for Ben and me would be the most important shift for the two moto guys. It would be the most important and deciding six hours of the race. The final battle for them and us. The Legends vs. Innovation Africa.

14 RIDERS ON THE STORM

Thursday the 19th. We were roughly 2,700 miles into the race after five days straight. Ben and I fought for the lead all day long. We were waiting at the team transition point for the Daves at time station#6 in Grafton, West Virginia. I think it was early in the day, maybe 9:00 or 10:00 am. There were many people out as it was a regular workday for normal people. Many of these regular people were watching us with undeniable curiosity as they went along their normal tasks for the day. The sky was growing dark and a storm was moving in. I hoped to be struck by lightning to wake my legs up as lightning did crackle the sky far off in the distance and we could hear and feel its thunder as it just started , there on Highway 50 at the cross street of Victory Ave. As we waited, the radio buzzed with details. The race was neck and neck. The road coming in descended from the opposite hilltop into the traffic signal and just across the street from me. Team Innovation Africa's rider came in to the stoplight first, just ahead of Dave Mirra. Dave moved up and parked next to him. They were side by side, waiting for the light to turn green. They did not even look at each other. Ready to take over from Dave was sitting on the east side of the light, just waiting.

There would be no riding easy and waking the body up with a good warm up. Not that day. Green light and we go.

[AS CLOSE AS CLOSE GETS: This picture tells the story. Dave Mirra and the Innovation Africa rider coming into time station #46 in Grafton, West Virginia, side by side. I am waiting across the street. This is where Ben and I will take over for the final battle. 2,700 miles, 5 days straight and we are head to head. The closest race I have ever had.]

It is a full effort for me just to stay on pace with the Innovation Africa rider. The road went uphill right away. Then it was a series of rolling hills, ups n downs. I was sluggish at first and dropped back about 100 yards behind the Innovation Africa rider. It was not long before we hit some real climbs. Ben had agreed to take most of the climbs. The rain wasn't that bad, yet. I thought about accelerating harder to close up on them, but knew I had nothing left in the tank. So I tried to stay right at my maximum effort, thinking it would be better to be steady for the whole shift. I took my first break and heard from the driver and navigator, Stephen and Will that Ben wanted the climbs again... Ben was amazing! Again, he lifted his pace to chase down Chris Demarchi, who at this point was the strongest rider on the Innovation Africa team. I was more than happy to take the descents and the rain. "I know what will help me today," I thought. "Riders on the Storm .The Doors .Press play."

I could tell that we were in West Virginia. It was very green; Trees covered the rolling hills that lined a very dark winding road. We were under a canopy of the trees most of the time. This skinny two-lane road was wet and slick, covered with leaves and moss. The road really had no shoulder, making it a battle for positions of the crews' cars for both our teams as well as the riders. The shifts for Ben and I would be short and full efforts that day. Full effort pedaling and no coasting downhill. The two teams watched each other, we raced hard to advance to the front, and we talked to each other when passing on the road, sometimes shit talking and we offered support or respect to each other. During our transitions, Ben and I urged each other on in our own way and in our own words. In the transition vehicle, I shared strategies and ideas with the crew to catch and pass those damn Innovation guys. Ben and I messaged through the crew to each other about where to do the transitions and sections ahead that we wanted to ride strong and where we could be faster. We had a constant cheering each other on thing going.

After a few transitions, we noticed that Innovation Africa was relaying three riders. Their plan was working well and they seemed to have had a plan to hit us (m Ben and I) hard on these rollers and climbs. They may have known that I had been getting sick and suffering. I hated to feel that I had become the weak link, but it was true. I had not let up on my efforts; I had just lost my strength. This was the last real place for them to attack us. They were riding super strong and we could only stay with them. Then they have picked up their pace and made it even harder—those smart, cruel bastards! On a long winding climb, Ben and I are able to close the gap on them. Ben took most of the climb and I did one small sprint in the red zone to give him a break. I could taste blood in my mouth again and felt good for the effort. My effort did not close up the gap but I do not think I lost any ground either. Now we were right behind them as we started a technical and very wet descent. I was willing to go all out and I did. I passed cars, trucks, and their follow car. I was all over the road using as much asphalt as there was. After the thrilling risk-filled descent, I finally managed to pass their rider just as he had pulled in for their rider exchange. Damn, I could have used more descending and less climbing. As soon as it flattened out again I was at my max speed and effort. Their new rider was closing in. I had my road bike but really needed the TT bike to ride these flat sections. The TT bike could have made a big difference. But who knows? The transitions to climbing in this area would have required more changes. Because the other team had three riders, it was working for them to have the option for bike changes too.

I heard the distinctive swooshing sound of a carbon TT bike on wet road coming up behind me. I could hear each powerful pedal stroke. I could tell this guy had to have quite a set of legs. That rear disc wheel, all carbon fiber; the sound is stuck in my head. Even now, I can hear it. The Innovation Africa rider works his way by me and all I could do was keep pushing and, stay steady. Drafting isn't allowed, so I just watched him go by, slowly pulling away while continued to give it all I had. I felt helpless as the gap grew, but I kept looking for a section of twisty, downhill road to gain back the time lost. However, nothing comes together like that. The roads are becoming more TT and suited to the Innovation Africa people. I looked for our transition and hoped that I could maintain my effort. The densely wooded terrain wound through some hills with a river. On each bend I looked for them and I look for Ben. The radio had no coverage. In this type of terrain, you have only line of sight.

The sky was still very dark that morning. However, for the moment it had stopped raining. I heard the occasional thunder crack in the distance. The road continued to follow the river and through some little West Virginia towns. We were in and out of the denser wooded areas and riding down fence lines of farms and country homes.

As we raced along there were moments that our two battling teams see each other when the road is longer and straighter. It motivated us to push harder I tried to keep pushing hard even when I could no longer see them

[TAKE ME HOME COUNTRY ROAD-Ben Bostrom charges through the West Virginia Mountains chasing Innovation Africa. A defining moment 2,700 miles in to the race]

There were a few short but steep hills and my legs were so worthless I dreaded these hills even though on the downhill's I could pull back some time going down the other sides. Anything going up was tough for me at that moment. There were some moments where I would find myself in a small town and caught at a traffic signal and I could enjoy the quiet, if only for a moment. It was if I was out on a solo training ride. Then the light would go green and I was back racing again, going flat out. Our transitions were getting a bit sloppy and we would lose a few seconds here and there, as I fumbled to click my cleats into the pedals. Later, after RAAM I would find that I had worn through my left foot's brand new cleat, breaking off the nose in five days' time.

The shift would be so long this day, with seemingly endless suffering. There was also added stress. Throughout our shift there was a car following us and filming us for most of the day. Occasionally it was very close to us and a distraction. It was not a RAAM film crew or an official. It was a group of Team Innovation Africa's crew. They were keeping an eye on us and sort of pressuring us. "What is going on with this?" we all asked. Both Ben and I only spoke of it briefly through the crew and we thought, "They must be total dicks!" Later we would learn that a few of their disgruntled crew actually tried to protest us for the following offenses; Holding onto our own cars, indecent exposure (really?), for having such good looking rider kits and for stealing their girlfriends. (I actually made that up about the team kits even though they were damn cool). Their claims were laughed upon and rejected by the RAAM officials. They had no proof because we never did any cheating. We were always decent too, even when we were undressed.

We have no ill will to Team Innovation Africa. In fact, we think very highly of them, but it is too bad that they had a few sour apples in the crew. It is rare to have this close of a race in any type of racing. I still am amazed that we raced this close for five-plus days and 3,000 miles. It is so hard to imagine, really. Anyway, at this particular moment in time I was too tired to give a rat's ass what anyone else was doing and after a while we stopped caring about them and then it was as if they weren't even there.

The course had now become like a highway. I got my TT bike for a few shifts, which was nice, but then I had a rear flat and changed back the road bike. (Amazing to have had but one single flat over a 3,000-mile bike race!) Ben was on his TT bike and making great speed. We managed to keep the Innovation boys in sight. On the longer sections of the highway and that felt good. We seemed to be pulling back a little time. When we drew close we could tell that they were just like us---really exhausted. Now this race is all will and guts. That helped me feel a little better. Now it was just a matter of who wanted it more. Who was willing to hurt more to win this thing? Then Ben and Rick Tillery got on an exit and turned onto a highway interchange by mistake. This costs us a few very valuable minutes, as Ben has to come back around to where we got off course. Two minutes, that was all and now we cannot see them anymore. They were just out of sight, five minutes maybe. Not much.

The remainder of this grueling shift was in rolling hills; steep uphill's to suffer and nice descents to rest. Ben and I were giving all we had to come back to them. I had a few short climbs where I could not get my body to jump. I had nothing left in my legs. I cursed out myself a few times, but only managed to get myself winded followed by more meditation with a slight bit of crying to God for mercy. Finally, we rolled into the team transition. It was in a small town at a roadside gas station. Ben and I came in anxious to explain that Innovation Africa was just a mile or so up the road. Dave Zabriskie took the relay. Mirra, before taking off in the transition vehicle, told me that Innovation Africa had not been through yet and that they had gone off course. Lauren, Dave's wife had been watching Tractalis and had told Dave that we are now leading again. There was an interstate highway a few miles back that had two right lanes. One lane went right onto the Interstate and the other went across the overpass then right onto the service road that was the RAAM course. They went hard right and onto the interstate.

Whew, desperation quickly turned into elation and an opportunity to close this thing down for good with only 270 or so miles to the finish. While the Daves roll into their shift both Ben and I really hope that the Daves are strong and well rested. Ben and I quickly tried to rest and regroup. I was really trashed and only wanted to eat and rest. My body, my legs in particular, were totally finished. I knew that our next shift would be hell and that I needed a miracle to recover. I believed that the Daves were going to go out hard with this slight advantage, really gap the Innovation guys and drive them into submission. I really hoped to wake up for the last shift of RAAM with a huge lead. The Daves really did put in a huge effort to attack them and pull away from them. However, the Innovation guys were strong and responded. The Daves gained some ground, but it was not as much as we had hoped for. The Innovation guys fought hard to hold on and stay in the race for the win and they were still right there. I cannot begin to tell you how much respect we all have for the Innovation Africa riders. They were so surprisingly strong. The strategy they used was very effective and may have been paying off more now when they could rally three riders to our two. They seemed so strong and committed.

At this point in the race, we were all physically and mentally just ready to finish and end the suffering. Can you imagine how totally trashed we were? How would you feel after five plus days nonstop? Can you just imagine riding a bicycle as fast as you can across the USA? We were 2,800 or so miles into the race and in a neck and neck battle with no time to rest, no milking it in to the finish line. This was a sprint to the finish. Both our teams were still alive, still ready to battle it out. The whole team and crew of both The Legends of the Road and Innovation Africa were still close. Any little mistakes at all could change the outcome of the race at any time. All it would have taken was any miscue like going off course, a flat tire or broken chain, a crash. We had to be sure to stay on course and make no mistakes, and to be fast and strong.

While Ben and I were trying to sleep and recover Dave Mirra and DZ were holding strong. Robson, Wayne and our crew readied for the final push to the finish. We had been set up at the team transition point at time station #50 in Rouzerville, Pennsylvania. We were still out in the lead, but Innovation Africa had hung tight. The gap was not as big as I hoped it would be. Robson and Wayne had been monitoring the separation between, but it was hard to tell where they were exactly because the Tractalis transponder is in the follow car and it could be getting gas or changing out crew. Innovation Africa's follow car may be closer to us than their rider, so you really cannot count on Tractalis to be 100% when things get this close. . Out of our last sleep and Ben and I were toasted. Ben had bags under his eyes and looked to be in a blackout style consciousness and I was just a wreck. My wheezing and congestion was worse and my legs were done. Again, my legs held water and my lungs had fluid. I was really praying for a miracle of healing from God.

My body has never been so stressed out and shut down, physically and mentally. I could barely speak, move, or breathe. I would have much rather had a broken leg to deal with. I needed only one thing, I just wanted to know how big our lead was. I barely had the energy to speak. I'm not kidding. I had asked how things were going on the road. I believe Robson told me that we were leading but it was still close. That was not the answer I was looking for. As I thought of how I was going to do this, to be totally honest, I was so sad. I could not stand the idea that I could ruin this beautiful race. I did not want to let everyone down. I was terrified. Why did I do this to myself? Why did I try to be more of a cyclist than I am? I was so very sad. Then I would just say to myself that I asked for it…I thought," well, fuck me I deserve it. I deserve to suffer like this." Then nothing more, no words, no thoughts, just an acceptance of my fate.

I was in a special, miserable lonely place; so mentally and physically beat down that my mind was silent. I begin to speak clearly to God. I could hear clearly my thoughts and instincts. I thought of Brenda and my kids and of how I wanted to be brave for them. I knew the place I was in and I knew just how short life is. I know these moments pass quickly yet they remain the strongest memories forever. There was only the truth and I am not a superman. I am a fragile human, just a man. I should not be asking for miracles in this place, a sporting contest. But, I did. I felt that this was my moment to take my medicine, to learn the hard way. I knew I deserved it. Then I just sat with it. It was God's will. I had accepted it. I accepted what I had to do. And with the end so near, only 90-ish miles to get to the finish, faith was reborn. I would not give up. It was not over yet. I was destined to learn a new level of pain and fatigue as if I had not learned enough yet. This would be like my 200th wind. I started to believe again. And by some miracle, my prayers would be answered.

[READY TO BE DONE: Here I am waiting to start my final shift, feeling so desperate and fearful that I would let my teammates down. My body was completely finished, as fragile as a 100 year old grandma.]

A miracle? Dave Mirra called in on the radio from the transition vehicle and asked to do a double shift. He was feeling strong, he knew I was miserable and the Innovation guys were still close behind us. Mirra did not want them to get back in it. Wayne respectfully asked if I was cool with that. Would it be ok if Mirra took a double shift? It would mean that Dave would join Ben and me and take the pressure off me. As if I might not be cool with that. I was relieved. Totally relieved. I almost wanted to cry. The Daves arrived. DZ was first in the transition vehicle. He was out and telling us it was still close. We were not in the clear yet. I would hop into the follow vehicle with my bicycle. Dave and Ben into the transition vehicle where Dave could keep shifting. I would later do one extremely painful shift and then get back in the follow car and stay there unless I was needed again. My lungs were so congested now that I coughed most of the shift. Both Ben and Dave were riding really well and it was nice to see Mirra ride. Ben and I had not seen either of the Daves ride other than during our transitions since the start five days ago. We had only seen each other briefly for a few minutes at a time. Mirra and Ben both have extremely competitive spirits. The two of them challenged each other like brothers do. It was good to watch.

I began to monitor Tractalis and watched as Team Innovation Africa's signal faded back as we began to slowly pull out and away from them. Even though our lead began to look bigger, it would be hard to tell as the updated positions on the RAAM website posted. The posts were scattered a bit and hard to get a true read on where exactly they were. We thought that they may be jumping back and forth with the follow and transition vehicles because they might be rotating all four riders. Or maybe they were trying to come up to find where we were to see the gap between us. Either way we could not be sure just where they were. What I was starting to feel was the excitement growing. The Legends of the Road were going to win this thing, this monster endurance race, this seemingly never-ending endurance race.

Ben and Dave continued pushing the pace each and every shift through the late night and soon the Innovation Africa team began to drop back even farther. At around 1 am Dave Zabriskie would joined the group and take a few shifts We were all awake and we were all here and It was nice to have all of us together for the finish that was just ahead. After the whole buildup of the idea, convincing these guys to do this and building this team, all of the work that went into sponsors and supporters the awesome volunteers who were now like family, the training camp and hours and hours of training, it was looking like this was it. We had this thing.

Time Station #52 in Mt Airy, Maryland. We are 2951.2 miles into RAAM. The final moment of truth. If we had any penalties this time station would be where we would serve them. Racers with a time penalty have to sit here for the duration of that penalty before they can continue to the finish line. Had we been penalized? There were so many accusations or rumors that we had been protested. Team Innovation Africa had claimed we cheated. Robson and Wayne had addressed each one as they came in through RAAM officials. However, it is still a race here and with so many questionable "what if's" you just never know what to expect. At this time station, every single RAAM finisher must phone in for permission to continue. We all held our breath when that call went through. Robson made the call to the RAAM officials who, somewhat quickly, confirmed that there were no penalties for The Legends of the Road. Then a collective group exhale and then there was simultaneous loud applause from our crew on the radios from all the vehicles.. All of us as a team were all wide-awake and focused now. It was also here that we learned that our lead was steadily growing. Now, less than fifty miles to go and we knew we would win this thing. We would win RAAM. When we got a little closer all four of us got out onto the road to ride together as a team. Five days after starting together in Oceanside, we were chatting and laughing again and reflected on our journey as we pedaled in to time station #54, Annapolis to take the official finish.

[FOUR FOR ROAD: All four of the Legends finished off this amazingly incredible journey together. It had the feel of the start. It was hard not to goof around a little. However, we were so tired we just grinned and giggled a little bit until we made it to the finish line. Yes that is the moon.]

Our finish time was 5 days, 11 hours, and 4minutes with an average speed of 22.90mph. After you cross the Line at TS 54, your time is documented. Complete. Then you are escorted to the finish line arches and ceremonial stage for the pyro technics, champagne and this is when the trophy girls are waiting to kiss you. Well, not exactly. But, who cares? We did not need any of that. We had just won it.

We were greeted by Fred and Rick Boethling, the two big men of RAAM, to be escorted down to City Dock, the site of the ceremonial finish on Annapolis Harbor. The four of us rode slowly through town and onto the dock. We were oozing with relief. I personally was VERY relieved to be finished and to not have to suffer anymore. I could now really rest. There was a small crowd gathered there waiting for us. Not a big crowd at all. It was around 3:00am. We could almost share the same thoughts without speaking at all. Then again, we were so tired we could not really engage each other or bullshit too much anyway. We just stood there and smiled, like a group of happy sloths, just meandering about in slow motion with giant smiles, totally relieved and extremely happy we had won.

15 WINNING

[MISSION ACCOMPLISHED: We posed together shortly after finishing. There is was so much satisfaction and relief at that moment. We knew that it was over. We won and we are done. I love these guys. Now beer me!]

Under the finish line arch we paused as a team in total relief. Mirra's wife Lauren and his two girls were there to greet him and us with a warm welcome, flowers and gifts. I had known that Brenda would not be there but I still had to look around for her anyway. My mind was so tired that I seemed to just stand and smile and repeat a thought of, "we did it." Soon we were on the stage with George Thomas, RAAM's official announcer and host of Over the Top online radio. I am not sure what was said but it was funny, happy, and good. At least that is what I remember. I also remember Rick placing official finisher's medals on all four of us. "Damn, I am a RAAM finisher now!" I thought, and I could feel it. I knew the feeling in my body was from the work. I knew I given it all I had, every shift, every pedal stroke. We all did.

It was almost dawn, the bars were closed, but there were a few beers around and I would drink them if I could only get my hands on them. As a team, we took photos and more photos with the entire Legends crew. There is such a sense of accomplishment that washes over you while standing there as a finisher. As a team we stood together almost glowing. We all were smiling ear to ear. There is a tradition for finishers to jump into the bay to celebrate the crossing from the Pacific Ocean to the Atlantic Ocean, or more accurately, Chesapeake Bay

[FAMILY MOMENT: Dave Mirra was greeted at the finish by his two daughters.]

[WE PEDALED TO THE MEDALS; RAAM finisher medal. Does it mean a lot to me? I wanted one ever since I first knew of RAAM. I will get one someday for solo RAAM too, but I will always cherish this one, I promise you.]

The bay being much colder. And it was around 4 am, so we decided to break that tradition. And just when I thought it could get no better, Laura Kindregan showed up and handed me not just one but a couple of beers. I learned later that Laura and Brenda and my good pal Carl Harris had been posting updates to the Legends of the Road sites to keep the followers up to date on the race. I have since been able to see how many people had watched us and supported us along the way. I have tears in my eyes thinking about that. Laura had all four of us riders ushered off to the hotel for some much needed and long overdue rest. And the crew did the same, following close behind.

[THE LEGENDS' RAAM FAMILY: The Whole Team. The Legends of the Road. Cannot believe it is over and that we won. How relieved are you to be finished after 5 days, 11 hours and 41 minutes? Pretty dam relieved! I love this picture too because everyone is so happy and equally excited. All of us did it together.]

Once in my hotel room I had to take a bath. Hotels baths are freaky so I steam out the tub and room real good before

I filled it. A steam bath helped open up my lungs a little bit too. You never know what might have gone on in there lately. Breathing in the steam really felt good. After a proper bath and cleaning, I tried to sleep, but I could not. I began to reflect on everything and I could feel the decompression or the depression coming on. I wanted to call Brenda but it was too early to call anyone on the West coast. My mind was extremely lost to my emotions, happy, sad, regretful, sorry, angry, paranoid, and tragic. I was jumpy and sweaty. My body temperature was high; as though I might I have had a fever. I had not ever put myself to this level of physical extreme and to feel this sort of reaction was scary. The emotional high that came now was days in the making, was then followed with this intense release of emotions. How is it that could have such an emotional high that it was sad and low? I tried to stay on the high side and focus on getting rest. I knew it would be best to just sleep, but I really could not.

It was close to 6 am. So I got up and went down stairs to breakfast. My legs had swelled up again and were hard to the touch. I never had the water retaining leg thing and it feels strange. I was wheezing as usual, and talk about grumpy. I was not my normal self. I was the only guest at breakfast. The servers had just put out the buffet and said sit anywhere you want. I ate a lot of food and liked it. Even after I had had my fill, I continued to eat out of boredom. I knew my body needed it. So there I sat, all alone in a hotel in Annapolis Maryland. I cannot say why but everything I looked at seemed to have a yellow haze to it. I relived a few thoughts of the last week and thanked God that I did not have to take another pedal stroke. I thanked all the heavens and angels that pedaled with me or for me and for us and kept us safe and helped us win. Humbled to a point of tears, I began to feel alone. I missed the ones that I love the most and wanted to be with them now. This terrible sad feeling made me want to curl up in the fetal position and cry. "Wow," I thought, "If this is the result of extreme fatigue, how will it really hits me now that I still have Pikes Peak to do before I can go back home?"

After breakfast, I walked around in and outside the hotel in a yellow haze over the next few hours until I found myself back at the hotel bar having beers. It was 10:00 am. I would not see anyone I knew until around 1:00pm when a friend of Rick, Fred and Wayne's picked me up to go see a doctor about my lungs. After a few tests, they found I was 40% compromised in my breathing and completely worn out. My lungs were not doing well they said and I told them of the last five or so days. The doctor said they would not release me like this and put me on a Nebulizer. After two sessions on the Nebulizer, they released me with a prescription for more meds and I was off again to see the crew at the hotel and see what was going on. There was a full-scale work effort to clean and reorganize the motorhome and rental cars. Robson and Wayne looked a lot better but they were still working. All I wanted to do was keep moving. If I was stuck in one place for too long I got twitchy and depressed. Robson and Wayne were recruited to take me for my prescription at the pharmacy. It would take too long for Robson and he left me and Wayne and went on his way. Beer was starting to sound good, so guess what I did. I kept moving toward where beer was. I walked across the street back to the hotel and went to the bar again. I ran into DZ for a minute. We just looked at each other and smiled in awe at what we had just done. Dave and I sat and talked about Dave a little and his personality shined through reconfirming that he is genuine and a good friend.

Later that day the Daves and Ben had gone to motocross and Freestyle legend Travis Pastrana's with Jim De Champ from the Nitro Circus who had also been at the finish line. They were learning the motorcycle backflip or something like that. We would all reconvene at the RAAM awards banquet. The four of us riders with the addition of Lauren

Mirra and his little girls had an early dinner at the hotel before the banquet. We sat around a table just reflecting on highs and lows of our race. We wondered about Team Innovation Africa and how they felt today. We also hoped we would be able to see them that night; shake hands with them for sure. We talked about some things and just sat together, happy to watch Mirras little girls playing while we shared an unspoken peace of mind. It was that "basking in the moment" thing that we had earned. This was to be our last night together before saying good-bye and even though we were super wiped out; it was nice to be together at the banquet, not just us but the whole Legends of the Road team We needed it to be this way. We had all earned this moment to celebrate.

RAAM puts on three banquets because there were still riders coming in to become finishers of RAAM. The cut off times varied for the different classes, there were still solo riders coming in to finish. The solo riders had 12 full days, the team classes had up to 9 days depending on the class. We attended the first banquet on Saturday, June 21. All the Legends team and crew were there, missing only Meg, as she had to leave early. We got a very nice corner table and had a super slow and relaxing celebration. The Legends riders were called to the podium many times to receive awards presented by George Thomas who made us proud. There were many happy finishers there that evening, but none as happy as I was. I only regret that I had not the sense about me to bring all the team up together; all the riders and crew.

After the banquet, the Legends riders and crew broke into groups to celebrate and reflect on the huge adventure. I was not able to go out and party on this night. I know they were in good company all night and that made happy. I needed to pack for the next day's flight to Colorado for Pikes Peak. After some slow and sad goodbyes, I was back at my room packing for my early flight from Baltimore, Maryland to Denver, Colorado.

I was a little nervous about going back into high altitude. In the last few quiet moments of this RAAM experience, I was focused and clear; at least for the moment. I have bonded with my three teammates in a way that words cannot explain. I have also bonded with the crew. All have a brighter light in my eyes and we share a wordless connection. I felt that it was over. This feeling will last forever. My heart and soul will have a place in them that will always have room for these amazing people.

[ROBSON BUTTERKNIFE HANDS: Robson is ready to eat and Paige is mid post at the Banquet.]

In the morning, it was a hard and slow struggle to get moving. I headed for the lobby with my stuff. I am new and different and I know it. When the elevator doors open at the lobby I see Dave Zabriskie there smiling as I drag out a huge couple of bags that I have strapped together to navigate swiftly though the airport. Dave walks over and gives me a hug, and tells me, "Travel safe." I say, "you too, " Robson was coming to get us you know, but DZ had already called for a cab and the cabbie had arrived. The cab driver was walking around in the lobby looking for Mr. Zabriskie. DZ has a look on his face that says, "maybe I won't tell him and I'll ride with you guys." Finally, DZ tells the cabbie, "I'm him" and now he is committed to take the cab or pay the fare. So, Dave Z is off to airport. Paige and Will show up just as Robson arrives. Robson was chipper and motivated to get us there on time. Robson asks, "Where is Zabriskie?" I say, "I don't know, but we should get going or I'm going to miss my flight." Soon after a couple of awkward moments in the early morning clumsiness, we get on our way to the airport.

When we were about half way to the airport and somewhere on an interstate highway we get a call from Stephen asking where we are. Robson in his Aussie accent, says, sorry mate I forgot you but you were not there at the call time anyway, so just grab a cab. I can hear some tension through the phone but Robson talks him through a backup plan. We did a quick pit stop at the train station to drop off Paige so she can go on to a cycling clinic and then on to the airport. At the airport we split up, check into our flights and head to our gates. More awkward good byes. Eventually I get through security and begin the walk to my gate. I pass DZ on my way to my gate and we laugh for a few moments. It's always funny to me that there will always be a ground point where after all the highs and lows, after all the hero moments and death defying or grave moments, we all revert to being children inside and out. Everything is funny; everyone is innocent and harmless hiding behind a shit-eating grin. The simple things in life again take over. I love that.

I am off to Denver. Once into Denver I started a 2-hour drive to Pikes Peak where I will immediately become a motorcycle racer again. I needed to start to transition into that frame of mind. First, I needed to rest. With my lungs I am going to need to heal quickly. PPIHC starts at an altitude of 9,000 feet with the finish line sitting at 14,400 feet. How the heck are my lungs going to deal with this I thought as I grab a coffee and sit at the gate to once again reflect on the past week or so? I am a mass of happiness and I am terribly sad that it is over. I can feel the depression kicking in. I already miss riding my bike with Ben and the Daves and it really hits me how much I miss Brenda now. My movements are instinctual for the next hour or so acting on pure instinct. Legends….. Every now and then, I will just whisper that and smile.

THE LEGENDS OF THE ROAD, PART TWO, PIKES PEAK

16 THE MECCA

During the flight to Colorado my legs were twitchy and kicking about on their own. I had the middle seat. Damn good thing it wasn't an International flight. Arriving in Denver I took my time to deplane and walk to the baggage claim to pick up my bags. Right away, my breathing was challenged and I felt the altitude. I was lightheaded and a little dizzy. All I could do was walk slowly through the airport toward baggage claim. I could feel the extreme fatigue in my legs too. Once I had my bags, I walked like a zombie, slowly and deliberately, to the rental car office and picked up my car for the week. . "And what the hell is wrong with my tooth?" I thought. The root canal tooth was now super sensitive. Fighting off the discomfort I made my way through the airport and managed to pick up my new teammate for the weekend, Don Canet, who arrived a few hours after me. Don was riding the second Ducati Multistrada and he would be writing a story for Cycle World Magazine. Don is a writer and a promoter as well as an ex- racer. He is quite a good road racer, though I had no idea how good he really is. He is a chatty guy and kept me enthused to be there as we eased along the scenic two-hour drive from Denver to Colorado Springs, the base of Pikes Peak.

I think I was talking more about RAAM, how we had won and how awesome that is. Can you believe it; he was ready to talk more about Pikes Peak? It was instantly clear that we were in different gears and eventually I would come around to focusing more on the next race, Pikes Peak. But for the moment, we were from different planets. Don was telling me he had been playing the video game to learn the hill better and I was telling him about pedaling through Kansas. When you are a new racer at Pikes Peak, you have a lot to learn. Your life depends on what you know about the racecourse not just your race speed. The video game is a great training tool for memorizing the racecourse. There is a very detailed rendition of the course design on the game that can be memorized by playing over and over. I hear that the road looks a lot bigger and wider on the video game. I don't play video games so I have no actual experience with the game and don't know how close it is to the real thing. Don is a rookie at Pikes Peak. This is a very special race, one that is more treacherous, more dangerous than any other in the United States. As a motorcycle race at high speed, anything can happen. Even a small fall on the Peak can have grave consequences.

We were on our way to Mecca, Not that Mecca. It is a motel named Mecca in Manitou Springs near Colorado Springs, my home for the rest of the week. The Mecca has been my temporary home for each of the six years that I have raced Pikes Peak. Liz and Gary Salinas, the two most awesome hosts and the nicest people you would ever hope to meet, run it. They have become more like old friends or family. I was really ready to rest now. Like right now and this was the place for me. The Colorado scenery was amazing, even sitting in traffic. I gazed out at rolling hills stretching out to massive snowcapped mountains and clouds lightly sprinkled across clear skies that the sun shined through to create warmth that would soon be hot. I was really looking forward to the rest I was going to have for the next 24 or so hours. The Mecca has been a refuge from all my stresses over the years and I needed that now.

We arrived at the Mecca at about 3:00pm on this fine Sunday, just 40 or so hours after finishing RAAM and got a warm reception from Paul and Becca Livingston. They were both looking all official wearing Ducati race shirts and hats. Paul and Becca are the official organizers for the Ducati Pikes Peak race team. They are more like my parents although we are almost the same age. I guess what I mean is that they are capable of taking care of me more as they would one of their own children. Maybe that did not come off the way I really feel about it, but trust me they make me feel as if I've been wrapped up in a super hero, safety bulletproof blanket.-. They are supportive and detail oriented. With them everything is, was and will be running smooth and professionally. Paul is this thin attractive type of guy with the brown grey shadow/beard. He looks good in hats, is always full of purpose, yet has the ability to observe and laugh at all the humorous things that surround us. At times that may be you, or me. And Becca, Google "perfect woman to marry" and you'll find a picture of Becca. Paul may refer to her as "the boss, "but only because she is. Together they make an impressive team, an impressive couple and an inspiration. There is something special being in this team.

FACING MECCA: My new home away from home. I love this place.]

The Ducati race bikes were set up on work-stands under EZ-ups in the Mecca parking lot and the crew from AF1 Racing from Austin, Texas, was going through a check list and cleaning them up. The bikes looked awesome, red and white with a ton of carbon fiber bodywork around a black body that had some incredible curves to the frame and swing arm. The swing arm is single sided and is shaped like the naked torso of a supermodel lying sideways. It looked like an exotic, racehorse. An Akrapovic exhaust system of Titanium with a short and to the point muffler. You really have to hear this motorcycle run at race speed to understand what is a Ducati. If you are not familiar with this particular bike, please Google "Ducati Multistrada R Pikes Peak" Edition. I hop onto the bike and just sit and relax. I tell myself I belong here and this is where I am most happy. The bike feels damn good. A lot different from a bicycle.

I felt as skinny and light as a child would on a big motorcycle. I had to start feeling attached to this exotic motorcycle. The Ducati Multistrada starts out as a sporty, high-dollar touring bike available to the public. Our race bike is a super streamlined, high-speed version of that, but is much lighter and produces a heap more horsepower. Brent Davidson is the actual tuner for our bikes. He was with us the previous year and due to a freaky infection resulting in compartment syndrome, he was forced to miss the 2014 race. He had put so much hard work into the bike in early 2014 that his work employer, the company AF1 picked up the slack and sent some of their other best. Ed and Ted filled in for Brent as my mechanics. Hard to forget the names, but in the beginning I called Ed, Ted and Ted, Ed. Both of the guys together were busy with two race bikes and a spare bike just in case there was a problem with one of the race bikes. I finally dismounted my bike, the number 43, and let the two guys continue their work. The vans, with the three bikes together under the Ducati tents, looked very impressive.

[THIS WEEK'S MOUNT: The Ducati Multistrada is stripped down a bit, but is still a hefty girl and it is quite a change in two-wheelers from the Cervelos to the Ducati.]

Liz, the manager of the Mecca Motel approached me from out of nowhere. Liz looks like a living Barbie doll; the Snow White edition. Liz and I hugged and said hello. It is always a warm and sincere welcome. She gave me my key and said, "You look like you could use some rest." She knew exactly what I had been doing for the previous week. I said, "Thanks, and yeah, you're right. I do." Quickly I dragged my bags and gear from the rental car and began to put my stuff into my room. I had three big bags that traveled there with me that day and some gear that was left there a few weeks prior when we were there testing and practicing. There was still more gear that was shipped while I was doing RAAM and it was in boxes already in my room. After dragging it all and tossing it into my room. I was again reminded of the altitude and my challenge was just to breathe. I was gassed, sweaty and worn out. I just collapsed into the bed and I tried to get some rest.

Finally, I was lying down. I was fidgety and sort of beside myself, but at least I was resting. As I lay there, my mind just would not shut down and let me sleep. Looking around the room in its 70's style décor with a box TV sitting on a large white wash dresser and my bags and gear spread sort of neatly, I could feel at home once again. I felt all tucked in and safe as if this was a good place to be right at that moment. Even though I was lying totally still it felt as if I was running in place, as if I was at the ready for the sound of the gun to go off at any moment. I could feel and hear a buzzing sound in my ears, a constant ringing. I took my meds and some Motrin and ended up watching some

TV. I replayed a few things in my head about being here at this moment once before, so wasted from the physical fatigue that rest should come on easy. The mental wear and tear has brought my inner self to a new place, with new eyes, viewing a world set in my own slow motion and specific ideas. Like living in a daydream. At least I seem to believe I deserve that feeling right now. That steady buzz going on in my head will not stop until I can turn the inner dial hard left until finally, I fall asleep or something very close to it. I got like an hour before waking up in a pool of sweat, overheating. The AC was on and it was cool in the room. So, WTF? Soon I would have to get up and go to race headquarter for registration and sign in with the team. Now it feels like I am being rushed and I am grouchy on the inside. But, what can I do?

Three weeks prior, I was here for the one and only test on the course. It was the only practice we had on the new bikes and on the Pikes Peak course. Testing the new bike was good and more importantly, I felt good on the bike and course. It was also Don's first ride here on the mountain. Riding with a teammate here is valuable. You can share and compare everything from the bike set up to the course characteristics and even the weather if you want to. The new Ducati had most of the settings from the old race bike transferred over to it so it was pretty well suited to the course except the engine braking was too strong. It had too much compression. The engine braking determines how much resistance is sent through the rear wheel when you shut off the throttle and my bike had way too much. The rear wheel would slide or lock up a bit when I let off the gas during braking if I did not use the clutch to ease through each gearshift when downshifting.

We had come here to take the final of only two yearly scheduled and expensive practice and test sessions. We got to ride the course and test the bikes, the tires, exhaust, gearing, suspension, fuels, etc. We spent two days with the bikes in a more non-formal test session. There were only 15 or so other motorcycle and 20 or so cars, so we could really concentrate on the course and the bike. Because we did not have Brent at the test we were a little challenged and a bit unable to make any big changes. The test was very successful despite one small crash. On day two in my favorite section of the course, I made a mistake and went down. Rider error. My favorite section is the lead into Engineer's Corner, a very tight uphill left-hander coming just after a 120 mile an hour flowing uphill. It was a sad moment for me. My favorite section on the entire mountain. I believe that this is or was my strongest section on the course. I really loved to slide the bike in while hard on the brakes. I would leave 200 or so feet of black slide marks that would stay all week and be visible for the race too.

I scared myself good when the bike got really sideways on the initial braking. For this corner, it is the hardest point of braking. You really need to mash the brakes then ease back after you slow the bike enough for the corner. The braking zone is uphill and sweeping to the left. It is a high speed section, like 120 mph to a 20 mph corner and you also cross the paint lines and that was where the rear really stepped out. I had to let off the brakes to gather it up and regain some control before I grabbed more brakes. I was able to get it back under control but ran out of road in the process. It's spooky when you know that you can't slow down enough to make a turn. "OH, FUCK!" is about what you have to deal with. I was running into the turn way too fast and had to lay it down. The bike and I slid off the road into the dirt but did not hit anything. I was a little sore but unhurt and the bike only had a few scratches; nothing major. The crash was a wakeup call. RAAM was coming the very next week and an injury with no time to recover would have been terrible. I did finish the test with some decent runs and good times on the lower section. I did feel good about the motor setting and left the test ready to come back and race.

The team was very happy with the test even though the computer technician was not on hand to change my engine braking I wanted less resistance because the rear wheel was locking up or chattering on the brakes, though I could ride with more finger work on the clutch lever to compensate. So I was happy to start where we left off at that test. There was always the chance to make some changes and get the setting right during the week of race week practice. We had also spent a day at California Speedway with Paul Thede from Race Tech Suspension.

Paul Thede and I have made many improvements to the Ducati over the last few years and the bike handles as good, or better, than you could ever expect from such a big girl. Paul is one of the most unusual and amazing people I know. He is genius when it comes to motorcycles and the specifics of their engineering. His mind has this computer-like speed to evaluate, assess, and respond to any challenge or wizardry that may be possible from his eyes. Screw the trouble shooting, he doesn't need it really he just needs good input from the rider. He is equally responsive verbally in any social setting and has a memory like an elephant, so look out. His wit is legendary and seasoned in our time in motorsports, but could easily transcend to any time or place. Together we have achieved much success over the years, laughing all the way toward victory or nothing spectacular. It is so fun to be around him. At the California Speedway test, we managed to make more progress with the Ducati. Paul can ride well, and I mean really ride well. So we can share thoughts and feeling at the same time.

His infectious passion for even the most general pieces of the motorcycle makes you aware of the overall magic that is motorcycle racing. Paul is a designer, creator and racer. He holds many records including a Bonneville speed record for the fastest battery motorcycle speed at over 200 mph as a rider. He has countless other achievements as the mastermind behind suspension in off road, motocross, Supercross, road racing and specialty races like Pikes Peak. Sadly, Paul would not be with us this year at the race and we missed him. I would break into a Paul Thede story to share with the team to keep him close during most of the days we were there. The stories always are good for morale and to make us all laugh.

Racer registration is held at the host hotel across town, Hotel Elegante. Colorado Springs is by my estimation a perfect town. It is almost the perfect size. Downtown is near the interstate, roads run east to west and north to south and you can get around easily and quickly. Buildings are older and established. GPS is almost unnecessary because you can find almost everything without it.. A short ride on the interstate and we are at the Hotel Elegante. After waiting in a few lines, grabbing coffee, hearing multiple languages like French and Italian, catching up on small talk we get to the business, the official business. "Sign here and here and then here and we can get the rest of the forms for you to sign." It is fairly quick and painless to get us all taken care of. "Good thing we got there first," I thought. As soon as we could, we made our exit and were on our way to do an official and off the clock dinner. I was so happy to have a regular dinner. Paul, Becca, Don and I would need to decide on what to eat and where to go. I was easy and hungry. Feed me... anything.

We settled on "The Front Range BBQ, "as it was just between registration and the Mecca. We parked and quickly rushed to the entry to find we were looking at a 15-minute wait because the place was busy. "Damn," I almost said aloud. But suddenly, we were being seated and I thought it was because we were all official looking with our bright red Ducati shirts and hats. It is funny as my entire wardrobe over this two-week stretch between RAAM and PPIHC consisted of spandex and team uniforms. What I wouldn't have given for a pair of shorts, T-shirt and to be barefoot walking on a beach or some soft grass! I could not wait to be naked and in my room that night. Sorry, I digress. This seems to be a common occurrence among RAAM competitors; A.D.D at its best not to mention I was feeling the meds. I couldn't help but look back on RAAM and all my experiences of the previous week and began to imagine the bands song as the music score to the end credits of a film. I could hear Jim Morrison singing, "THIS IS THE END," as the sun was setting on my first night in Colorado. I had now made the change over from RAAM to Pikes Peak.

Pikes Peak has one of the most ridiculous weeklong schedules of any race in the world. Vampires keep better hours, Fisherman are late risers compared to a Pikes Peak racer. 3:00 am is the standard call time on all of the scheduled practice days as well as race day. It has been that way for as long as I have attended this race. Once it felt somewhat special to have such a crazy schedule for this one of a kind event but now it just seems ridiculous. You are exhausted at the end of the week feeling as if you really endured something beyond a normal "extremely intense" weeklong race. I am sure that I am not alone in this sentiment. Surely, it would be better to get to set-up at dawn and then ride throughout the day, during the sunshine, in the warmth of the day, and most importantly, the full, overhead light of the day. It seems ridiculous to test tires when the road is at 38 degrees then have to race when it is between 60 and 70 degrees. Our tire testing data is flawed at best.

I'm a morning person, I really am. However, I like to get up and have coffee, then ease into breakfast and then get into full motion. That is possible at 5:00 or 6:00 am, no problems there. But to get up at 3:00 am and do coffee and breakfast is not at all good. It is quite a shock to the system. It's just not possible to trick the body and mind into functioning at this hour. We had to be at the park gate of Pikes Peak at 3am, which meant we were up at 2:20am dressing and leaving the hotel at 2:30am. I usually get up just at before the moment we leave. A gentle pounding on my door will cue me to exit. Then it is a dash for my seat and all of us get tightly packed in a race vehicle to drive up the massive, high altitude mountain on a winding road. The timing is the hardest part, fresh from a warm bed, stumbling out into the cold, dark morning. Will I get carsick? You can bet I will not enjoy this nor have I enjoyed this part in previous years.

In the past, I have tried to sleep on the drive. I am usually halfway dreaming anyway, or you try to be somewhere else in my dreaming mind as the crew does the driving, parking and set up while I will stay quiet and warm inside the race vehicle. It may be strange, but most of my thoughts are sexual. Why, I have no idea. Honestly, the only thing that I would be happy about at this hour would be sex. I could go for that. Anyway, this is what we do as racers, or at least that is what I do. I stay out of the way and stay warm because as soon as we start riding we are dealing with freezing fingers and stiff, slow-moving muscles. Being warm allows for good movement and clear thinking about riding the machine and the course and nothing else. That is important. I do not want to think about being cold and stiff or anything else. I need to think of my bike, the road and me. The way the tires are gripping, the motor and how it is running and most importantly, the way I am seeing, marking my braking points and turn-ins, picking my lines and generally riding on the road that I am racing.

This year was very different from all past years I have raced here. Number one, it was hard to get to sleep. I was groggy and tired but sleepless at the same time. My body temperature was on the fritz. I had dropped to 150 pounds from 175. I was cold all the time that I was awake and as soon as I did get to sleep, I over heated. In addition, I had a bronchial cold and the altitude was really getting to me when I was on the hill. This is usually my strength when I am in Colorado because the altitude has never affected me the way it usually affects others. This time I was having issues with the altitude from the moment I landed. How would I be able to ride with altitude sickness? I hoped that it would pass as soon as my body recovered.

All of this seems crazy to me right now, as I look back on it. Oh yeah, I did tell you that I was49 years old when I was there at Pikes Peak?. Seems my prostate is going just like my eyesight. After a mostly sleepless night with multiple toilet trips, I was awake and looking for coffee completely pissed off. It was Monday morning---a big day for the whole team. This was the stress filled social day with the officials and the competition. There was some fun to be had, like seeing all the race motorcycles and the cars close enough to touch and seeing the few riders and drivers that are cool people--my old friends and a few new ones I want to meet.

17 TECH AND THE TEAM

Technical Inspection is somewhat complicated at Pikes Peak. This race is so special. It happens to be collaboration between automobile race federations, motorcycle federations and Colorado State Parks and who knows who or what else? It is technical and time consuming. We also had a separate riders meeting and a few other obligations as motorcycle competitors and as the Ducati team. It was just a few of the many hoops to jump through, but it is simply part of the racers program and must be attended by all of the team. This was another day with a heavy need for coffee. Rod Faulkner flew in late the night before. Rod is the partner of Paul and Becca, (Faulkner and Livingston is their company and race team), a fixture for me to be there, as well as the owner of Dumonde Tech, Rod's oil company that makes cycling oils. So guess who sponsored the Legends of the Road during RAAM. Rod and I have developed a super solid, symbiotic relationship and I need him here to keep me focused and safe. That is first and foremost. However, for the moment, I needed him to keep me straight and nice. I am short-tempered with all this pre-race stuff and I could simply snap and start acting like a little crybaby at any moment. I had refuge and the protection of Rod, Paul and Becca to keep me safe. I felt an additional ease come over me with the crew surrounding me.

There were a few more key team people coming in that day. Michael Larkin from Akrapovic exhaust Systems, our hero and sponsor from the previous year. He is a very likeable and generous guy that has supported the team for many years and has a keen sense of humor. We also had two Special Forces guys from Wounded Warriors joining our team, Yaunce and Chris. It was something special to share our experience with them. The two guys quickly turned that around by sharing their experiences with us. That is what is so very special about this crew; anyone that is part has equal respect and acceptance. All voices are set at the same high volume. I have known this group of people as my God given friends because I believe that is what they are. They are the ones that were placed here into my life by his grace.

Throughout the day, we worked together as a whole team, going over each person's roles, working with the bikes, practice sessions, tires, motorcycle set-up and schedules for the next few days. The bikes were mostly sorted out. Over the last few years of development of the race bike during practice and races the bikes have become really dialed in.

[GADGET INSPECTORS: Both Ducati's make it through inspections. Thanks to the race starter as well as chief technical inspector Frank, is the fellow there in grey going over the front end.]

We had the Ducati Multistrada motorcycle working so good that this was just making small changes based off our previous test session at the mountain a few weeks ago before RAAM.

As the official Ducati race team we completed our attendance at the technical inspections where bikes are weighed, checked for all compliances, thoroughly scrutinized and cleared. Our riding gear was put through similar tests and also passed. We were perfectly timed to get through it quickly and cleanly while it was still early and the officials were still calm, relaxed and had good attitudes. Chalk another one up to the planning of Faulkner and Livingston. There is another detail for every competitor that must be done in order for the racer to be eligible to compete. Each rider or driver has to have a physical performed by a licensed physician. It has a list of items that are a little over the top. I understand checking the status of your heart, lungs, motor reflexes and eyesight, but the exam calls for the usual prodding and poking of my penis and testicles. I am not sure why as it states on my birth certificate that I am a male and have been one all my life.

Guy Martin made his name at the famous Isle of Man TT, a British event first run in 1907 where racers speed around a 38-mile road course temporarily closed to traffic. With it being run on streets normally used for everyday traffic there's little in the way of safety measures other than a few sections of air fence and the occasional hay bale. It's a super-beautiful event that's also super-dangerous—many riders have had their last rides trying to go too fast around its 200 turns. Martin was here with a project bike to compete in his very first Pikes Peak. Guy was wielding some of the largest muttonchops that I've ever seen. He is

British, full Brit, and he is known to speak with such a heavy accent that you cannot tell exactly what he's saying. Sometimes when he is interviewed for video, they insert subtitles—it is that tough to follow his words and phrases. I hope that I can get to know him because he seems so cool and interesting. Guy is riding a bike that I believe he engineered solely for this race. It has dual turbochargers and a special, fabricated....everything else. It is rumored to produce somewhere close to 300hp when at its 100% open throttle with full boost.

Jeremy Toye is a well-known and respected American road racer. He too has competed in the Isle of Man and was voted rookie of the year in 2012. He is a likeable and very interesting guy with an easygoing attitude, a great riding style and an extensive variety of uses for the word "fuck." Pure road racer. With him came Team Kawasaki with a 1000cc Superbike. He was at the test a few weeks prior. He was very fast right away. The bike sounded impressive too, lots of power in that thing. That bike could be heard from anywhere on the mountain. I am not riding a superbike. I think I should be now. There were also a few French newcomers and a few "oldcomers" too. Fabrice Lambert was another very fast rider that was out for the training sessions making good times. His speed was impressive. He would also be on a superbike, a Ducati 1098R. As a rookie, he was there for the record and we suspected he would be super-fast. He is also a very nice and optimistic guy. I enjoyed getting to know him and seeing him at very odd ours of the morning.

The car racing division is like it is at the Indianapolis 500--history, amazing legendary history. It has a very distinguished past. Many famous drivers have competed here over the years. Mario Andretti; Bobby, Al, Louie and Robby Unser, Rod Millen, Dallenbach, Tajima and Sebastien Loeb, who holds the current record and many more great drivers have driven and challenged the Peak. One of my favorite people racing was ex-motorcycle division racer and champion Greg Tracy, back for his second year behind the wheel in the electric division. He drove the Mitsubishi MIEV Evolution III. On a motorcycle, Greg was fast at Pikes Peak and has competed for many years winning titles in multiple classes. Greg has also taken a few massive crashes there. Maybe it is safer for him in the car now. We have raced here as teammates and rivals (you are both in this sport). You want to straight up win, beat everyone and then be a super nice guy. But you want to win first. I have only good vibes for Greg and I wished him the best for his race.

After an hour or four, we managed to get all our official business completed as well as the typical BS that is a standard with this crowd of people. It is just good to see the other guys and would be a shame not to get to visit just because. I also like to see the nervous people running around all stressed out about things. The general stress that hangs in the air there is strange. It is a mix of bundled up energy and outright panic. You see people become totally locked-up and almost paralyzed. They are usually the ones just in front of the long line, and then there is always some guy running through the crowd like OJ Simpson through the airport all panic-stricken--running and yelling for something left behind or forgotten. Good times.

I was happy to leave get back to the hotel. This was my rest day and still hoped to log some rest hours. I can feel the need to lie down again, to try once more to sleep. I am starting to feel better. My lungs still feel pretty phlegmy but I am breathing a lot better and have started to lose the hacking cough. I seem to be letting the bod shut down and have slowed down mentally. I think for the last few hours I have been in a slow motion state. Moving slowly and speaking slowly. I do want to lie down now but it is only like three o' clock in the afternoon. It is said that to stay awake long enough to adjust to the time zone is the best thing to do. I think the haze is on for the rest of this day so who cares what time it is, I just want to sleep. As soon as we get back to the Mecca, I try to get into bed with the TV. Let's just say I watched a lot of television, stretched out and tried to keep productive and organized. And I did get some rest in there and some genuine sleep.

18 FREE PRACTICE DAY 1

Tuesday is day #1 of practice, five days until race day. Tuesday morning is an early one. 2:30 am is the call time when I must be ready to get up. The entire Ducati team would load into a couple of Sprinter vans and head up the hill. At 2:30AM when I woke up I could feel my body slowly trying to repair itself. Strange, it just felt strange. Better I think or maybe worse. The truth is my whole body felt unlike anything I am used to. Sluggish and weak. I didn't speak much because I just didn't want to and I knew that would only slur or moan like a drunk. To try to make things easier on myself I dressed in my riding suit now instead of later. Better than trying to get dressed on the gravel shoulder of the road next to the van in 30-degree temperatures at 12,000 feet. I slipped into my Kushitani leathers, (black and badass cool guy looking) put on my Sidi boots, an extra big jacket and a beanie. "Knock knock," says Rod as he taps on my door. I gathered my ride food, vitamins and meds into a backpack, and stepped out into the cold morning air and climbed directly into the van to stay warm. We first drove through the 24 hour AM/PM gas station on our way to the highway near the Mecca. There were many people out, drunks, bums or tweakers, no offense. And to think that we were the ones that looked out of place.

After a 35-minute drive from the Mecca with at least five thousand feet of altitude gain, we arrived onto the course at the start line. Today we (the motorcycles) were scheduled to practice on the upper section of the course starting from Devil's Playground. We climbed an additional three thousand feet on the winding course to the designated parking area. Can you say vertigo? It was a practice moment for Don as he was in the front seat shadow riding the lefts and rights along the road as we climbed to Devil's Playground. I think I even heard him mouthing the gear changes and motor revs. For me I could not have cared less and tried to keep from getting sick.

Devil's Playground sits on a plateau at 12,000 plus feet elevation—more than two miles above sea level. Despite the name it does not resemble any kind of playground. In fact, I think it was used as a landscape to film a few parts of Planet of the Apes, the older films with Charlton Hesston. It is a rock and shale covered ledge with zero vegetation. On this day, only a couple patches of snow added some color to the rock. Riding there would not be so pleasant at this time of the early morning. I think that it has its place in the race as the final push through the dead zone or the final desolate challenge to the finish. It is not the safest place nor any bit forgiving if you were to crash up there. All the motorcycle riders, crews, teams and everyone else with anything else going on up there were herded into a makeshift parking lot that was anything but level. Cold, very cold. It was nearly 3:45 am when we arrived and the crew started setting up. I was acutely aware of how thin the air was and how carsick I was feeling. I was ready to puke at the smallest movement. Each time stillness settled in and the heater stabilized to warm the inside of the van, someone opened a door and wrecked it. "Be still you bastards," is what I wanted to say out loud, but I knew it was all necessary

Practice days were broken up into three groups and three sections of the course. You never ride the whole course complete during practice. The only time you run the full racecourse is on race day. I have raced Pikes Peak six times and have run the full course five times, as I had a crash last year and did not run the full course at race speed.. Sections vary in length but it is approximately broken into thirds. The cars make up two full groups, motorcycles one group. I could not guess why we had drawn the top section for day one. I do not enjoy the top section at all. It was so cold (freezing), so dark and damp (frozen) that morning. When there are no clouds, the sky was clear this is "THE" place to witness the most beautiful sunrise you will ever see, period. It is an emotional experience to see it. However, that day it was just too cloudy and we did not see the sunrise. Damn. I was looking forward to that.

My inner time clock was on the fritz and my body needed to release pressure. To be perfectly truthful, I had to take a shit. There are no out houses up here. "Well that's just f-ing great," I say aloud as Don looked on. All I could do was grab a handy roll of TP and walk out to the edge of the pit area, pull off my suit and squat one out in the extremely cold thin air. Climbing out of a leather suit is hard work at 12,000 feet, especially with vertigo. It was still dark out so I only go about 50 feet from the van to do my business. I wondered how funny I would look if the light was suddenly up. This is never the way to start your day, but I could not hold that in all morning. A small matter of personal hygiene also makes this kind of gross and wet wipes are again my way, my salvation. Love those things. Doing my best to contain the waste site I returned to the van almost gassed and sort of sweaty but, with a sense of relief in my exhausted weak ass body.

There was a lot to do to get things ready for the crew and it becomes like a fire drill. Likewise for the other teams out there in the dark. I tried to remove myself from all the commotion and focus on riding and staying warm enough to do it well. Don joined me and we talked about a few things before we would ride. It is hard to just ride, memorize and rehearse the course up there because there are so many things going on and so much commotion and we are on a very treacherous mountain peak. Don and I talked about the section up top and the different corners. Don is obsessive about this road course. He has memorized each section to a freaky detail that has me feeling more able to talk about with him. He says to me something like, "The dip at Bottomless Pit, the right-hander, has a double apex third gear floater with an on camber braking zone and uphill off camber long right in second or third gear exit. It becomes a blind entry to the next left and you must wait for the apex at mid throttle. Right?", "Ah, what?" I think to myself, acting as I know exactly, but in reality, I am sort of confused. I just nod because I am not really speaking too much yet. This will become somewhat common for Don and me. His over exuberance and his attention to details will keep him safe as he has been, so well-rehearsed that he will be able to remain safe and fast. I only leave him with this, "You should ride at 75% for all these practices and study the hill at a manageable and safe speed. You will not have a good race if you crash out in the practice sessions."

Paul, Becca and Rod were on top of setting up. Parking is limited but they handled it. Maybe that is why we are always up so early? They have a great relationship with the race organizers, the officials and the starter. We always seem to get the best of everything; parking included. After a 5:00 am riders' meeting and a prayer we waited for enough sunlight to start taking runs. The build up to start running creates movements in the pit area that are somewhat comical. There is always so much nervous energy, macho energy. The deal up there is this: you can talk brave and even act as brave as you want through sign-up and entry or at the restaurant, the bar, with your team and in your safety zones. However, when you are finally there on the Peak, when you finally hop on the bike up there and start it up, lower that face shield and open up the throttle you had better be ready to live it. You'd better be ready to be brave and man up in this place. If you are not up to it now, while there is no heat, no grip, and no safe and nice road to cruise at a comfortable speed, you will no longer be recognized as a racer and you will be lost in a world of fear and doubt. You will be unable to take in all the feedback from the road and the motorcycle to make improvements or to change a bad set-up. It is at that time that it gets very, very real up there.

After I was fully dressed and ready to ride I took some time with my bike. I just sat on it and got used to how good it felt. I simulated riding it in my mind and where I wanted to be mentally when I would begin to ride it. Sitting on the bike as it is perched on the stands with tire warmers and all, I visualize my movements and stretched back and forth and up and back. The bike felt so much bigger and heavier than my bicycle. I was so thin after RAAM that I wondered how strong I would be. I had not ridden the bike since I got there. I also wondered how much faster I would be that before that same reason. Lighter and faster. I think of how good it was going to feel when I would be riding hard, riding fast and smooth. I was ready for that great feeling. Loud horns signaled that the starter and course marshals were ready. The sweep riders are ready too. Sweep riders are escorts for the competitors. They are our lead-out guys ahead of the racers like a pace car. Safety first as they can communicate with eyes on the road and radio communication. They also follow the racers or sweep after all the riders have left the start area. These official riders wear reflective vests and flashers. They are easy to spot and stay together as two riders or four.

The first run is a sighting run and is designed to be a safe ride on the course at safe speeds. Not every rider sees it that way so you must look out for these fools. There are guys out there that are nervous and twitchy. Theses riders are mostly rookies that want to win this thing right here and now so you had better stay well clear of them. Some guys are so nervous they just cannot help themselves. There have been many crashes due too over exuberant or nervous riders who did not heed the warnings of the road and weather and most importantly their own limitations. You must respect this mountain and this race like no others. This is a very dangerous time and crashes can happen going up or coming down. There will be accidents during the practice week, there always is. Some of the worst accidents happen during practice. Riders will get hurt and you do not want to be one of those. As a competitor, you must deal with safety, speed, comfort and fate. The first run is for a sighting and feeling of the course and that is all.

After we rolled out on our first run, it took a few moments for me to feel myself adjust to the bike. The motorcycle was so amazing to feel. The road was very cold and slick. After a few miles I began to run the bike harder

[BRIGHT AND EARLY WELL AT LEAST EARLY
Getting ready to take my first run from Devil's
Playground. How cold is it?]

when there was enough gap to the next rider. Just a few punches to feel how the motor was running. I quickly figured out there was a problem with the electronics on my bike. To make matters even more challenging, there was ice on the upper section just before the summit. This is what I meant earlier about manning up. The road was covered with a white coat of ice. I rode slowly to the summit and parked within the group of riders and next to

Jeremy Toye. All he said was, "WTF." Riding back down it was so cold my hands and fingers felt frozen by the time I returned to the starting point. Back at the pit area I my mechanics Ed and Ted the news about the bike. They got right to work to fix it. Don and I hopped back in the van and turned up the heater. My hands and fingers turned into frozen sausages on the ride back down. During the practice days we usually get four to six practice runs per section with usually about 25 minutes between the times stopping one run and starting the next run. That is all the time you get to make changes to the bike or try new tires, or as in our case, try to fix a motor/electrical problem.

Due to the ice on the Peak, the officials have lowered the turnaround point to a section below the summit called Boulder Park. This was a relief. Slicks on ice? Toye, said it best, "WTF!" On run two, the first run at speed, I quickly realized that the changes made to the bike by Ed/Ted did not fix the problem, but may have made an improvement. I rode much faster and started to feel myself becoming tuned-in to the bike and road. The upper section is the straightest and fastest, but there were still many blind corners and bends. There is no run off anywhere, there are steep rock embankments to one side and boulder covered slopes that fall away steeply on the other side. Speeds are on average between 75 and 90 mph. With my Ducati electronics in limp mode it was a bit sketchy to ride hard at half throttle, so it was back to Ed and Ted.

The guys tried doing a recalibration of the system by plugging into their laptop computer, then they tried turning it off and back on again like you would a home computer.

They checked the fuel, plugs and a few other slight changes still didn't solve the problem. So we ended up spending the entire practice chasing after an electronic problem without much improvement. The bike remained in a limp mode.   I was unable to go above 4000 or so rpm's. It was getting frustrating as well as becoming a bit dangerous because when the bike was under power it would pull and then just shut off. I had tried to just ride through it initially but the bike would not have it. I got a good hustle through a couple of sections and then the motor would shut down again. Ed and Ted made the best of the turnaround time between runs to make changes quickly to the motor and electrical system.

[TROUBLE SHOOTING: Ed, Ted and Chris attend to the bike between runs. They worked hard to get the electrical issue fixed by trying many different things. There is not a ton of time to work with though. 9:00 am is the deadline. The bike will be ready for tomorrow.]

Everything we tried was not able fix the problem and we finished the session without a clean run. It is unwise to force anything up there so we maintained our cool and rolled with it. We knew we would fix it.

I had a hard time trying to get my mojo back under such conditions. I was hoping to get all cozy and friendly with the bike that day, setting up my week like a champ. I felt happy that we did get to ride the bike and that I would get one more practice session on the top section in a couple days. I was struggling with the altitude and my lungs were still congested. Paul had brought canisters of oxygen and I did use the hell out of them. I did not seem to feel all that much better though. I needed to figure out a way to rest over the next few days for my body to recover before the race and for my mind to get it together and get into it. I felt way to lethargic and lazy. It seemed impossible to snap out of that detuned feeling. I had to think about the bigger picture and accept that we would get up to speed slower than normal. Under the circumstances, it is probably best that I just give into this mentality. On a positive note, my legs felt good and I had normal feeling in the muscles, I was no longer retaining water in my legs and a spring of new hope and faith were again strong in me.

While the team cleaned things up Rod and I discussed what needed to be done, the tires we want for tomorrow, engine brake. What can be done regarding the backpressure on the rear wheel into the corners off throttle, fuel type, etc.? The sun was coming out and it felt good to warm up and to be finished. I was very happy to be heading down the mountain in one piece and to a good breakfast. There was also an effort in place to try a new Pirelli front tire that day. We did manage to accomplish a good test of the tire. It was a rain / slick. It was impressive on a very cold, damp, paint-covered surface. The timing results from practice were as expected and we were fifth fastest with a slow time. More than ten seconds down from the fastest time. Day one times: Fabrice Lambert 2:42, Jeremy Toye 2:46, Bruno Longlois 2:46, Don Canet 2:51, and I was off the back just a bit at 2:55.

After a smallish breakfast on our way down the mountain. The mechanics, Ed and Ted had already gotten after the electronic issues. I circled about for a few minutes to wind down. Soon, I was trying once again to get some sleep. This week would normally put me in a haze after multiple sleepless nights, but in my case after RAAM, I was there and then some. My body wanted to shut down but my brain was fired up and every time I went to asleep my dreams were of a panic situation as if I was still on RAAM. "It's my turn to get on the bike," "Where are we at" and the worse recurring dream was, "did I sleep too long? I better get up," making me pop up stressed out at any given moment. I seemed to be dreaming more relative to my daily life and current tasks than to some fantasy type of dream. It may be more of a busy mind than anything else. Hello paranoia. .

After I got up I was having thoughts that during RAAM, I had fallen asleep and no one woke me up. I realized that I do not remember a certain section of the race therefore, I must have been asleep or blacked out or something. This is the when I had called Dave Mirra and accused the team of leaving me in the bunk as they raced on without me. It seems that I am able to realize it is just a mental block. I know it is not true, but I could not seem to shake it. Wait... I become worried or paranoid is a better word for this feeling. Like a switch has changed and now I am suddenly worried about my relationships, I remember and regret the past. I worry about my kids, I worry about Brenda. Even when I tried to pray I could not focus on the topic for long and I would not finish the prayer. I'd get off track and start to think of something else. Depression washed over me like a wave that I did not see coming in. Finally I just said "F it," and got up to go looking for coffee and distractions. Funny how any type of distraction will do to get my mind off things. It really is incredible how emotionally fragile you are at this level of extreme fatigue. These are the effects of RAAM

I messaged my kids by texting. It is the best way to get through to them. If I call they will usually answer but in a way it is better to text them. I looked forward to seeing Hunter, my oldest along with my daughter Ronni who would be coming to Pikes Peak with my mom and dad in three more days, driving there in a small car from California. All of them are troopers for sure. In addition, my soul mate, my muse and motivation, Brenda Lyons would arrive on Thursday evening. She was in Denver for work today but, she would be coming to be with me through the weekend. It was important for me to have them all with me.

19 LIKE A FAMILY VACATION, PAST PIKES PEAKS RACES

Hunter, Trevor and Ronni are my three amazing little kids, not really so little any more but they will all ways be my little kids. Hunter is the oldest. He is 21. I was a kid raising him. He is a man now and that is strange at times. He is so smart and artistic, much more than I am. He is going to college and is working too. He makes a dad proud. Then there is Trevor, he is 19. His light is so bright, endless and pure and he has a big giant heart. Trevor is my dirty-faced boy, the middle kid with the skills. He's so stubborn at times. He had a late growth spurt and he is now the tallest. The skater kid still working on the kick flip. Then, Ronni, my little girl. She is so sweet that it makes me cry. Of course, she and I have the father/daughter bond. It was given to me at her birth. She is my princess. Two of three of my kids were coming and that had an additional emotional effect on me. It was our place, our race and that sets Pikes Peak apart from all other races that I have ever done. That is how we started coming here before it became a much more dangerous race. The feeling I get when they are close to me is a release of anxiety, I am connected and not missing a thing anywhere else. There is no other place that I would need to be if they are here. I do not live with them anymore and I miss them every day. But, they will be here and that is all that will matter to me. Maybe together we can recapture what we once felt here.

2005 was my first race at Pikes Peak. I brought the kids. All four of us drove up from California, road trip style like a vacation. Together in a suburban with the All Access trailer carrying all the bikes and parts. We met my mechanic Glen Grenfell who had flown in from his home town of Iron Mountain Michigan. And of course, fate would have it that we started our traditional temporary living situation at the Mecca Motel. We all stayed at the Mecca for the week and had the very best time ever. The boys had little battery powered motorcycles and we built a track around the parking area and buildings. We could not keep the little bikes charged up long enough. The bikes were Honda mini road racers. The bodywork was beat up after the boys began to beat on each other and eventually one of them broke off a foot peg. From the inside of my room I could hear them slamming into each other followed with laughter. There really was no need to leave the motel because they were having such a good time.

The swimming pool is where Ronni and I would hang out after the early practice sessions. I had more need for rest, but it was so fun that we really did not sit around too much. While Glen and the other mechanics worked away on the bikes, the kids and I kept active doing all sorts of fun things. The Mecca would became a yearly home away from home. After the first time we had stayed at the Mecca in 2005, the place had made a lasting effect on all of us. After returning to the next school year at home, Ronni had a school writing project and came up with this very detailed fiction about living in Colorado. When I went to her open house, her teacher actually asked me how long we lived in Colorado and how did we like living in California now. So, it must have had a positive effect on her. I think that the way my life was following these crazy wild adventurous schedules as a motorcycle racer made our lives more like a fairytale. Regardless, the Mecca is a magic place for us.

Paul and Becca, Rod, Paul Thede, Glen and many others have been living at the Mecca for the week-long Pikes Peak event ever since. It has become the place to be. It sits just below the Garden of the Gods (a park full of incredible rock formations) and closer to the peak than the other resort hotels in town. Tension leaves your body when you are there. There is no need to rush or stress about too much.

Once, motorcycle racing legend Malcolm smith and I sat at the pool comparing old racing scars and winding down on a timeless afternoon. I have known Malcolm for a long time, but this is the only place around that we have had time to share these kinds of moments. He has met the kids too and has been there to support his son Alexander many times. He is both an icon and a very funny and cool person to be around.

[YET ANOTHER LEGEND: Anyone who's ever seen the iconic motorcycle movie "On Any Sunday" know who Malcolm Smith is. He and I enjoy a conversation at the Mecca pool, comparing scars and stories.]

The first year in 2005 at the Mecca there was an Indian woman that was always in the Jacuzzi—all day long. She was covered in tattoos, had a Mohawk and suffered from Tourette's syndrome. Sheila was her name. She would be in the Jacuzzi for six or eight hours a day. Every so often, she would have an outburst, yelling randomly a mixture of things and thrashing about. She never used profanities though. The kids were a little scared at first, but they got over it. At times, I was trying not to break out in laughter. She is a very strange but a very interesting person. There was something sweet and endearing about her. She also seemed to be ok with the kids and I and that was good. According to Liz and Gary She seemed to like us and accepted us just fine. On the second trip out there in 2006, she began to mix in with us racer people and I learned that if she liked you she would buy things for you and place them in a trashcan near your room. Again, I learned this from Liz and Gary. She had left me some cologne and clothes in a bag. That is according to Liz and Gary. If Sheila did not like you, she would not face you. She would just show you her back.

One time during a busy late afternoon while all the racers and teams at the motel were working on bikes and gear, there was this big mouth, big drinking macho man that was riding Pikes Peak for the first time and staying at the Mecca. His name is not important. He was throwing his awesomeness around the Mecca one evening after he had sucked down a few cold ones when he and Sheila came together near the front desk. Sheila immediately turned her back at him. He was not discouraged and tried to come around her to show is awesomeness and she just kept on spinning away from him one way or the other until he finally just gave up and moved on. Paul Livingston tells the best story as he and Becca were watching it play out from a distance. Sheila lives at the Mecca now and has become part of Gary and Liz's family. Sheila eventually took over my favorite room at the Mecca. The one with the big flat screen and the Jacuzzi. Go figure. I have so many great memories of the Mecca through the many years I have been racing at Pikes Peak..

During that first year, we had to pack up all three kids and drive up to the course daily before dawn. It felt just like a family vacation and Groundhog's day. We were all stuffed in the Suburban heading into the mountains. Ronni would get carsick each morning. It was so tough for her to stomach that drive up the winding road. She was placed in the center of the back seat to view the road, but mostly to have a bucket in front of her in case she needed it. She got sick most every day. The boys just slept away or fought with each other as brothers do. I felt good knowing that they were more worried about sleep or finding some other thing to do like look for lizards rather than worry about what I was doing. My little Ronni would be so sick she looked green at times, but she never complained. By the time we were back down to the Mecca we could all have some rest then breakfast, usually by 10:00 am so the whole day lay ahead for us.

Directly across the street is Amanda Fonda's, a good Mexican restaurant. The place has been there forever, it has an indoor and an outdoor seating option, and both have super cool atmospheres. Yes, we love Mexican food so how nice is that? Amanda Fonda's is a blessing and a curse because it is so close and easy. Our diet consisted of 70% Mexican and 30% snacks and drinks with a roll or two of Rolaids. It was common for us to have two meals a day there. It is the meal stop of some of the fondest memories I have from Pikes Peak. Like a song from the past that instantly projects you to that moment again just as it was. Some of my best memories are not of being on the motorcycle, but in the other things that we did. We made trips to the zoo, Seven Fall (a series of seven cascading waterfalls of South Cheyenne Creek), local lakes and tourist spots like Garden of the Gods. The zoo in Colorado Springs is one of the best I have ever been to. Ronni and I did the whole afternoon there one day and did not get to see it all. The giraffe exhibit lets you feed the animals from a high spot. Like, right at their heads. The gorillas and other African animals as well as the local cats and bears were more active there than at other zoos.

In 2007, Ronni and I went to see the Seven Falls. It should be called stairway to heaven without oxygen. This place is amazing and a great workout as well. Stairways climb next to the falls like ladders. At night, they light up the falls and cliffs with multi-colored lights. It is worth the work to climb it. Once on top there is a huge park to hike and explore. After such amazing options of things to do you might think we are spoiled and needy for the extravagance, but no. It is most often more fun to go to Denny's with this group. We really do not care that much. We just like to make an adventure wherever we are.

My very first trip to Pikes Peak was to do a test ride in April 2005 with Gary Trachy a fellow racer and great guy. It was months before the race. He talked about it being really an amazing experience and he said it was super fun and that I would love it. I had heard it was super dangerous and that people had died up there. He said come with me to practice and decide for yourself. That trip turned out to be one of the funniest weekend trips ever. I got to ride the course for the first time with no pressure at all. It was still damn fast and scary. I had driven up the hill with Gary. He showed me the road and the tough spots, the good sections and the dangerous section. He showed me a couple of places that were deadly if you were to go off there. It was awesome and it was scary to see it like that. The course had dirt sections then and actually, there was more dirt than paved sections—it was not all paved until 2013. The dirt was pea-size gravel and was kind of slick yet smooth. Gary and I had a great time riding for those few days. We got to know each other and had a few laughs.

Gary is really a good guy with a great sense of humor. He and I talked nonstop during the 18-hour drive. We told a few stories of the most embarrassing things we had ever done. I cannot remember my story but his was funny as hell and had me laughing uncontrollably. He explained how one night he and some friends were all drinking throughout the day and spontaneously decided to go to Catalina Island in California. One of the guys had a boat and some money. They sailed over and spent the evening there. While on the island, they were in a bar and started doing shots. Gary said, "I don't do shots," but did anyway and threw-up all over his shirt and was being thrown out as he pleaded to stay. He claimed he would buy a round for the house if they let him stay. Apparently the bar tender saw the need for the money and relented. Later as he and his friends were walking back to the harbor to the boat, they became a bit rowdy and macho. He said as they were walking down an alley a small half door caught their eye and Gary decided to kick it in as a show of young man's strength. As he walked away feeling triumphant a voice snapped out "hey you" stay right there… turns out it was the access door for the harbor police department. He had a tough time coming up with a story in such a pinch, but told the police that he and his friends were just playing around and one of them pushed him into the door and accidentally broke it. The policemen asked him which friend had pushed him. Gary pointed at one of his friends, "Him. He pushed me!". The police arrested both of them and they had to spend the night in jail. The guy he pointed at was the guy who owned the boat. Gary is a super funny guy and we did have an amazing few days of riding, but in a way the rest of the trip is what the experience of Pikes Peak was so worth coming back for.

After making the initial trip with Gary I did my first race at Pikes Peak in 2005 aboard a KTM 610 Supermoto unlimited bike. I won the 750cc class, set a new course record and I was rookie of the year. The race week was more practice for me to memorize the road and to get my first taste of the ridiculous time schedule. It was with my mechanic Glen Grenfell and my team, All Access that we first came together as a team. The motorcycles used to race in a group of five riders at a time. You lined up at the start line five wide for a flag start. It was tight racing I think I prefer it that way. Gary rode the 450cc class that year so we did not have to race each other. After testing out my leathers a few times in the practice sessions with small crashes, I made it to the start line ready for the race. I started in front and pulled out a lead on the pavement section. I had a few mistakes on the dirt like going off the track once at the end of the straight before Gilly's Corner (a hairpin left after a long straight that was still dirt at that time) without a crash. I went past the corner in a skid/slide and down a little embankment and through some bushes. I was able to get back on course pretty quick without being passed. I saw second place rider Jeff Grace coming into the corner as I took off. I continued racing and just after the brake check booth at Glen Cove at about the halfway point there was a fire engine on the course where a rider had crashed. I slowed and rode around the engine, there was a red flag but I could count on Grace coming in and passing me if he could, so I raced to the top of the mountain. It was actually snowing at the top when I crossed the finish line. At the start it 75 degrees and sunny, but 12 minutes later it was cold and snowing on the top. It was just the icing on the cake that we had also set the course record; 12:12:00

After that race in 2005, I was hooked. As a promise to the kids, we had planned a fishing day for Monday. Just as we were heading out to go fishing, we were told of the awards banquet. We almost missed the awards banquet! I could not miss it because I was to receive awards. We popped in to make an appearance, and yes, to receive awards. It was another big bonus. There is never enough time to do all the things you want to do or need to do I guess. The kids had earned a fishing day. So, on the way home we stopped in Copper Mountain and went fishing. Moments like this show me that God really loves us. There really is very little money for winning Pikes Peak. Some things are more about the real experience of it and not a monetary reward. The reward is in the experience.

I came back in 2006 and had an epic duel with Gary Trachy and got beat by 1 second. Gary and I had a great race for the win, passing each other a few times and dogging each other shamelessly. We were never more than a bike length apart the whole race. Gary rode a Husqvarna 660 and I rode the 610 KTM again. We were so evenly matched. We did go faster than the previous year and set a new record 25 seconds faster than 2005. The official finish time was 11:47:00. Gary now held the record for the 750cc class.

[ONE TICK FROM A WIN: This is Gary and I racing head to head in 2006. We used to race five at a time. We had a race long battle that I lost at the finish by one lousy second.]

In 2007 it was a completely new Pikes Peak experience. That year BMW would field the biggest motorcycle effort ever at Pikes Peak. I had just signed a contract with the German company to help develop a 450cc motorcycle for motocross and Supermoto and they also had ideas of conquering Pikes Peak. Gary and I rode BMW 1200cc beasts called the HP2 Mega motos, road bikes, big ones, with a lot of horsepower and top speed. The bikes were super heavy, German metal

The road was still a mix of dirt and asphalt then and Gary's brother, Greg Trachy, a German road racer named Marcus Barth and a Supermoto rider named Casey Yarrow also rode the big BMW's. It was a BMW race. The course surface had been changing. There was more asphalt each year, but there was still many dirt sections. We raced together three riders at a time still using a flag start. It was beginning to get a little tight with these big bikes now. Plus the higher speeds on the paved sections was getting friggin crazy in a group.(in 2012 a single rider time trial start was put into effect for safety reasons) I ended the race without a transponder and was given a time. Third position.

Before the race, I would throw my qualifying run to get a slower time. Each run during qualifying I would stop and wait for 20 or 30 seconds on a tight corner and then ride slowly to the finish point. I would end up getting a time that would get me a later start grid with the slower riders. I believed that in a fast group Gary and the faster guys would follow me. It is easy to pace off another rider as long as he does not ride off a cliff. You can follow a fast rider and use him as a brake marker and a corner mark. You can draft him.

[LOTS OF MOTOR, LOTS OF MOUNTAIN: 1200cc Mega Moto BMW was the biggest bike that I had ever ridden anywhere let alone at Pikes Peak. That year was scarier than it should have been.]

It seems now that I was helping riders quite a bit during practice to pass on the gift. On race day, I wanted to be alone. On the actual race run, I thought I was on a real flyer and believed I would win but the transponder on my bike did not register at the finish line and so I was given a time based on assumptions that was just slower than the time that got the win. Bummer.

In 2008, I rode in the 750cc class again and had another epic battle up the mountain changing the lead. This time it was with Davey Durrell who nipped me on the top section in the dirt just before the finish to win the race. Davey is possibly the winningest motorcycle rider in Pikes Peak history. As funny as this sounds I rode the same Husqvarna 660 that Gary had ridden and beat me on in 2006. I had the pleasure of having Paul Lima from GP Motorcycles and Cristiano Menga "the little bastard" there as my team and mechanic. Malcolm Smith gave Cristiano the nickname as a term of endearment that year. I was healing from a compound fracture and compartment syndrome to my lower right leg and a right shoulder that had serious nerve damage. I was sort of a mess and I probably did not have any business racing or riding for that matter, but I was mentally ready to move on and make it happen again on a motorcycle. I cannot explain why, but I believe that during this time for me it was very important that I race there. There was also so much going on in my life on personal levels that were driving me. I had a real feeling of urgency. It was one of those times in life that you must do it or you will never do it again. "Ride or Die" was on my mind.

Durelle rode an Aprilia 550. A twin cylinder with fuel injection. We had a great race. First Davey led and I passed him at Engineer's Corner around the outside. It was a nice pass. I was able to pass him around the outside on the brakes while sliding in nicely. This pass was possibly hard to accept for Davey. After the pass, I did not gain much of an advantage and never pulled out any kind of a lead. He just waited for me to make a mistake. If only the course had more asphalt. On the upper section above Devil's Playground Davey was stronger than I was. He and his bike were just better. I had a few slow entries to sweeping sections between mile 17 and 18. I really tried to hold him off and keep a good pace, but he eventually got by just before Upper Gravel Pit about a mile from the top. I tried one last time to out brake him into the tight right-hander before Boulder Park and nearly went off the mountain. Davey won and set a new motorcycle record as I rode in his dust just back and out of the win. Second at Pikes Peak is more disappointing than any other place you can race.

I would not return to Pikes Peak until 2013. It was not for lack of interest or effort. I did make the usual calls and requests to sponsors and race teams. Truth is, there was no longer a Supermoto series. The economy had taken a hit and motorsports funding was all but gone. What little money there was in the sport was now focused on the Supercross series or in motocross. Then there was my job. I had taken off into the Nuclear Cowboyz show and a couple of other work projects in 2009 and my priorities had changed. I still wanted to race Pikes Peak. I truly missed it too. I kept in contact with Paul and Rod too because they had become the Ducati team. The road was now all pavement and the bike classes had become ruled by the 1205cc class. Overall times on the hill were very close between the cars and the bikes. It was getting more dangerous with higher speeds and many of the original riders like Gary and Greg Trachy were deciding to never do it again. Many of the original bike racers were finished as well.

Carlin Dunne was now the outright motorcycle record holder. Carlin had quite a gift for riding up on the Mountain. Carlin is also very brave and fearless. The bike of choice was also a branded Pikes Peak Edition Ducati Multistrada. Recent developments had taken my life to a place where my fitness and my focus had made me a racer again. I began to contact, or more to the point, bother Paul and Rod about coming back to ride. First, we discussed the possibility of riding a Kawasaki Ninja 600. This was exciting and possibly perfect news. I was pretty hopeful that would work out. It didn't. The next possibility was to ride a battery-powered bike and at first I was not too optimistic, but after some thought it started to fit my other plans and make good sense. I was feeling good about this new challenge. Paul and I spoke of the counter angles to make it a big interest to my current projects. Sort of a win, win situation. Then that fell through. I had begun to accept that Pikes Peak 2013 might not happen.

Lucky for me there was Paul and Rod. The two of them had been committed to make it happen. As I kept the faith that it would eventually come together they did the work and came back with Ducati. Paul had asked Michael Larkin of Akrapovic if he would be a part of this team and support it with his own bikes. Michael had the same bike that Carlin had ridden in the previous years. So with Akrapovic as the sponsor and with the Ducati bike we would race the 1205cc class. And so the team unfolded. There would not be too much in the way of practice time on the bike and there would be no trip to Pikes Peak for the scheduled tests prior to race week. I would need to take it all in when I got there.

As for my schedule, I was still full-time with the Nuclear Cowboyz and I had also started working on the 2013 RAAM as a video host, covering the race with "Riding the Line." The week prior to RAAM, I would be working from a car while driving across the country with the race. I was also training for RAAM by putting in lots of training and a fair amount of pedal time. So the week prior to Pikes Peak I was doing 16 to 18 hour days. I would finish shooting RAAM and fly directly to Colorado for the race. With Paul, Rod, Michael, and the rest of the team we really had a good chance to have a great result. I just had to show up ready to get the riding part done. The general rule throughout the team that we wanted to have fun with no hard emphasis on winning or record setting. There would also be a new start schedule for the bikes this year. The motorcycles would go first. It sounded good really, at least in the beginning. After a good week of practice and a good qualifying run, I was top qualifier in the 1205cc class. This had me as the very first rider on the schedule. I would start first. All things looked super good. We had a chance at going for both the win and the record time.

I had ridden my way into feeling confident and ready to put down a good race run. I believed we had a good shot at the record or to be in the under ten minute club. I was feeling brave through the confidence now. You try to manage your practice runs while riding fast and hard but never riding too hard. You want to save that run at 100 percent with all the risk taking for the actual race run. No need to tempt fate the entire week at this place. Stay at 75 percent and stay in one piece for a strong and fast race. The bike was amazing and the tires were good. So far, the course was pretty clean and consistent. Overall, we were ready. After the final day of practice, the qualifying on Friday, we got some heavy rain. Then on Saturday the day off, we had some more rain. We woke up to rain on race day. Suddenly being top qualifier sucked and I would be racing on a questionable course. I would be the first rider or vehicle out on a dirty course. Who knew what I would have to deal with up there. Wet pavement, sand run off from the rains, rocks, there could be anything out there.. Surely, any rubber that had been left on the course would be gone. I was scared to think about it. I honestly was not feeling good about it.

I got dressed into my suit and riding gear in the van. All of our team members were quiet and there was a tension in the other teams and riders as well. Paul, Rod and Michael were quiet and serious. Everyone else was a bit tense. Brenda was with me. We stayed away from everyone and together in the van as long as possible. I did the usual pre-race ritual of sitting on the bike and visualizing my run, my movements and rehearsed the course. I went to work removing fear from my mind. Now is when my faith will hold me steady. This is how I am able to ride up there. You must be able to focus on the course and to ride hard without hesitation and be fast. I love and trust in God. What else is there to do? Whom else can I trust? I must say that the feelings that you have to work through to race there are tough. There is an excitement that runs through you like no other. This electric buzz in your body tingles in every cell in your body. To be able to focus well you must be able to accept the possible consequences. I tell Brenda that I love her and that if anything were to go wrong that she means the world to me. Brenda did not want to hear this sort of thing from me at this time and made sure that I knew it. We walked together to the start line and I got ready to start. There were a few delays that challenged my concentration. Paul and Rod kept me calm and Rod told me the things I needed to hear. Finally, we were set to start, some 30 minutes late.

[MY WORLD: Brenda and I have a beautiful intense moment before the start in 2013. It was the only time that I was truly scared to death and the first time I have crashed during my run...

The start. I think I was holding my breath as I made the left/ right onto the course and hit the rev limiter in second gear and again into third. Then I relaxed and made the next gearshift before the right on top of the hill at speed. I felt better and shrugged off my apprehension. The next few minutes went very well. I was riding well and pushing hard on a very dirty and slick road. Into Engineer's Corner, I hit my marks with a sliding entry and was really cooking. A few moments later, going hard into Heitman's Hill corner I crashed. Sort of out of nowhere, I was down. I slid out on the low side and went sliding across the road. Dirty surface? Paint? Who knows? Quickly I was up and back on the bike, accelerating hard, losing only ten or so seconds. For an instant, I thought that I could still win this thing. So I started to push very hard to make up the lost time. But I pushed too hard too fast and got disoriented long enough to forget the course for just an instant. I overcooked the entry for the corner called Sump, which is a second gear, tight corner. I hit it tapped out in third. I had no choice but to lay it down and crash a second time at a higher speed (like 80 mph). This was pretty much the end of any hope of winning the race. I am lucky to have fallen there because recently there was some grading of dirt on the outer part of the corner to fill in a drop off. It was a sand embankment that stopped me from going into a rock garden. I did get up and finished the run. I continued to the top with a broken front end and no real injuries to myself other than my pride and my sadness for the team who had worked so hard. Out of the first five starters three of us crashed. There were others that followed throughout the morning. Two riders in my class were hurt seriously.

[THE DAMAGE DONE: 2013 was a tough day for these riders. They were not as fortunate as I was to be able to walk away from crashes and still finish.]

The dirty surface took its toll on the racers who went early. I was disappointed, but also felt lucky to not be hurt. I had never crashed out of a Pikes Peak race before. There is no second chance. You get one run and you have to make it count. There is one fact about the road/race course here: you get what the mountain gives to you. The conditions of the mountain will be your limit for speed. The weather will be the limit., the road will be your limit. You may be at your best for any condition that may present itself, but the road will determined what you can do with it and what your time is going to be. If the road is fast you will be fast and if not you will not. It is one day of the year and it will be what it is going to be.

It hurts a lot when something goes wrong. I was going to have a heavy weight on me about this race. I felt like I had to come back to redeem myself and to make it up to the team. I wanted my day in the sun again. I wanted that feeling of peak performance, of being spot on. I wanted to share it with all the team and with Brenda. That is why I was back. I wanted to have my great ride, my great race. I want to have the all-out motorcycle record. I want to be the fastest, the king of the mountain.

20 THE RIGGLES

Each year during race week Don Riggles hosts a dinner at his amazing house in an upscale neighborhood of Colorado Springs. It is nestled back into a mountain and above the valley. From his deck, it's been said that you can see Missouri. Riggles is like the SNL character Bill Brasky.. "He goes about 7'8, 450lbs and crystal shatters when he talks." He and his wife invited the whole Ducati team to his humble abode for dinner. This was the fun, low stress event of the week, one that I really needed about then. I could let go of all the stress and have some serious laughs. My body and mind were both happy to be there. We first sat out on the deck looking east, snacking on cheese and nuts and drinking a beer. The evenings there are really long and peaceful. The warmth of the day holds into the evening only to be interrupted with an evening shower, which is almost a daily event in June. We had just gotten comfortable when the rain hit. Poor Don was tending the barbecue and that is exactly where we left him. We all got up from our chairs and moved inside. After a short time, the rain had gone, the sun had returned and we could once again move freely around the deck and take back our seats.

Meat was on the menu, and lots of it. "It's what's for dinner." I was actually feeling anti-meat that night, but Don's beautiful wife prepared snacks and lighter fare for the meal that I could eat. As I watched her preparing the food, I wondered how Don could have gotten her to fall for him. She seemed clearly way out of his league. The whole meal and experience was perfect. The men took to the garage area to discuss politics and beat the living hell out of Bruno's street fighter muffler. (Bruno Langlois is one of our competitors and last year's winner in my class. He is a Frenchman from Corsica with a Ducati Streetfighter motorcycle). They, Paul, Ed, Riggles and our military brethren, Yaunce and Chris, were actually removing or trying to remove the baffle from inside. Bruno wanted that thing to be louder than it already was, and it was loud already. It's a Ducati. So making it louder will have no effect on performance, just sound badass.

Don's garage is immaculate. Don no doubt takes a lot of pride in his stuff, manly stuff. There are some pictures on the walls and some artful posters, souvenirs and other keepsakes that could be housed in a museum. And of course Don has a macho set of tools; chain saws, axes, an assortment of rifles and other manly things are hanging on hooks, others displayed in cases. The truck parked center of the garage is a big, full duty diesel. The Ducati crew, Don and Paul, took turns with the muffler. Using an assortment of different tools made little to no progress to remove the baffle until the drills and torches came out. One by one the other men filled up the garage. Each new arrival asked what we were doing. A slight error with a hammer and screw driver made an exit hole out the side of the thin aluminum shell followed by an F-bomb. Now there was a shift in the atmosphere. This change prompted a mass exit out of the garage and back into the house.

Don Riggles has been very active over the years with the motorcycles at Pikes Peak. A racer himself and motorcycle enthusiast, he is a fixture for us because he opens his home and his heart up for the race or any other motorcycle race or event in Colorado. One year at the riders' meeting Don had the responsibility of addressing all the riders regarding the schedule and some of the safety issues. During his speech, he was brutally assaulted verbally by Eddy Mulder. Eddy is a legend in motorcycle racing to say the least. He is well respected and more experienced than anyone else is there. I was amazed at what I was seeing and hearing. Seated in the back row Eddy sat back in his chair, arms crossed with a toothpick sticking out of his mouth. With a very self-righteous point of view, he blitzed Riggles repeatedly about every safety topic. Don tried to get through it quickly but Eddy just kept hammering him on each topic. He would not let him go. I could see the sweat on Dons forehead. All I could do was sit in awe, like a high school classroom where the art teacher and the football star clashed in a verbal battle. I could see that they both were heated at the discussion but they also had a sense of humor and became aware of themselves at about the same time that smiles could be seen rising from each of them, as the room had grown quiet and confused. Don would take it in stride and joke about it later.

I have known Don for as many years as I have been doing Pikes Peak. We have made many new friends through mutual friends along the way. Ron Heben (KTM team manager at the time) had introduced us. I was with Ron and KTM in Copper Mountain testing exhaust systems before a Supermoto race there in 2004 or 2005. Ron had told me all about Don over the phone prior to my arrival. Don had been a tour guide for Ron during the preceding week that I had arrived. Don had taken Ron fishing up along some amazing secluded river. I was the lucky one to hear the fishing stories. It was like John Wayne pulling at me to sit down and listen to this, "White fish, over there was all business as he readied his pole to cast out," Don said, motioning to Ron as Ron looked on. "Heben thought he was going to show me how to fish. When he wasn't getting snagged or snapping his line he would get all excited, casting out and then working his lure while reeling in," Don said as he mimicked casting out and reeling in. "And then he finally hooked a fish. Now he was showing me. He had caught the big one and was working hard to land the beast. Yeah, well you know what he pulled up? A sucker fish! White fish." Then Don laughed uncontrollably. Ron would dispute that the best he could as Don and I would be feeding off each other's laughter. It made for a very enjoyable testing session. Even when I was turning fast laps, I would just start laughing inside my helmet.

Over the years, I have come back on many different bikes with different teams. Don has always been there to invite us to his home and to his hospitality. He and his family and friends are just givers. All I can give him is a jersey or a poster. I have even left him with a broken leg one year from Fan Fest. He would try to kick-start the Husqvarna race bike during the press event in front of a crowd of people. In Riggles fashion he man handled the 660cc bike like a toy and showed us his power to kick-start it and the bike back fired and kicked-back hard, breaking his leg. Don walked it off the best he could but must have had a few months of healing to remember us by. Meanwhile back at the Riggles, things were intensifying around a discussion about whether the motorcycles should have a cash bonus for winning. But of course I thinking, "Make it big like $100,000. And a big ass silver cup. Yeah. That sounds good."

The other people who had gotten this discussion rolling thought they did not need a purse and the race was more of a prestigious experience. I began to wonder if these guys have ridden a motorcycle up there lately to even understand the risk that it takes to go fast enough to win. I knew that I would be competing either way but still believed that it would be much bigger and much more prestigious with the money. This opinion had ruffled some feathers. There was also discussion about safety and for the most part, I tried to stay out of it, but I just couldn't. Each year there are slight changes made to keep the risks for the motorcycles to a minimum. There is no way the organizers can take care of everything and there is that damn Murphy who always seems to have something up his sleeve. For Pikes Peak, it is a major job to cover the whole course with safety barriers, hay bales and now air fencing, not to mention safety crew. And consider the safety of the spectators. We all have our opinions about what is best. I have exceptional ideas that might require more funding than what is available. Sad really because with a proper budget one might change the ridiculous practice schedule to more closely simulate race day conditions. Hint, hint. Maybe all you would need is a Friday, Saturday and Sunday rental of the course to have more than enough time to run two days of practice (2 course sections, upper and lower half) and race day. And if the park needs to keep it open for tourists on the cog, the race organization should receive commissions of ticket sales. These are only thoughts in my mind that will not be brought into tonight's discussion. "Ahem!"

After some interesting and at times heated discussions with other dinner guests, we said good night and headed back to the Mecca. Paul, Rod, Becca, Don Canet and I were all together amazed at the beautiful standard for the Riggles, larger than life, warm and friendly and blessed with a variety of friends. On the drive back we mulled over the events and topics of the night. It was fun to visit Don Riggles for sure. The scenery is familiar and pleasing as the sun had not gone down behind the mountains. Then, finally, I was resting alone. I thanked God for the last few weeks, the adventures, the challenges, the quiet times alone with him and the special people who had given me so much. I begged for the heart and eyes to see my way through this crazy, amazing race. I wanted to achieve my goals and finish under ten minutes. I tried to calm my mind and control my thoughts. I really could use a good sleep. It seemed like so long since I had slept well. It felt crazy to be so tired yet having to try to sleep. How could I be so tired and unable to sleep?

21 THE W'S

Wednesday, Practice Day 2 call time is 3:15 am, the middle section. The W's. It's four days before race day and the routine is the same as the previous day. I woke up as if I had just closed my eyes and was not really rested at all. Again I dressed in my room, grabbed my stuff and got into the van. We drove up that winding road to the middle section of the hill and parked in the spot that was saved in trade for a cold pizza; a deal Rod had made with Frank the parking engineer. I am not sure how long this deal has gone on but Rod brings Frank a cold pizza every day we practice. It is an odd arrangement but we were all happy to benefit from it. Frank sure drives a hard bargain. Today the motorcycle pits were at the parking area in Glen Cove, which is at the halfway point of the course. It is also known as "The Brake Check" by the tourists. There is a ranger booth in the center of the up bound lane and the downhill lane. It is very tight parking here. We were packed in like sardines, so it is a good thing the pizza deal was still working. Today I would ride the old bike if the new one still had any motor issues at all. They called the old bike "lawn dart," a term of endearment from an incident a few years back with Alexander Smith, Malcolm's son.

Alexander had a bit of a get off, impaling the bike into the ground like a dart maybe. I rode this bike last year when we were the Akrapovic Ducati team. It is also the test bike from weeks ago and is really a great back up bike despite the name.

Sonny Anderson joined us that day. Sonny is one of the very most important people ever to volunteer, build, promote, organize, manage, start and run the motorcycles at Pikes Peak. He's retired from that now, but he and his partner Bill are the salt of the Peak, the good old boys. I was honored to have him with us that day and I always feel better when he is around. He knows more about this hill than anyone else does and he has given me some super-secret information over the years, all of which have improved my times and kept me safer than I would have been. He is a super nice guy and it's a real confidence boost when he's around.

Today we need a good result from practice. We can only hope for the best from the new settings on the bike. Ed and Ted with Rod and Paul told me that the bike was really feeling good. They had come up with a new mapping for the motor and told me the problem seemed to have been solved. They were confident that it was fixed. I ran the sighting run on the new bike, getting all warm and fuzzy, as it really had improved. I returned to the pits with the good news and we immediately decided to focus on the new bike and only the new bike. Before each run we'd have the tire warmers on until the tire temperatures were warm enough to give us good grip. Without warmers you would have no grip, period. There would be riders all over the ground. The temperature on the road is like 38 degrees. On the first run the motor felt great with the updated computer setting. It was better, much better. Don, my teammate, would also inherit the new computer setting on his bike. It was an Improvement from where the bike originally was. The crew had turned a setback into a step forward.

The middle section is the shortest of the three sections and has quite a few hairpin turns. There is a huge altitude gain in short distance by way of the W's, a zigzagging climb up the steep ridge to Devil's Playground. There are a couple of fast sections that are a bit scary too. There are several places on the hill where bravery and memory can make a big difference; four of them are in this section. One such section is a long sweeping right hander called Elk Park where you are blinded by the morning sun as you sweep right at . 90 to 110 mph in fourth gear. The turn tightens up a little just as you come around a blind bend. This really is a BLIND BEND. This section is scary. You have to hold the throttle on and wait till you see this road sign that is the brake marker for a first gear, hairpin and a right turn with a very permanent guardrail to stop you if you miss your mark. Problem is that most of the time the sun is right in your face just before you get there. It is a hard braking zone. Sliding in heavy on the brakes I have left a few black marks on the entry, and even a few more heavy marks in my shorts.

The W's are a serious test of your memory and your braking skills. There is nothing more surprising than preparing for a longer section ahead at full throttle and then suddenly finding out that you are in the shorter section. More cars and bikes seem to make these types of mistakes here followed by crashes and the occasional flying off the hillside crash. You really have to know where you are at all times because the braking zones are very important to get right as well as the acceleration out of the corners. First gear corners followed by clean shifts to top speed and then braking back down to first gear for a hairpin turn and then repeat. Nine of them in a row with a few other bends and sweepers mixed in. I usually like to slide the bike in the braking zones to help my rhythm and turn-ins. But I was not really feeling it this day. As much as I would have liked to it was not in me. The engine braking was too hard and I was still too sluggish to ask for such skills at this time. Damn.

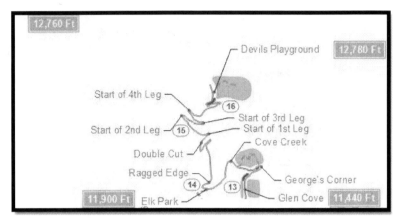

(The Middle section is from Glenn Cove to Devils Playground. The W's. Nothing flows through this section. Heavy breaking and hard acceleration, steep and tight.)

I was feeling a little better, especially now that the bike was running so good. Though in my fatigued state it was easy to get ahead of myself. I talked with Rod about how things were going and asked him to please help me by reminding me to stay well under my limit. The truth is that I was very slow and sort of weak from RAAM and still needed time to recover. If I could rest while building my pace slowly, I would be able to get stronger and more alert and then I could get back to full speed. Rod was there for me the year before helping me to be smart and pace myself, to ride into race shape. Rod gives me confidence, he gives me support where I need it. He makes me feel like I am more important than anything else. Rod knew how tired I was, both physically and mentally and that week he will helped me to ride and to rest safely at the same time. Together we communicated honestly and without distractions from anyone else. What this means is that I could ride accordingly to my condition each day and I would try to stay at about 75 percent of my maximum effort. Rod was consistently there to tell me "Go easy, stay safe." It was the best way to manage the week and make the start in as good of shape as I possibly could in my condition.

I was sort of conservative on all my runs—at least as much as possible. Today's practice starts on the middle section from the Brake Check booth. It's an uphill start point. Every twenty or so seconds the flagman sends a rider one at a time. When it's my turn I accelerated away, first gear, second gear, third and then turn right on an off camber turn with a rock wall on the outside. Next is an uphill and mostly straight section of maybe 800 feet before a 180-degree left-hander named George's Corner, a first gear knee-dragger.

[FAST BY GEORGE: George's Corner is the first left-hander after Glen Cove. A first or second gear hairpin but, not one of the W's. The W's are all first gear 180 degree turns.]

The next section is an uphill fast right, a short straight to a fast left-hand sweeper that is a bit off-camber, a third gear long turn, a long knee-dragger that really starts to climb uphill. The course really gets fast here and is an around the mountain style turn with a long right bend to Elk Park. The next section is a blind entrance to a first-gear turn with a very prominent Armco barrier. By the way, in the morning this section also has direct sun light right into your face.

These corners are among the good warm tire zones where I can trust my tires' grip, making this section one where I can judge the bike's performance; braking, grip, acceleration, speed etc. If you can get the bike working well here it is a great start. There is also a section that starts at 4thLeg and continues all the way to Devil's Playground that is very important for the bike set up. You must have these sections well-rehearsed to be fast in the mid-section of Pikes Peak.

Bike set-up is the difference between fast and not fast. Yes, it's very important. Tires, fuel, engine settings, suspension settings, all of it is so important. A bobble can cause a crash and a crash up there can have very severe consequences. Taking big risks up there is best saved for the one and only race day run. Anything can happen on the mountain, and I mean anything. Today, on the way back down from our 3rd run I was following a rider on a 450 Honda Supermoto bike. (A 450 Supermoto is a motocross bike with slicks, a 450cc, light and agile bike with 50 horsepower. I rode a similar style bike in 2005, '06 and '08).After you sit for 15 or so minutes your tires get cold and hard. We had been sitting for at least that long before the sweep riders appeared to lead the whole group back down to the starting point. The rider on the 450 was just in front of me and was turning right going down toward 4th

Leg around a sweeping right turn and just slid out at about 60 mph as if he had hit an oil slick. I watched him and his bike slide helplessly off the edge and disappear. I slowed to the edge of the road to look for him. As the rider cart wheeled to rest about 100 yards down the steep slope in a heap, his bike cartwheeled out of control, gaining speed all the way down to the road below about 300 yards before it clipped another rider causing a second crash. The crash can be viewed on YouTube, search for "Honda from heaven." Holy shit I thought as I heard myself start laughing in my helmet. (It's a nervous habit I have to deal with seeing this sort of thing) Jeff Grace was the poor innocent rider below that was hit. Well, damn, it couldn't have happened to a nicer guy.

Practice ended before 9 am. Bruno, Don and I were all within one second of each other (2:43:00 plus or minus) on the timing sheet and the two riders on Superbikes just ahead by 5 or so seconds at 2:38:00. Don and I rode Ducati Multistrada's and Bruno was on a Ducati Streetfighter; all production bikes with upright handle bars and seating positions. Jeremy Toye and Fabrice Lambert were riding Superbikes. They were lighter and had more horsepower and yes, they were faster than us. Bruno had won the 1205cc class in 2013 on a Multistrada, He and I were the fastest riders in the class last year. I went first onto that slippery course and you know how that ended. Bruno started second and went on to win. He is very fast at Pikes Peak. Jeremy Toye is a much respected Superbike racer and his experience from Isle Of Man TT must make this seem normal. He is an amazingly talented road racer with that extra bit of bravery. Finally, there is Fabrice Lambert. He's French and full of so much enthusiasm and youthful energy. Fabrice also is fearless and very talented. It is strange to see each rider's personalities shine through while racing there. The coffee smells different, the colors are brighter, and the clock ticks slower. Everything else in life fades away just a bit for all of us. The present is easier to focus on and demands your full attention. We are warriors and we are brothers, extremely brave, but honored and humbled. Yada, Yada, Yada. You get the picture.

With practice day 2 in the books we headed down the mountain. Bon Tons for breakfast. Coffee, Yeah Having coffee-time with Rod is like a present to myself. We have such great talks about everything and nothing at all. We took our time and talked about simpler things like Brenda and home. Breakfasts on these terrible early mornings are long and without any rush to start the day because we just finished the hard work of the day already.

["AND SO ZERE WE WERE..." Fabrice Lambert was always so excited and good to be around. Not sure what we were talking about here, but surely it was an awesome story.]

Often Rod and I would just relax through the late morning with no need to rush. There was a different understanding of time going on with me then. So beer just felt more right. There was a coffee, an OJ, a water and a 16-ounce Heffewiesen sitting in front of my plate of eggs, hash browns and pancakes. Minutes feel like hours here. We were tucked away from the outside world, tightly packaged inside the dense patio seating area of wrought iron fences laced with flowering vines. We were under the shade of a Corona umbrella centered in our table. A fountain played music like a mountain stream next to us as I gulped down a beer with breakfast at 10:00 am. It had been five days since I crossed the finish line for RAAM and I was not the person that I had been here in the past. I was happy just to live in the right now and I wasn't planning too much for later. That would be wasted time out of this glorious picturesque moment.

Don and I had a few interviews that afternoon with, KILO Radio station and ESPN. They are not my favorite thing to do but they are good for the team and the sponsors and the event. Sometimes interviews became enjoyable as most everything else does at Pikes Peak. I usually have some agenda to speak about but not that day. I was acting on instinct in a Q &A regardless. Other than focusing on Pikes Peak and the motorcycle I can't remember what we spoke about. After we got rolling there was no shortage of things to say and things to promote. The race by itself is pure racing the clock with a double shot of adrenalin. Most people that know Pikes Peak can conjure images of speed and danger, legends and history. I had remembered a 1988 video of a French rally driver running up the mountain with a helicopter and on board cameras filming the run. It was called "Cloud Dance." The road was all dirt back when this was filmed. You must really have a look at it because it is awesome. The feelings in me run pretty deep about the race, its past and most of all the past racers that have graced this place or challenged the Peak. We do not actually get that deep in these short interviews, but you get my drift.

After wrapping up and taking a few photos it's off to the Penrose Heritage House for a quick peek at the new Museum of Pikes Peak. This is a must-see if you love racing. Pikes Peak is almost 100 years old. The museum showcases famous drivers and race cars; time periods and the evolution in the automobile. The racers are a who's who in all of the history of racing in the United States. We came back to see the Museum in its entirety later, though it was fun to get an early peek.

Next we bolted over to Johnny Martin's Car Club; a local VIP automotive club for a meet & greet. We ran in to a few other racers and talked some smack. La Dee Da. There was lots more car stuff going on and some fun video simulators of the hill climb. Some press had shown up to get a few sound bites. Our bikes were set up for the club members and VIP to look at.

Finally when our posse of Paul, Becca, Michael and Don were ready for dinner we split. They were indecisive about what to eat. I had told them about a place called Adams Mountain Café just up the street from the Mecca and suggested we try it. They said, cool, so we went. Turns out it is sort of a vegan place that kind of suits me, but not all of us. Once we went in and were seated and looking through the menu it became clear to me that the crew were a bit uncomfortable. I asked them if everything was ok, Paul smiled and said it was the granola crowd that was here. I looked around the room and noticed a more earthy group of people. So what if the woman leaning back in her chair next to me had hairy arm pits and a faint beard. It was good food; vegan food and beer. They were all troopers and stuck it out, Paul and Becca had soup & salad. Michael I think had the mac & cheese. Don and I both Had the vegan Lasagna and I think he liked his as much as I did. It was really good. On the way back to the Mecca somebody said, We won't be going back there again!" Actually Paul and Becca had just moved from Mission Viejo, California to an off the grid in Virginia City, Nevada. So in a way this may have been good practice for them. The locals up there in Virginia City may be very similar to these folks. Bon Appetit.

22 DEVILS PLAYGROUND, PRACTICE DAY #3

Thursday, Practice day 3. Only 3 days before race day. The 3:00 am departure from the Mecca Motel was crowded today with the addition of a film crew from Pirelli Tires. They would be filming us and a few other Pirelli riders. "People, we got ourselves a convoy.: We were back to Devils Playground that day to run the top section. Back to 12,000 vertical feet. Cloud cover again ruined the world's most amazing sunrise. I thought, "Today, I will get a proper practice on the top section and that will help my confidence and give me a second chance to make the bike set up better." I felt that I needed the most work on this section of the course. That day I felt less affected by the altitude. I was getting better. I had lost most of my cough and had clearer lungs. My dizziness was going away and I felt like I had rested. I wanted to believe it too. I wanted very much to know I was clear minded and agile like a young kid. Not a 49 year old guy that just is getting old. Same old program to get dressed, get up the hill.

[COLD TIRES, COLD RIDER: Brrrr. 12,000 feet is so cold at 5:30 am. This is waiting in line for a practice run. We sit in line while the tires get up to temperature and then we quickly jump in to take a practice run. Without hand guards your fingers freeze by the time you get back down.]

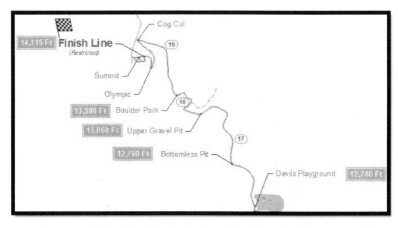

[TOPPING IT OFF: The Top Section is from Devils playground to the finish line. This section is full of blind spots and higher speed corners, most of them off-camber. Just after the right kink is where you will see the mountain in the distance as your turn-in marker.]

The top section is very fast and deceiving, flowing and steady between third and fourth gear for a while. No trees up there, no obvious markers to see or memorize to know when to brake or turn in. The flowing sections have rises and dips, long lefts and rights circling around the right side of the mountain counter clock wise (the upside or peak of the mountain is always on you left) and that makes it hard to find braking points and especially hard to know when to turn in. When you exit from the W's onto Devils Playground you hit a flat straight across a plateau. This is where we start from during the practice sessions. Even though we get a handful of runs during practice it's not enough to develop any muscle memory. It is straight, fast and flat. You just touch fourth gear at around 100 MPH and then it bends to the right where you get to fourth. (It's more like a kink) You can stay on the throttle through there. The road then climbs a bit before it crests and turns left with the mountain where there is no visual warning of where to turn.

There is a distant marker if you know where and what it is. It is a bit tricky, but it works. If you stay far right at the fog line and keep an eye to the distance just above the road you will see it. There is a mountain peak approximately a mile away that will come into view as the road levels out and turns left. It is the same moment where you must drop the bike turning left to make the turn. When you see the peak, turn left at full throttle. Miss it and you are off the road and likely a dead man. You do not want to blink here. This is one of those things that have been a secret (Thanks Sonny) for a handful of motorcycle guys and now everyone who reads this will know. But just because you know the secret does not mean you can or will use it. (Not to be used on a cloudy day.) There are three sections that are left turns circling around the mountain counter clockwise. They run fastest to slowest in my experience. The three lefts do not have any names that I am aware of but they are all fast and have terrible consequences if you were to go off the road at that speed. When you do them right the feeling is really incredible. Probably like walking a tight rope but in this case it's just hitting a brave apex at maximum lean angle.

There are two downhill sections with right turns at the bottom. First there is bottomless pit. It is an off-camber third gear corner that seems way faster than it is. Imagine turning a cereal bowl upside down and trying to go around the outside of it as fast as you can. It also has a deep drop-off to the outside of the corner. That's why it's called bottomless pit. The second is called gravel pit which is a Gout (gravity pressing you down into a dip) right-hander where you are really moving; fourth gear and maybe 120 mph. After the fast right you have straight uphill run into a tight first-gear corner where you're very hard on the brakes. It is hard to get this one right because the lack of an obvious brake marker. All you see coming in is a guard rail. Most of the time you brake too early and have to coast a bit. Once you have made the right turn there's a second gear section that is a left, right, left into what is called Boulder Park. The road becomes extremely bumpy through Boulder Park and you are at maximum lean angles there. The left, right sections are smooth and have good pavement, but the next left and right are bumpy as hell and usually covered with new asphalt. That is where the road gets fast again. Then there's one more fast and blind section around the left side of the mountain with a steeper cliff-like ledge on your right and some really bad bumps in the middle of the fast line ending with a long straight to Cog Cut, a hairpin left hand turn. You are really hard on the brakes into this corner. It has no brake markers so you have to guess and that means better safe than sorry. This usually means you hit the brakes too soon. After the left the road inclines steeply around the right side of the mountain top and a second and third gear blind sweeping turn that is really bumpy to a first gear hairpin right called Olympic and back around to the left to the finish line—bumpy all the way

The sun was out after the first few runs and it was particularly difficult to see. Practice went well that day. We finalized front tire choice, took some good solid runs, and felt that we had a bike that was running like a champ. By the way, my vertigo was gone and I was feeling so much better. I didn't take full hard runs, but I was starting to run hard through some sections. "Small bites" if you know what I mean. No big ones. I pushed hard through Boulder Park a few times to make sure the bike's suspension was stiff enough to push hard on the bumpy sections and that the tire choice was right. We were still fifth fastest time in practice but all five riders were closer than on day one. I also tried to get the corner at 19-Mile and the braking point right at Cog Cut better than I had been going through them. Into Cog cut corner the road has a rise before the corner so you can't see the corner till it's too late and I finally moved the braking point to the rise. I did one entry so hard that I locked up the front wheel while riding a nose wheelie. It scared the hell out of me. Other than those areas I kept it well under the limit and finished up solid. Fabrice was 2:36, Toye 2:42, Don, Bruno and I were just a few seconds back at 2:44.

[THE TEAM: The amazing group of people that makeup our Ducati/Faulkner and Livingston Team

After practice our whole team gathered for group photos. Tage the camera man (yeah that same Tage from Riding the Line) got a few hero shots. In the practices that morning we had on-board cameras pretty much every run. We enjoyed the work we got to do together and did a few creative shots for his film for Pirelli. There was a much more pleasant feeling in the air for our team that day. I'm not a huge fan of the upper section so I was glad that we were done with it until race day. The whole team was goofing around a little and making it fun to be there. We were the official Ducati team and we were the life of the International Hill Climb for sure. I love team events much more now than ever before and this one was special because we were all acting and feeling equally important and that goes a long way for everyone.

After practice we headed down the mountain. I tried to lead our group of guys back to Adams Mountain Café for breakfast. As we pulled in the feeling was good. But just out of the car I got Punked. There was no Bacon on the menu and this crew knew it. The grumpy, sleep deprived meat eaters were spinning circles in the parking lot mumbling and grumbling and looking for trouble. I caved-in to the pressure and we all got back in our cars and headed back to Bon Tons once again for a more suitable, greasy feeding. Again back to my new rituals. I felt so much better that day that there was no need to deviate from the previous day's meal. I had a beer with breakfast. Yep, and it was good. I was starting to really feel somewhat normal again, at least psychologically. My twitchy mannerisms were calming down. I felt steady and relaxed. I do love having breakfast. Even with the beer. I got some looks for it, but who cares? I was replenishing calories for a recent loss of body weight and I was done riding for the day. What is up with the Adams Mountain Café? I can't believe that no one liked it. Was a becoming a cyclist/roadie/vegan-ish dweeb?

I tried again to get some sleep after breakfast. I think I was a bit anxious to see my beautiful Brenda and that put thoughts in my head. Yummy thoughts. I think I passed out for a bit, not too long and I got some rest, you know the kind of rest that makes you realize that you are really tired and need to keep resting. Well that was the kind of rest I had. All too soon I was up and just a bit grumpy again. Once again it was time to go to the next event which was a reveal of the Pikes Peak wing at the Penrose Heritage Museum. Stumbling out of my room I grabbed some clothes. Outside the door it was raining again, but still pretty warm. So no need to change clothes. I saw my rental car and it looked like an official team car after Rod had dressed it with big magnetic sponsor logos that screamed " VIP parking" for sure. We drove over in my newly dressed sporty sedan through town catching glances all the way to the event. Yeah, we were official yo!!! We parked for free and checked out the museum. I'm going to have to remember to bring the magnets the next time I'm trying to find a parking spot in L.A. or San Francisco.

The Pikes Peak Museum is very special and amazing. It's so cool! There are many displays; cars, bikes, pictures, videos and more. The history of this race and the peak are well represented with donated cars and bikes and there are some very authentic photos of the history of the race. Many of the top racers for the 2014 event were there as well as some legends and celebrity types. The presentation was very nice. They announced the riders and drivers and had us all line up together for pictures and such. I had lost a lot of weight, my pants kept sliding down. I needed to go without underwear so my backside could heal from all the seat time I've had over the previous 10 days from RAAM and then Pikes Peak in leathers. I needed to be careful not to expose my plumbing. From the museum we went back to the Mecca to rest and regroup for a bit before we needed to show up at another event function.

The crew then migrated to the VIP reception at the Penrose House where our motorcycles were displayed. Brenda Lyons was meeting me there, finally. I had not seen Brenda since I left for RAAM 16 days prior. She wasn't late, which is unusual. I was nervous to see her and had some butterflies and a special feeling in my, heart. Brenda was there waiting by her rental car when we pulled in. She was wearing a work shirt and shorts--little shorts. She is only 5 foot tall and is so sweet, so nice. She had worked all day in Denver and drove in just now. Her hair is straight and black. Her legs are so nice. She has such a big smile and big dark eyes. And yes, it is so good to see her. We spent a little time hugging and kissing. She smelled so good. Our reunion was nice and felt so good. But we cut it short as we needed to attend the ceremony right then and we started moving toward the tent across the court yard in a hurry in order to keep Brenda's on-time streak going. We tried to get some of the food being served before the speaker took the mic. I watched her move through the group saying hello to my team and I watched her reactions to people with a warm curiosity. Tom Osborne, the chairman of the board for the hill climb, was speaking from the podium; profoundly and demanding about something that I can't remember. With my rock finally by my side, all

I could do was take in Brenda and feel the calmness come over me knowing that she was finally there. Tom was also at the riders meeting and at the Riggle's house for dinner. He is another larger than life person and a Ducati rider; one of our posse. Brenda and I duck out to spend time alone together. It had been a long time to be away from this woman. I cannot explain how lucky I feel with her. Just lucky to know her and that she loves me back in the same way that I love her. We were together finally and I planned to relentlessly smother her for the next several hours. As soon as we could we left the reception and looked for a nice quiet place to eat and in the process we ended up at the Adams Mountain Café for dinner. Brenda liked it and we ate well. And did I mention that they had a great beer selection? We soon returned to the Mecca. Brenda would not be making the early call time for the next day's practice and had planned to sleep in. We settled in to the room and just laid down immediately. Loving on Brenda was long overdue. Nothing else in the world mattered anymore, her warmth took me for a ride to a distant and special place. Home. Thank you God.

Sadly, morning came way too soon. I wished I could stay in bed and sleep right there with her, all spooned out and locked together. It was so cruel to have to move away from there. She rolled over as I get up to stop the alarm from buzzing. I was awake and moving despite the overwhelming urge to just stay with her and hide from the outer world until a tapping at our door told me that would not be possible. They were all out there, the whole team, and they were waiting for me. 3:00 am is a nice change from 2:00 am...or not. Today we will be on the lower section of the course so the call time is for 3:15 am. We grabbed coffee and snacks from 7-11. Morning humor is key to making it a good day. As we drove up the hill I replayed the last few hours. I could still feel her and smell her on me. The drive up the hill went by much faster than usual and we arrived at our special parking place.

23 QUALIFYING, FINAL PRACTICE #4

Qualifying, Practice day 4.Two days before race day. The lower section. It is my favorite section on the hill. Most of the pavement has excellent ride surface and the grip is very consistent. The road has some of the most flowing bends and corners on the whole mountain. Tree cover disguises each section by creating a tunnel vision thing so you ride from memory. I believe that I know this section as good as or better than any of the other riders. The road section for qualifying is too long to play it out quickly in your mind so you must trust that you know it. I am pleading the Faith on this one. You must know that you know it so. As you start your run it will come to you as you are moving. I mean that there are so many turns and bends that to try to be super analytical of everything is asking too much. It is best to focus on the first couple miles critically and then have a looser grip on the details of the remainder of the course. You will have details once you are there if you have faith. You will know your points of braking, turn-ins, exits, gear shifts, etc.

The start location and procedure are like this: You sit alone facing a flagman at the start point. It is on the end of a straight section of road. From the start point there is approximately 75 yards to a left-hand turn. The turn is about a 80 degree left-hander and then to a small straight where you go through a big steel starting line archway made from staging truss. From the start point you cannot actually see the archway until you have come around the left turn a bit. The arch is also where the timing strip is and your transponder is triggered. This is where your time starts and you will be on the clock. The left and straight are a run-up to go across the start line. You really want to be moving at full speed when you trigger the timer and this is how I ride it. A rolling start from the flagger in first gear, shift to second gear, then through the left, try not to slide the rear tire and accelerate hard through the timing strip. Shift to third gear and bend right into an uphill straight away shifting to fourth gear then fifth gear. At about 130mph you will crest the top and go right into a double apex right hander where you cross the paint lines while dragging your knee with the bike leaned over pretty good. You should be at around100mph. You then dip downward through two long lefts. This is not quite flat out through here but it's very fast and you use the whole road. You are crossing paint lines that give the bike a little wiggle each time but the grip is always pretty good due to your tire warmers having done their job. The course basically weaves left to right at high speed for a couple miles before reaching a top speed of 145 mph through a sweeping right to an uphill left into a tight left-hander called Engineer's corner. I used to slide the bike there on the brakes and leave a black mark all the way up the hill, but after my crash a few weeks prior and the engine brake adjustment it was still too hard for this I was just not into it anymore. I use the term "not into it anymore" to make myself sound cooler, when in reality it's a pretty scary section. This is one of the fastest sections on the hill entering one of the slowest corners. It is the slowest corner since you have left the starting line and it breaks up the monotony of just switching back and forth at speed.

Next is a tight left and right where I use the edges of the road, the whole road. First, second and third gear around a fading right-hander, then building speed around a long left, back up to 130mph and into the long and straight run called the Halfway Picnic Grounds. Many spectators are there during the race. This may be the longest and most open straight section on the hill. At the end of this straight you have a third gear left-hand turn. This corner claims a few riders time to time as the corner is a hard braking zone that is kind of slick. It is usually a bit dusty or dirty. After the left it is uphill again weaving uphill on an off-camber on the throttle in third gear and maybe fourth. At the top of the hill there is an odd left-hander where you are braking as you set up for tight right-hand corner. Brown Bush is a sharp right 180-degree corner with a steep but short hill just after it. A couple of turns later there a short straight followed by a hard brake zone for a right-hander that again has a steep uphill section to Blue Ski, a triple apex left-hander that you are dragging your knee the whole time in second gear. (This is totally awesome section that makes 4 corners into one corner) Then into some switch backs before you hit what Paul and Becca call "Micky's Corner" ,the scene of my 2013 crash (first crash) the one that got me. That leads you into another fast section before another hard braking zone into a first gear 180-degree left. It is one of the hardest braking zones on the hill and multiple paint lines to cross while on the brakes. The trees feel really close to the roadside making this fast section feel really narrow.

After the tight left you head uphill to a 90-degree right-hander at Ski Area or the Ducati Zone (for the race day it is the Ducati VIP Zone). There are many other notable and key points like bumps and cracks in the race surface that you must be ready for or just avoid by staying wide of them. A couple more rights and lefts at speed and then you're into a fast right-hander called Sump, a fast right-hander at first that then tightens up to be a sharp turn before heading uphill (My second crash site from 2013).From there the corners tighten up and have some camber to them so you have got to keep your toes on the foot pegs so your feet are not getting pinned between the bike and the road surface. Our bike has special foot pegs that sit up almost 2 inches higher than the stock Multistrada foot pegs and they are just a bit narrower, but they still touch the ground on occasion during maximum lean angles. The finish for qualifying is a transponder stripe just below Glen Cove. Today we will try to go fast, within 75 percent or maybe 80 today, and more importantly, to the limit of course.

We were able to park just where we would on race day, allowing us to simulate our roll-up to the line, sort of. There is a random first come first serve during practice. You have to be flexible and then quickly assert yourself to get what you need. I didn't want rub anyone the wrong way, but also didn't want to start behind riders on smaller cc bikes or slower riders. They would get in my way and slow my run down. As I had mentioned earlier that the gaps between riders is approximately 25 seconds. During qualifying it's closer to 40 seconds. You can also hold for a couple extra seconds at the flagmen to give just a bit more distance between you and the rider in front of you. We were at the lowest altitude for the race and the bike actually feels faster there even if that is close to two miles of altitude at 10,000 feet. A low fog made things a bit moist and vision too was a little concerning, but it was starting to lift.

For qualifying we only have three runs. We should have gotten more but a few crashes will ate up a lot of time. I still needed Rod's help to stay at 75 % and he didn't let me down. He was in my ear right before my run. He is all ways there for me and at times his nervous concern makes me feel really good. Telling me to ride smooth and safe. Before my first run Frank, the starter, tells me to look out for elk at Halfway Picnic Grounds because a few were seen moving through there just a few minutes before. I wave the next guy in line to go ahead of us and he does. I want him to scare the deer off and we gave him extra space so he wouldn't hinder our run. Could you imagine hitting a full size elk on a motorcycle at 100 mph? Not me. Then I took my turn.   I try a second gear start from the roll-out and it is smoother through the left right. Catching third gear is also smoother and I was making more speed. I was riding just under the maximum limit, the pressure was off and I was able to just ride without too much stress. I was riding a bit better and it was still early and I

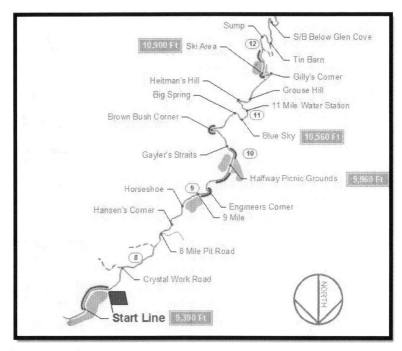

[THE LOW DOWN: The lower section. My favorite section. Flows like a road course, has the best surface with the best grip and a mix of fast and slow corners]

could pick up the pace in the second and third runs. I had a smooth and clean run. Nothing too special, but all good. I scraped the pegs often and I was hitting the frame on some of the dips in the road while I was leaned over. And if I didn't get my toes on top of the pegs I'd pin down my right foot between the road and my bike until I'd eaten away my boot slider and worn a hole in the outer toe area of my boot. Yes, I was pushing a little bit…here and there. After the first run I had the set the fastest time. Upon my return to the starting area I saw Rod. He had a little smile on his face. He calmly told me that I was the fastest. His smile is contagious. I was also thinking that the run didn't feel all that good and I was laughing just a little bit on the inside.

There is always tension around the start line that oozes off the flaggers, starter, riders and teams. My bike sat on the stands, front and rear with its tire warmers on., I wanted to make sure the temps were right in my tires then it is up to me when I run. I picked my time and asked a rider in the line-up to give me his spot and to my surprise it turned out to be Mike Ryan. Mike drives a big-rig race truck. He had a big crash the day before, going off the hill at Blue Sky, destroying the truck. The fact that he was alive and in one piece was a miracle and it was a bit of a shock that he jumped back up on the horse and was there ready to race a day later on a motorcycle. He very graciously gave me his starting spot and I thanked him and said "I owe you one". That's what is so special about this place and the people racing there. Pikes Peak racers are just a little bit different than athletes in other sports.

On the second run I improved on my time but had also missed two critical gear changes. After the second run we were second fastest behind Fabrice. During Jeremy Toye's second run he crashed hard and got to test out the air fencing at the Picnic Grounds in the fast left-hander. It's very fast there, like 130 mph before the corner. It's a bad place to crash. He wasn't hurt, but his bike wasn't looking very good. It is a reminder of the penalty of a crash. On the return ride back down the hill I saw the marks his bike carved into the asphalt. I also saw Jeremy walking over to the rescue truck and knew he was ok. I could tell that he had scared himself and was shook up a bit. Later I saw him and heard him tell of the crash and its effect on him. He is as brave as they come and to hear him talk through it was scary. Falling off anywhere on the hill is scary, especially at high speed when you know you will be hitting something. In 2013 a rider was seriously hurt in the same spot. It was a good thing or a lucky thing that the Pikes Peak motorcycle group had set up the air fencing there.

Back at the pit Rod was trying to pull in my reins, but after seeing Jeremy's damaged bike return on the rescue truck I think I got it. I was thinking that I should just relax a little. We would all get our runs on race day. Who cares if you're the first rider to start or the tenth? It really does not matter, but I also had the urge to let it ride out in an attempt to win qualifying. It is in my DNA. I lined up for my final timed run. After rolling out and running through the transponder strip on my third run I felt fairly good and start hauling the mail. The next few sections flowed together pretty nice and now I'm thinking I should open it up and go harder. I felt that special feeling with the bike when almost out of nowhere I tucked the front going into the Hansen's corner left hander. I had to press pretty hard into the ground with my knee to get the front tire to regain traction and keep the bike upright. I tingled all over thinking how stupid that was to push hard then. I could just see the whole week ending with a stupid crash. I immediately let off of the intensity and eased through the rest of the run without any problems.

So, after the third run we were a few seconds faster but qualified third. Fabrice was first with a time of 4:13:00, Don was second with a 4:17:00, and my time was a 4:17:20, just a nick behind Don for third. Don Canet had picked up the pace and put in a fast time in the last run. I am still surprised at Don's ability to pick up the pace so quickly. I guess that video game must be some simulation. Don was riding really good, the guy has some stones too. I mean, it is just really rare to see someone ride Pikes Peak this hard and be able to learn the road so fast. So, this will be the start order for the race. After looking at the times of all three sections together my combined time was 9:45:00 (the three sections do have little breaks between them so additional seconds will also apply to make the run complete) a good place to meet the goal I had set for this race. I didn't expect to beat the two superbikes, but I did expect a good run and to be in the 9 minute class with Carlin Dunne and Greg Trachy. My teammate Don was also looking poised to be in the 9 minute range and in his rookie year, which is pretty impressive. A sense of relief came over me once we were finished with all the practice and qualifying. I can tell you that you feel like you just cheated death or tested fate again and now you want nothing more to do with it for the rest of the day. There was only the official race that lay ahead. There was a sense of release of all my nerves. I looked forward to the time before my start for my body to rest and recover to be better for the race.

Next it was down the hill for a repeat of Bon Ton's after we picked up the amazing and beautiful Brenda Lyons whom may have been still in bed. Laying there in only her sweet little panties? Probably not, but the image in my mind was gorgeous. Sonny would also join us at breakfast for good measure. We were happy about our qualifying success and that the equipment was better than ever. There was hope for more, as there always is. I always think that the mechanics will tell me that they have found 20 more horsepower or that Pirelli will show me a set of tires that are better than the rest, but these are only pipe dreams. Still, there was the chance I'd wake up Sunday morning with that special feeling--that feeling of knowing it's going to be my day. I could always hope for that. Mike Ryan was sitting in Bon Ton's with his team. He has qualified on a motorcycle for the very first time ever in his long relationship with the Peak. It was not what he was hoping for but was an amazing last-minute back-up plan to make the start. Rod and I sent him a beer to say thanks for the cut in line that morning and to wish him the best. It was 10:00 am. He was there the first time I raced in 2005. The big rig he drives is a monster making thousands of horsepower. It is just scary to see it in action. Thousands of horse power.

This would be the last real breakfast of the week. It's sort of strange that I am so fond of this ritual. It seems like a transition point from stress to rest. Happy hour after a long day of work at 10 am. I like the mornings there to last, no racing through this breakfast. The Heff was still on my mind as well as eggs, toast, pancakes and coffee. I love these moments, sitting and reflecting. I had missed Brenda all morning up on the mountain and it was so nice to see her at breakfast.. She was so warm and smelled so good. I pawed at her a bit as we positioned at the table. I wished that she had come to qualifying to see me ride. I ride better when she is there. Or when my Dad is there. I thought about these things, many things, during breakfast and even though I was immersed in one topic or another with the group of amazing people, I had gone into a quieter emotional place. So, thank you Jesus, life is just awesome again. I knew I had more time to rest, more time to think and to clear my mind and I felt good about things.

Soon my journey would be in its final moment and that realization made me both happy and sad. I didn't want it to end, yet at the same time and I wanted it to be over. I truly felt the strain of my all out efforts and my lack of sleep or rest. My body and my mind were still pretty wasted. I was still in a state of repair, but wasn't yet finished. I would need to take a whole month off when this was finally and really over. For the moment I was happy to just relax in the calm before the storm again. I knew the main race was still ahead of me but for now it can just wait. "I love the friends I have assembled on this thin raft... I prefer a small feast of friends to the large family" (Jim Morrison, "The Wasp"). I want to stay here in my little world and in this moment.

Fan Fest in downtown Colorado Springs was that night. Fan Fest is a very cool event. Main Street is closed off and becomes a street festival with food venders, music, radio, arts and entertainment. All the teams racing at Pikes Peak display all their race cars, race bikes, side cars, quads. Fans can meet the drivers and riders, get autographs and take photos. It's a family event that is for all ages and it is pretty entertaining and after a long week of practice and qualifying is a relaxing break. I used to be the one trying to get out of it. I'd make my appearance and slip out the back to be alone, but not anymore. Partially because there was beer! The street side restaurants and bars were all open and mostly packed. We had arrived around 4:30 to the Ducati booth. Our outpost for the next few hours.

Don and I were there to sign autographs and be available for photos and general BS for anyone who stumbled into the booth. There were also a few beautiful Ducati hostesses posing for pictures and applying temporary tattoos. I realized my age at that moment as they were younger than my own kids. Anyway, they had the interest of many of the male fans of all ages and this made the booth more welcoming and busy.

Of all the motorcycle racers and teams   positioned together on the same street. We were not the only team to have put work into our presence and appearance. We saw that some of the riders we saw in the pre-dawn times of the day could actually clean up pretty well and pose as regular people. My friend Wes Agee with Rich Kearns and a few other top freestyle motocross riders were doing a demo for Red Bull with a Freestyle ramp set up on Main Street. Brenda and I would sneak away for a little while to see the demo and say hello to Wes and the boys. He looked good and it was good to see him. We worked together on the Nuclear Cowboyz Tour. He was on the show for four seasons and was always one of the good guys on tour. He's a very talented freestyle rider, a tough competitor, and a great guy.

Freestyle MX is still a pretty huge part of my life. Starting in the mid 90's to this year I have been making a living on many different facets of motorcycling and FMX is the biggest one. I have dedicated many years to the sport. Starting with the freestyle films like Crusty Demons of Dirt and Organ Donors, to name a few, I was able to develop a bit of a niche for myself as a designer or a conceptual guy. There's not much money in it but, it was super fun. Eventually I began to tour a FMX jump show on the Vans Warped Tour in 98 and 99 doing a ramp to ramp freestyle demo. In 1999 I worked with MTV Sports and Music Festival and LXD FMX Competitions. In 2000 I built the courses and ramps for the X Games in San Francisco. Later, there would be many more FMX events and shows like the Tony Hawk, Boom Boom Huck Jam and most recently the Nuclear Cowboyz. Nuclear Cowboyz is a theatrical FMX show that I wrote for Feld Motorsports in 2009. In 2014 the show was in its fifth year of touring as the most complete FMX / theatrical touring show ever designed and it was still my day job.

The Ducati I rode for Pikes Peak was so different than what I am used to. I am very new to this type of motorcycle, which for a brief moment made me question what exactly I was doing there. HMMM. I was first a motocross and Supercross racer and that is where I am most comfortable. I then went to Supermoto which is racing on the asphalt with a few dirt sections added in on basically the same dirt bike with road tires, massive brakes and stiffer suspension settings. Baja 1000 was also sort of similar, but through the Mexico desert in an endurance style, point to point with GPS or mapping. Baja is a long distance enduro race with teammates. Road racing or Pikes Peak road race is on totally different motorcycles. These bike have three times the power, are a lot heavier with much differently engineered set up. They are totally different types of motorcycles that require totally different riding styles and techniques. I have been lucky to get the opportunity to do this. I do like this kind of bike. To be honest I have always been comfortable operating machines in general. Any kind of machine.

When Brenda and I return to the Ducati VIP tent we found Dean Golich, (My coach and trainer for the previous year) and his girlfriend Ashley. After RAAM it was good to talk with him and share with him the actual experience. He said some really nice things about how far we came to achieve the goal of winning RAAM. And I am happy to know that he had enjoyed working with me as much as I had enjoyed working with him. He is so knowledgeable and works with so many amazing athletes that at times I am a bit intimidated and nervous around him. I can't imagine what he really feels about me and my physical abilities or what he sees in my genetic makeup. In 2014 I was almost 50 years old and hardly considered myself a top athletic specimen. Thank God that deep down I do not believe in prejudice. I love knowing that so much. I know what I have become through physical and mental training and making dreams come true with hard work, pain and suffering. I thank God for the faith that lives in me like it does. That faith has been more than enough at times to see things all the way through to the finish. Dean has been a gift to me as well. A coach of coaches to be on my side. To guild me into a place of the purist athlete, one that I have been mostly just a tourist.

My family, my mom, dad and Hunter and Ronni arrived that day. Even though I may not have needed to duck out from there their arrival gave me a valid reason to make an early exit. Brenda and I took off and made our way back to the Mecca where they had just arrived. Liz had put them in a nice room. I found Hunter first just outside the room and I could hear a NASCAR race on the TV as I walked up. "How was the trip," I asked and Hunter gave me a look that says it was a long drive all cramped up. I nodded and said, "Really, that bad?" I got a look at the car they drove all this way from So Cal and spent endless hours in. A small car packed to the gills. I walked into the room to find that Ronni was not feeling good and had lain down. I walked in and lie down next to her and say hi, she said that she had a fever. I felt her head and she was pretty hot. My mom said she had strep throat and I quickly sat up and backed away, No way. Oh, Ronni, love you to death, but stay away from me. I can't get that. My dad Ray looked happy to be out of the car and asked how it was going. What that really means is how everything is going with the bike, practice, you know, the race stuff. I filled him in as we arranged for Hunter to stay in my room and we will leave Ronni quarantined in bed where she was.. Their cousin Darren, my younger brother Dave's son, was there too. It looked like Daren wore the whole group out. Hunter especially. After getting settled Hunter told me a few tales from the road trip. Yeah, troopers for sure.

As the day came to an end I could stop this feeling of running out of time from coming over me. I was back logging my life in pictures like I had connected with a piñata full of pictures with a wrecking ball and now they were just all over the place. Post RAAM emotions are a mix of highs and lows that come on out of nowhere. Thinking of my kids being there, all grown up was enough to make me cry. I held back from showing it long enough for Hunter and Brenda to get to bed. There are times that I really like to sit up when things are so quiet in my mind that I can dream and imagine all things like a rehearsal and I try to rehearse my run. I try to think of the things that will be easily lost in the excitement of the race. Those places on the course that I do not know so well and as many likely scenarios as I can imagine. Like rain or fog, oil or dirt on the road. Snow…Spectators or fire engines.

24 A DAY OFF? REALLY?

Saturday morning after a good, long sleep. This may have been the longest and the best sleep I'd had in almost three weeks. I was still the first one awake and was only around 7:00am.Thankfully there was no alarm going off at 3:00 am and the sun came up before I did. Brenda stayed in bed as I got up for a coffee and strolled around outside to see who else was up. The morning was really crisp and fresh with air so clean, new. I woke up Hunter so we could go to a bait shop just down the street and get him all set up for a day of fishing. Hunter is still pretty fond of fishing and it would have been really nice to have gone with him. He needed a good slow and peaceful day after such a long drive out in a little tiny car. I was obligated to other motorcycle-related events so I couldn't go with him. After we got the local scoop on where to go and the proper gear and bait I gave him my rental car with all the magnetic logos on it to drive to a local lake. Just before he left grandpa Ray asked Hunter if he wanted to take Darren fishing with him. He tensed up momentarily and said, "no no, I'm good, "then burned out like a mad man and quickly drove away. "Well, looks like he wanted to get there before the fish stop biting. Ha, so what will we do on our day off? We will go motorcycle riding," I think.

A line-up of new Ducati motorcycles was assembled at the Mecca. Paul had three Ducati Hypermotos parked in a row for us. They were all ready for the Ducati Group ride. Not quite a full day off, but this was a fun bonus activity and I got to drag Brenda into it. Don and his girlfriend Donna who had arrived the day before, Paul, Becca, Brenda and I would lead a group of about 30 Ducati riders up the Pikes Peak course. Brenda would get to ride with me on the actual race course and she was all giddy about that. First we'd ride off on our own, just the six of us and would meet all the other riders at the parking area at the reservoir just before the start line. We goofed around a little on the way up to the gate and it felt good to have Brenda wrapped around me and it was too much fun playing with the bike to make her hang on even tighter. Yeah I can almost always be the funny guy.

Paul led the group through a briefing about the ride, the history and of course, a short safety driven moment. Then the fun began and we started to share a story or two under the life size wood carved statue of Gary Trachy, This is one of Paul's favorite punch lines that started years ago by Greg Trachy if I'm not mistaken. (Actually it's a Bigfoot carved from a giant tree stump). And so we started the ride up the road through the start line and onto the course. The VIP guest riders got a chance to see the course safely, at the posted speed limit. There was a film crew doing a motor pace in an SUV with a cameraman in our faces leading us to Glen Cove for the first scheduled stop. So I wasn't able to really goof around too much with Brenda on the back of my bike--no wheelies or burn outs. But we did manage to have some fun. At Glen Cove the entire group stopped and we got into a few more detailed stories from past and the recent races and practices. Paul, Don and I shared stories of our own experiences and of a few other unfortunate riders. Some funny and some not too funny. I told of the first year I raced the Peak; the course was dirt in this section and when I raced through in my run a fire truck was on the course with a downed rider. I had slowed and went by safely, but there was a fire truck on the course!

After a little Q & A at the mid-way point we continued up the hill to our second stop at Devil's Playground. It was sunny and warm down at the start line and it was about 80 degrees but, up there at ay 12,000 feet it was windy and cold--about 50 degrees. I said to the group, "do you see that rock over there on the bluff?" and pointed over to the rock that was where I had to take a dump and with most of the group looking over to the rock, I lost my nerve, I said, "never mind. Let's just get moving before we all freeze." We all remounted for the final leg to the summit. To have a look around and see the landscape at a slower speed, you can really appreciate the beauty of this place. On the summit all of the Ducati bunch gathered for a photo at the Pikes Peak Monument. It was about 40 degrees up there and around 85 down at the start line. Brenda and I ducked out to get warm inside the gift shop and as is our tradition we ate a couple of doughnuts and looked around the place. From the Peak you can see pretty much any direction for 80 miles. America the Beautiful was written from this very spot by Katharine Lee Bates. Originally it was a poem called "Pikes Peak" and then became the anthem we all know. So, you can imagine the views by the words in the poem.

About halfway down the actual race course there was a special Ducati big rig truck and VIP tent set up for the riders to feed them for the day's lunch and for the race it on Sunday. We were planning to go all the way back down to the start line where the team was setting up, but it was so cold we just stopped at the VIP tent to get an espresso and a snack and warm up. It was so nice to take this break from the descending , so we stayed there a while. It is a huge honor to be a Ducati team rider there at Pikes Peak. Ducati is such a cool company and always has only the classiest set-up on the mountain. After thawing out and having two espressos and tiramisu we continued down the hill to the start line where the race team was setting up. Again the Ducati pits were in the most prime location and looked better that the rest. We soon left the group and took a nice ride back to the Mecca for some rest and to be free of any other responsibilities. Brenda and I could relax for a little bit before the barbeque at the Mecca.

The ride back to the Mecca is full of beautiful sights to enjoy from a Ducati motorcycle. Riding casually through the mountains is priceless really. Brenda was clinging tightly as we ripped around the descent to Manitou Springs. We cruised through old town Manitou which was populated with tourists that day. Feeling touristy but still sporty on a motorbike is kind of stimulating. I do not usually like to ride street bikes because of drivers on the road, but here it is a different feel. It feels less dangerous and more touristy and less commuter—more of an experience than a rushed commute. This was more of a "slow down and smell the coffee" ride. Dang, we should have kept riding a bit longer and farther into the mountains. After this very enjoyable cruise we headed back.

Back at the Mecca I took some time to get ready for the next day's race. This was the time to get it out of the way so I could have some quiet time. It's like packing for a trip. Why wait until the last minute? I planned for everything as usual like the weather, rain, fog, sun. I packed various lenses for the helmet, I packed under gear, etc. The door was open to my room and Rod came in to see how things were going. We talked for a bit while other team members were outside doing this and that. Rod told me that I'm his favorite and I returned the light-hearted, yet sincere words. This place and the vibe had the feeling of a family get together with all the relatives. I had to deal with the stress of the next day coming head-on and I was again feeling under pressure. I wished it was more stress free, but knowing what's coming is undeniably stressful and the possible consequences rattled me to the bone when I let it sink in.

Liz and Gary, or as they see it, the Mecca Motel hosts a barbeque each year the night before the race. There are so many racers and special race people that will show up to take part. The Mecca is not the host hotel, but this is still where we and even riders and drivers staying at the host hotel all go, along with Sonny Anderson and his son Brian, Tom Osborne, the Riggles, the Trachy families (all 3 of them), and the Italian and French riders and their crews usually come by. Sheila and her family were all there along with a host of others. My son Hunter was back from fishing; a little sunburned but happy that he went and he did say that he caught a bunch of fish but released them. Sort of funny that I feel more like a dad because he went fishing.

Ronni was at the pool and looked like she was feeling better. The Trachy's were there too and had set up camp in the pool area. I joined Gary so I could be close to Ronni. She's grown up so fast! I remembered her here when she was like 9 years old. She must have seemed to be getting big to me then too, but now she is a little woman. Gary has brought his whole family. His little girls are also much bigger now. Gary also had a cooler with beer and that was also nice. While Ronni swam with the Trachy's little girls I caught up with Gary. This year Gary commentated for live TV. So now I could relax and Gary told me another amazingly funny story; this one was about an incident in the subway years ago. Ray and Bev (my mom & dad) we were watching NASCAR or baseball on the TV in their nearby room. All of our team and crew settled in, the clock slowed down, and we had nowhere else to go. Each of the room's doors were open as most of us were out there together. It all felt pretty good right then. We shared some stories and some laughs and we all had to duck for cover and then readjust when we got a little afternoon shower. That just added to the unique and magical qualities of this place.

I tried to stop time a little bit in my mind and heart so I could stay right there for just a while longer. It felt like the sun was setting on me. Soon the thoughts of racing would be back on my mind eating at me. I knew that it would be hard to sleep and then it would be hard to wake up. This is the twilight of calm you have at this race. As soon as thoughts of the race enter your mind you can no longer relax. That feeling of the countdown starts to bear down on you more at Pikes Peak than any other race that I have ever competed in. Baja was the only race that was close to this in comparison by the way your mind battles against itself. There is a sense that washes over your entire being the night before. Your mind and body can feel the stress and the fear. I do not like to talk too much anymore once I am in these feeling and thoughts. It is better to just tune out or to watch and listen to the others in the group. I wished that my fatigue would just hit me hard so that I could just black out and drift off into a deep, deep sleep. But I knew that it wouldn't be like that, not tonight. Paul and Rod had laid out a schedule for race day morning. The plans were made to leave in the morning together with Rod, Brenda, Don, Donna and I. That is all that I cared to know. I wanted to clear my mind and rest now with my special people near me and nothing else to bother me.

25 RACE DAY AT PIKES PEAK

RACE DAY: It's 5 am. Brenda was up before me and was getting ready. I knew the moment had arrived. This was the day. I rose slowly and grabbed my things without a word. My thoughts were dancing about in my stomach and I kept them there to myself. Rod would drive me and Brenda, Don and Donna a to the Ducati pit area at the start line. We put all the magnetic team logos on the minivan rental and headed up the hill to our pit. All the spectators were also on their way up the hill. There was lots of traffic. We bypassed the long line of cars all the way to the gate and cut in nicely (Note to self: Do NOT forget to take these magnets with you to all future events). We arrived early to our parking spot and still had a bit of time to relax and that is amazing. I do not like being rushed on race day. I like to take my time, have some coffee and some breakfast. I do not like small talk, do not like jokes. I like quiet in the morning before this race. Brenda just sits with me and gives me space. I am not a pleasant conversationalist on race day and will likely be aggressive, and well, not nice. Maybe it is because my poor tired ass was feeling the total wear and tear of the last few weeks. It has all finally come to a head. I stayed still and warm I just tried to stay quiet and focused. At 7:00 am there was a riders meeting and a prayer, after which I could have more time to get mentally and physically ready to race.

At 7:35am they pre-gridded the motorcycles and at 8:00am they started the motorcycles; one rider every minute. The starting order begins with the light weights class, then the vintage class, then middleweights and then us; the 1200cc open class. I would not start until close to 9:45am if the schedule went as planned with no delays. I spent a little time with Rod and Paul to talk about things like road reports and timing of the start and our planned procedure. They were fairly calm, which was reassuring to my spastic mind. On the surface I may have seemed calm, but under my skin I was extremely anxious. Our pits were right in the center of the busiest section of the pits near the start line. Most of the spectators were moving through or gathering there. The emergency vehicles with flashers and sirens came pushing through the crowd on their way to sweep the course and get set up at their positions. Racers were staging, crews were pushing bikes on rolling stands with generators to heat the tire warmers. All kinds of were media snapping pictures and shooting video.

I took a moment to sit on my race bike just to feel it and I stretched a little while on it. Closing my eyes I could see the first few sections of the course and rehearse my lines and my shifts, my weight transfers and my head positions. I needed to be so tuned in, so present. I know what is coming and what I need to do. I recite the Lord's prayer to myself a few times because that is what I always do. As I start to let go of the intensity and find my Zen-like focus a helicopter buzzed over us, breaking my concentration. After a couple of minutes of that buzzing I went back to the minivan. Brenda was with me and she wasn't nervous this time--not like the previous year. Her confident and sincere look had me calm and feeling good.

I can only ride hard with my faith. I say with my faith because it is my faith in God that allows me to ride as hard as I can, pushing the limits for a record time. Ride without fear. I trust in him. I can focus on riding and the rest is God's will, I know. There really is no other way for me to ride there on Pikes Peak. You must be able to go hard and fast from the start to the finish even if you can only guess if the course is good and clean. This year it was much different because there were no surprises on course. I was riding well, not over the limit, and the bike was very good. Does that sound convincing? We were going to be on a warmer, cleaner course after many riders had already ridden and their tires had brushed away the dirt and dust and left rubber down for good grip.

At 7:35 am the race began and the first rider took off. Each time a rider takes off you can hear their full throttle launch and then you can hear the rider's motor going hard, going fast. You can hear the sound for about a minute and then the sound just fades out. Electricity runs through my body every time I hear that sound. The line kept moving forward, riders kept starting and things were feeling pretty good. The Ducati pit area was so close to the starting line we could pretty much see all that was going on. Rod came back to update us on the timing. We were coming up soon. I was fully dressed in my super cool black Kushitani leather suit and Sidi boots. I put on the Shoei helmet walked with Rod and Brenda to the staging area behind the actual starting line. There was still a couple riders in the middle weight class who had not yet started. Our mechanics were still at the Ducati pit with the bikes. When we were very close to starting they warmed up the bikes, removed the tire warmers and brought the bikes to us at the starting line. We'd rehearsed this all week and it felt normal so there was no stress for us.

Now it is time. Now is the time for us in the premier class. The 1205 class. Fabric was first and he was moving about nervously. He'd hugged me two times already, filled with excitement. All together the premier class riders and crews kept moving up toward the starter. We were now at the start line. Fabrice waited ready at the flagman, ready start his run. He revved the motor a few times and crouched over his bike, waiting for the green flag. However, before he could launch himself into his run there was a sudden red flag and a full course yellow. There was an emergency stoppage of the event. Our bikes had been called up as well so, we were at the front of the line. And now they calling for a race stoppage. Right away the team was searching for information to the cause of this course closure. Rod pulled me aside, said it was going to be a while and to just relax and sit down, that they will be sending a few riders back down to restart and that there was a crash on the summit. So I found a shady place to sit down. Brenda was with me and I keep her calm by saying, "I love you Brenda." She keeps me calm by being Brenda. She knowingly looked at my face and motioned toward the fence line by where I was sitting I looked to see Hunter, my Ronni and my mom and dad.

[A GROUNDING MOMENT: Brenda keeps me sane and focused during the delay. I was so thankful to have such an amazing and brave woman with me. Look at her color and her softness. Mmmmm.]

I moved to be with them and to be in the shade. I reminded myself that I have done this a million times, or enough times to know not to let anything bother me and it hasn't…yet. After 10 minutes or so the riders who could not finish their runs have returned to the start line and are getting reset. One of the riders is so shaken and worked up that he may not restart. Rod tells me they will send the helicopter to the summit to transport the injured rider. Hmmm. The Helicopter doesn't usually go to the summit. In fact, I do not remember it ever going to the summit. It means that someone is hurt critically and there is no time to wait for him to be transported down the hill to a safer elevation. I tried not to think about it. I said a prayer to myself for the rider that crashed and try to move on in my mind to a brand new place.

Thirty minutes went by, but it felt like an hour. Tension had grown. And now it was bothering me. Rod wore his poker face but I could see his worry and concern as he reminded me to ride safe and be safe. I could feel all the tension in the surrounding race teams, race personnel, and emergency personnel. I could only guess what is taking so long and I just didn't want to think, I just wanted to ride. To remove myself and my mind from the situation I had a song in my head. Over and over I could hear it. A woman's urgent, sexy voice, "Come a little closer, before we begin. "Let me tell you how I want it, and exactly what I need." The song takes my focus off the outside world and gives me a clear focus. I want a feeling in me that is like being horny and anxious to ride. I kept singing it in my head, "I'm here for one drug, I'm only here for one thing, so, come on and tell me, can you fly like you're free?" It is an "In this moment song. It was working a little bit and I could start to feel myself riding the bike.

Now the safety crews began to relocate to their positions. There was an all-out scramble from all the riders getting ready to restart. The official race starter seemed to be getting ready again. He signaled that we would be going green soon. The scene at the start line was so chaotic and busy with people moving in and out, back and forth and up and back, that an all clear at the start seemed crazy. Then all at once the race crews wanted to restart and the race finally got going again. One by one the five or so middleweights that returned all went off again and there was a little balance restored to the program. Again, it was finally time for the 1200cc class. We all moved up as a group in single file to the starter. Fabrice had taken off the warmers and was on the bike and ready to start as he revved his Ducati, cleaning it out. He is crouched over the bike stretching out his arms and hands in between the roll of the throttle; twitchy and looking anxious.

The Frenchman was ready, the starter pointed at him with the green flag then waved it. Fabrice rocketed away and rolled out to the right fairly easy, then cut left and opened the throttle to the stops as he disappeared from our sight. The 1200 cc big bikes make a lot more noise than the middleweight class and we could hear Fabrice's bike screaming out and tailing back to us through the distance. I could see the film crew on the helicopter above the trees chasing after him as if they couldn't keep up--it sure sounded like he was hauling ass. An electric and excited feeling rushed through me as I heard him at full speed racing away from us. Don was up next. We'd have a three minute time gap between each of us. While Don got ready I wished him luck. The gap between each rider created a moment of calm before the fuse was lit to fire the next one off. I watched as Don took off. Staying right he started in first gear then grabbed second gear around the left hander. His Ducati sounded so bad ass. I heard each of Dons shifts as he rode out of range with the helicopter in pursuit. Again this has me feeling electric and my anxiousness grew.

Rod hugged me one more time to remind me to be smooth and safe. I love these intense moments. "Here I am now. It's my time," I thought as I rolled forward and took my position on the start. I was ready to go, our time had come and each roll of the throttle was my mechanism to focus me where I needed to be--I feel more ready, hypnotizing myself into a calm and ready place; relaxed and ready. Suddenly the flag men yelled and signaled with crossed arms for me to hold. Someone had crashed. Suddenly Rod was right there with me. He talked to the starter and together they told me to cut the engine. "Really?

This has got to be a joke!" I thought. Somebody was definitely testing me. I had a few desperate words with God inside my helmet. Rod thought that it might be Don that is down. Now I paused a second. I needed to be clear on what had happened. Rod told me that he wasn't sure what had happened. Large exhale here. WTF?! Just when it looked like there would be another delay and I've accepted it and started to mentally decompress a little, the officials decided together that we were good to go. "Did Don crash or what?" I thought. "If so he must be OK because we are restarting. Fucken-a." Insert loud sigh here.

Again the recalibrating moment has begun. The singing in the head and feeling myself ride. Roll the throttle and feel the motor, check. The bike is singing now too "I must confess I'm addicted to this, shove your kiss straight through my chest." (Adrenalize Me, In This Moment) "Ok, enough of this," I thought as I said a quick prayer. "God please keep me safe, please watch over my loved ones, and please send your angels to ride with me and make me fast. I love you God, thanks for loving me,". I rolled the throttle a few times in my hand to focus. The starter was waiting on me now. He'd been waving the flag for a little while already. I nodded my head to him and he waved the green flag. Again.

I started in second gear, rolling out easy and smooth on the throttle and kept to the right before dropping into the left-hander across the paint line and opening up the throttle. The bike wiggled a little bit as I got on the gas. I caught third gear crossing the transponder strip and back over the paint lines to the right and up the hill in fourth and then fifth gear at about 130 mph.

[NO TURNING BACK: After multiple delays I am finally ready to start.]

I eased off the throttle for an instant and went full again, lean right, through the double apex right I got really loose, had a big wobble but stayed on the throttle because I knew it would be from the new tires. The next few sections went pretty good and the bike was working really well. I felt good. The flowing corners from 8 Mile Pit Road to Hanson's corner went very well. They are flowing corners and straights that feel pretty amazing because you are really smoking fast through there and hanging off the bike left to right. Then I am so fast through the section named Horseshoe and had such an amazing drive that I was sure I would be carrying way too much speed for Engineer's Corner. Going at it about 145 mph I got on the brakes early to compensate for the speed, but, was way too early and had to coast in and I lost some time. A feeling of urgency ran through me as I said to myself, get with it and quit fucking up!" Going through the left right flip flop in had great drive going into the Picnic Grounds. I noticed that I've been holding my breath and I am starting to gasp. "Breathe!" I said out loud to myself.

I settled back in, focused and get my act together, sliding the bike a bit on braking past Picnic Grounds into the left and had a few real good corners into and out of the tight right hander called Brown Bush, and the uphill left right after it, accelerating hard. I set up for the entry into the right hander at Big Spring with a nice braking slide deep and steady, then transitioned from right to left into Blue Sky and 11-Mile Water Station. This is one big left hand corner fully leaned over on my knee. I made sure to be on my toes so as not to pin my foot against the bike and road surface. I was in second gear revving pretty hard. It felt so amazing. I crossed the paint lines five times during the full corner and felt that I did it right. I pushed on and into the off camber left zone into the next hard right setting it up well and hit the apex perfect. I even felt the humor run through me as I nailed the right hairpin turn called Heitman's Hill. (Where I crashed the previous year).

Even though things were going fairly well I was feeling a very slippery rear tire. What at first felt like I was riding well and sliding the bike because I was fast later seemed like something wasn't right. The fast section before Gilly's corner is like 130mph to a hairpin left hand turn. I was going way to fast and I blew the corner on the brakes and nearly went onto the dirt. "Fuck," I yelled out loud, scrambling to get back on the gas up the hill to the right at the Ducati Camp at Ski Area and I went a little wide after the major bump on the inside under the fog line while I was trying to make up time. Easy through the tightening apex at Sump, this is where I went down for the second time last year trying too hard. I did it right this time and moved on. I was sliding the rear tire all over the place and wiggling across paint lines. The greasy feeling seemed like more than just a hot tire, but I still felt fast although a bit squirrely. I felt I was on a good pace.

I reached the half-way point at Glen. Past the toll booth and through the off camber right hander, I felt an urgency now like I may have been a bit lazy and I tried to make up some speed into the left hander going hard on the brakes into the corner, then on the brakes late I slid sideways into the left hairpin, George's Corner and messed it up pretty good. That is twice now that the rear has stepped out. I went as wide as the dirt on the outside of the exit and that is some 30 feet off the good line. I protested with a few more F-bombs while hustling to get back up to speed, all sloppy and panicked stricken. Finally back under control again and instantly into the next corner I set up for Cove creek, the big left hand sweeper. In third gear through the corner I felt perfect. Now, accelerating hard and at pretty much full lean I tried to shift into fourth gear but missed he shift twice because I couldn't get my toe fully under the shift lever. There was then no reason to even get fourth gear because I was almost all the way through it and now I'm really pissed. So through the sweeping right at Elk park I wringed the Ducati's neck to the rev limiter in third and stayed on the throttle, cussing most of the way. I stay on the gas as long as possible before the tight right-hander hard on to the brake, sliding in with a little rear wheel hop from the engine braking. I made the turn and accelerated hard and headed around the blind left to Ragged Edge. I really committed myself with all the built up angst and crossed the paint lines in third gear on the rev-limit hard. The rear tire stepped out but I stayed on it, smoothly sliding under power as I headed to the W's. That was scary and I am now full of adrenaline, but it was a sweet slide.

Into the first leg of the 3 W's is a long right off-camber braking zone that takes some patience as well as a good line off of the paint lines. This is the moment that I felt slow and anxious to get my ass moving. The corner is so tight and slow that I over compensated with the throttle and pulled back so hard to open it that I stretched out the throttle cables. The rear tire stepped out about 45 degrees on the exit and nearly tossed me. With feet off and legs splayed out I saved it and got full on back on the gas. "Is the tire going flat?" I thought to myself. "WTF?" There is no second run here. It's all or nothing, one run and you're done, that's it. I needed to pull it together right now. You must instantly forget about any mistakes and don't look back. Every second counts so you can't let anything go. The problem at Pikes Peak is that if you actually have a tire going down and you do not back off you're likely to crash.

"Get me out of the W's!" was all I was thinking. But I had a few more interesting surprises crisscrossing the mountain.

At the top of the W's I made the tight right hander and accelerated hard, tucked in. There was a long and thick channel of spectators alongside the road. The spectators had come out in droves. Once I was on the plateau of Devil's Playground I really got it together. I was fast through the right kink and smoothly set up for the left hand ahead. I set up on the fog line far right and I waited to see the peak in the distance to make my turn-in and this time I wasn't afraid to stay on the gas. I saw the peak reveal itself and dropped the bike to the left and through the high-speed corner without letting off the throttle and it worked perfect. Up there on the top section there were really no more spectators and I could just ride alone and open minded

This set up the remainder of the top section. I flew into Bottomless Pit faster than I ever have; braking hard and leaving a dark skid mark from the rear tire. I got through the next two big sweeping section clean but not too fast. The tires seemed to be working better too. At Boulder Park I was consistent and had good turns. There were quite a few emergency trucks and fans there waving encouragement to me. The long bumpy uphill went well and I got all that the Ducati could give. Coming around the mountain and trying to hold my speed as long as possible going into the last real hard braking zone at the Cog Cut hairpin I shut off a little early and then I did a repeat at Olympic Corner. All that didn't really matter as I was finally at the finish line, safe and with one final all out acceleration to the Peak I crossed the line and coasted in. "Phew!"

When you cross the finish line at Pikes Peak you feel so relieved and so completely drained. It is hard to express in words. I felt as if I had held my breath for ten minutes. After crossing the finish line I let go. I just have to coast it off, ride around in circles, get off the bike and walk it off. It's like when you have the Willies. Your body just wants to shake it off and all the built up stress of the entire week is something you want to take off like a suit and toss away. I felt deep emotions wash over me and I was almost in tears that it was finally over. My amazing journey had just ended. I was emotionally spread out, confused and extremely sad all of a sudden. I was ready to burst in so many ways that I even thought of accelerating to the edge of the cliff-like plateau and launching myself into tomorrow. But no, I just circled the dirt lot until I found Don and Fabrice's Ducati's and park mine alongside. I just sat there inside my helmet. I needed this moment to close down my own shades. I stayed behind my helmet shield and released my emotional tears.

My Journey of the last three weeks played back in my mind. I am at the end. I have finished my race. I sat there alone for quite some time. Or it least it felt like a long time. It could have been like an instant, but it felt good. And then it hit me. I started to wonder how fast I was. Was it a good time? Did I win? I was doubtful of winning and was more concerned about getting under the ten-minute mark. Were the mistakes I made too big? How much time did they cost me? After a few post-race interviews and trying to contact the team and Brenda to let them know I was safe, I looked for the time sheet. By the time I saw it I know that Jeremy Toye had won. Or was he celebrating for some other reason? Turns out he was a 9:58:68 and that is awesome for Jeremy. That didn't not look good for me though. I scrolled downward to find Fabrice Lambert at a 10:04:40 and below him was Don Canet at time of 10:10:10 and there I was with a 10:11:30. Eleven seconds over the 10 minute mark seems huge. I was sort of bummed. Yeah, bummed. I had wanted more and I had expected more. How could I have been over 11 seconds out of the 9 minute zone? Not only had I missed my goal time I missed the podium by one lousy second. I looked over the time splits and saw where my mistakes had cost me. In my favorite and usually best section, the lower section I sucked. In the middle section, pretty bad too. The top section was my only good section. Whatever...... I just didn't want to accept it. How could that crazy and scary run have only been good for a plus ten minute run? I know that I could have been killed or wrecked for what now seems to be worth nothing. I was pissed off. This was just hard to accept.

26 TRAGIC FINISH

As I replayed and reexamined the run, I looked for a reason for it to be so slow, guessed about my time and why it was not good enough. I stayed away from everyone. I was keeping it all to myself. I did not feel much like talking. I was just pretty pissed off about my time. One moment I was sad and relieved and the next I was pissed off and edgy. I went on a walk to find the van with my travel bag. In the early morning before the start of the race each rider may pack a bag to be transported to the peak. You can pack your phone, a jacket, food, drink and some money. In hindsight you should also pack a six pack of beer. You will be there all day and you will need a few things. It's a long day at 14,000 feet. During my search I passed a few of the other finishers. I overheard a few riders talking about a rider being killed at the finish line. "This was the reason for all the delays," I thought. Was Rod aware of this? Did he know? I knew something bad had happened while we were held at the start line. Now I knew why they kept telling me to just be safe.

It sounded surreal. I heard that a rider had crossed the finish with his arms extended in celebration, then he had a terrible crash into the rock field just right of the finish line.

At the moment you cross the finish the paved road turns to gravel and you are still near 70 mph or so. You are also still turning when you cross the line. It never seemed to be a big deal before now. Apparently there were a few riders that had been there to see him crash and stayed with him until the medics arrived. Those riders were pretty shaken and keeping to themselves. When I finally found the van and my travel bag I noticed a motorcycle in the back of it. It was the rider's damaged Triumph 675R . I could see by the damage to the bike that it was a bad crash. The rider was Bobby Goodin. I did not know him personally although he rode my class last year and we had been passing each other likes ships in the night for years. I wandered what exactly happened. I wondered if it was true. And then a sadness and an anger came over me. I was ashamed of my feelings. To feel jealousy for the winners, to have anger and dissatisfaction about my time suddenly was stupid To ask why, to ask God with sharp sarcasm, "why couldn't I have won today?" and be pretty pissed off about it.

[THE HARSH REALITY OF RACING: Bobby Goodin crossed the finish line in celebration before he crashed and was killed.]

I sat there for a while and just thought about the people down the hill waiting for us racers to come back down. To return to them and return to living that normal life again. To tell the stories of the race and to share the intense and special moments. To love each other. Who is waiting down the hill for Bobby and what are they going through or do they know yet? As I looked at his damaged bike I was overtaken with my emotions again and tears fill my eyes. I wondered what it would do to my kids, my family and friends. What would it be like for Brenda if I never came back down the hill? I have seen my share of major injuries and my share of deaths from motorcycles. I have lost friends and I have been affected in many different ways. I always feel bad and I always seem to respect and accept the consequences, although I do truly believe it is never going to happen to me. I have always known that. So, why do I have such a reaction to this? Where is my foolproof denial?

I raced this race for completely understandable and respectable reasons. I love racing motorcycles. The thrill of riding and racing, competition, it's pure passion to me. That present focus always outweighs the risks. It always has. However, there is also a reason that this race is special. I don't think about it too much and I don't talk about it too much. In fact I hardly ever do because It sounds so ridiculous. There is something that draws me to this race because to race it you must also accept the risks that are extreme and permanent. The danger is also a draw for me. Knowing that if I really screw up or if the bike fails or the tire fails at any time it could all be over. Understanding the consequences and acceptance of the consequences strengthens my faith. My faith in God. I can ride with that faith and trust it. I can live closer to God by giving in to my faith. I can walk the tightrope without a net. Being killed doing this is always present even though I really believe that it would never happen to me and that is in my faith. I trust in that. I am also aware that ultimately it is God's will and ultimately in his hands. So if he takes me I must be ok with it. That has been my reality being here, in this race, until just now. I am not happy about thinking any other way than that. In fact, I have only known glimpses of these thoughts before just now.

Throughout the remainder of the day my emotions jumped back and forth. I'm a racer. I'm a human being. And as both together I wasn't sure how to act, react or speak of it. I knew that after the previous three weeks that I was extremely frail and emotional; much more than I ever have been. We are creatures of habit. We act like we normally do most of the time regardless of what has happened around us. Shock has run through my body and mind many times over the years. It runs its course. We can feel pretty deeply at moments in time, then we just return to our "norm" My mind was skipping like a scratched record. I spend my time with other racers on the Peak. We talked about things race related, compared stories of our runs, we ate, we watched the updates, we people watched, we rested, and we walked around and in and out of the two buildings atop the Peak. But we rarely spoke of Bobby Goodin. I think it is strange that so little was talked about for the rest of the day. I jumped back and forth from sadness to anger to relief and celebration. Again, this was the end of my journey and it was suddenly very sad. My inner thoughts, or demons had begun to take liberties with me. I heard the voices in my head say things like, "Now that's the way to go. Just end this whole thing with a huge, fiery and poetic crash."

The race continued throughout the long, long day until all the racers had run and were all finished and parked on the Peak. My time on top of the Peak seemed to go by so slowly. It seemed to take forever. Once all the racers are finished, all the cars, all the motorcycles and all of the riders and drivers would parade their way down the hill back to the start line.

I desperately wanted to be with Brenda and my family. I wanted off this mountain right now in a bad way. As I got ready to parade my way down I learned that my Ducati has a dead battery., I'd left the key in the on position all day and now I must push start it. Don had a few ideas to bump start it. No real problem on a mountain peak. I had to let most of the other riders and cars go before trying to bump start it. The bump start worked and I rolled slowly away with the massive group of racers. As we moved slowly down the mountain we started to pass the safety crews in the upper section who were out on foot next to the road. Boulder Park, Gravel Pit, Bottomless Pit. They clapped and waved flags or their hats to all the racers descending the mountain. We the racers wave back. Again my feelings danced around as if I was in a mosh pit trying to find a place to land that would make me feel good about something.

At Devil's Playground there was a line of fans stretching about 300 yards long down the left side of the road. We slowed to a walking speed to thank all of the spectators. For the remainder of the descent the spectators and course personnel formed roadside lines to high-five us as we passed. Some of the riders did burn-outs and revved their engines to celebrate with the fans. These hardcore fans had waited all day. They'd been stuck on the hill since 3:00 am that morning with no way to exit until the race was over. I believed they deserve some recognition and it did feel great to say thanks. For a little while I totally forgot about everything and just sat on my bike and hid inside my helmet safe from everything else. I really appreciate the fans who have been here all day. They have been here for over 10 hours on the peak. Hard core fans showing support and I do take the time to shake hands and slap fives but, I really would love to just get on the gas and race down the road to be with my team. To see Brenda's face and see my kids. That is all I want right now and it is pure agony to coast down the hill at 5 MPH.

27 SAFE

Back at the start line a massive traffic jam of race cars and race bikes, team personnel, and fans had completely blocked the start area. I tried to be patient and wait my turn. All around me were people moving so slowly. I imagined myself throttling through the crowd like a bowling ball through the pins. I was anxious to get there faster and full of angst. My patience won out and I stayed composed. I finally rolled into the Ducati pit area and was warmly greeted by all the Ducati team. Brenda had changed into a tank top and yoga pants (one of the greatest female clothing items of the 21st century), instantly lifting my spirits. She had gotten tired of waiting and went for a run to relieve the stress and pass the time. I told her she looked like a piece of candy as I just held her for a while. She smelled so good. Rod, Michael, Paul and Becca and the rest of the crew were all happy and now I continued to be lifted up. Mom and dad had gone back the Mecca with Ronni and Hunter so I had to wait just a bit longer to see them. All the Ducati team was super happy. I did not win, I was fourth, but they didn't even seem to care. We regrouped again as a team and took photos for all of our different sponsors. We celebrated with each other as if we had won. At first I tried to explain my ride, but realized that it didn't really matter. I was relieved, felt the love and was so happy to be there with everyone.

There was a trophy and awards presentation after the racers had all returned. It was held in a huge white tent just left of the pit area and start line. All or most of all the riders, drivers, teams and crew gathered together; some on chairs and some standing in the back. Many were honored and recognized for their achievements of the year's race, class by class. As the 1200cc class is recognized I felt pretty sad that I missed the podium, but with Don there the team had its third place finisher. In fact Ducati finished second, third, fourth and fifth. It felt good to be with my team and especially with Brenda. As things wound down I was very aware that no one had mentioned Bobby Goodin, the rider that was killed. Emotionally I was sort of lost and a little angry again. I thought that someone should say something to honor him. Why is there no mention of him? I prayed in my head for someone to speak up. But, it never happened. Nothing was said about Bobby Gooden. Should I have said something?

I had an argument with Don on the drive back down to the Mecca regarding the way it was handled--about whether or not it could have been avoided or if safety could have been improved. Crashes, injuries and even death are consequences that each rider or driver has understood going into this race. Don said, "Bad things can happen up here and we know it." We all take that risk when we ride up there. There is no safety to protect us everywhere at all times. In my heart I think that all of these things are true and still, no one was quite ready for this. Can race safety be improved? It always can. It always will. It will always get better. But it won't fix everything. What still makes me sad is that no one mentioned him during the post-race gathering. No words were said; no somber moment of silence, no prayer. Why weren't we recognizing this veteran competitor who lost his life on Pikes Peak? This is where I am pissed off about our lack of compassion. Where had the humanity gone? Are we all really that cold, hard, macho? Race, win or die and show no mercy no sympathy. After all I know of these people here. All members of the organization are good people. I know they are, so what has happened? There must be more to be done.

The remainder of the drive was fairly quiet and I think we were all ready to get a moment alone and get cleaned up. As we pulled into the Mecca finally I saw my kids, Hunter and Ronni, and my mom and dad too. We did not speak once of Bobby Goodin. We were just happy it was over. There was little time left before we'd take off the next day. We had to make a move for one last group dinner. The group raced across the street to the Amanda Fonda's Mexican restaurant and were denied entry as they are closing. We ended up by default at a barbecue/gas station place; the only place still open on a Sunday night. Everyone was bouncing around the buffet style staging area and we finally made our selections and relaxed at our table. It was nice to have one last group dinner regardless of where it was. It was 9:30 pm and we'd been at it since 5:00am. Most of my day was at 14,000 feet and I felt so tired

Back at the Mecca we talked about the race even more and shared a few gifts for each other. Rod presented me with a surprise; a painting from artist Chris Woolley. It is an image of me on the Ducati accelerating in front of a rock face at top speed. Chris was there to sign it for me. It is from the previous year's race and is very beautiful. Many different colors create energy and provoke thoughts and feelings. He titled the painting, "Koan," which means "the unanswerable question." ko·an ˈkōän/ noun A paradoxical anecdote or riddle, used in Zen Buddhism to demonstrate the inadequacy of logical reasoning and to provoke enlightenment.

[KOAN: The unanswerable question.]

I was stuck in a Koan myself. Maybe I was just be too exhausted to deal with it, I didn't want to rest or sleep, but my body was starting to shut down. Soon Brenda called me to bed. "I'm coming," but didn't want to just go about my life as usual, as if it were any other day. Not this time. I have always come down from one huge adventure and raced right into the next one. This one was different. I thought, "I will attempt to savor in it, or to take more meaning from it, for a while at least. I guess for now I might just leave it there to stew for a bit longer. These 21 days passed like a marathon in multi speeds and in numerous colors, on many level with many layers. There will be lots of looking back even after the smoke has cleared away." And with all these thoughts I went to my room; teary-eyed I fell asleep close to Brenda and not far from Hunter or Ronni, or my mom and dad. It was a pretty good place to be.

July arrived, but I cannot say I was aware of that. This was the last day of this adventure, next was the journey back home. I awoke to the warmth of Brenda's beautiful curvy body. Damn, she has some nice legs. It was so nice to be in neutral. For a very brief moment it was like the whole world outside was blown up overnight and we were the only ones left. I felt no stress, no needs, and no cares. And then some asshole honked his horn outside, crushing my moment. Still there was no big rush. I only had travel to deal with that day. The trip home. It was a sad moment, but a good day that should be kind of fun. Why not? After shuffling with rental cars and buffing out scratches to the paint of Brenda's rental car we were finally ready to go. We had many sad goodbyes with family and friends and one last coffee with Rod. Coffee is always so good. Can you imagine having coffee any other way? As we wiped away our tears Brenda and I drove away from the Mecca on our way to the airport. Brenda with me now and that seemed to be all that mattered—I couldn't have been happier. Every day is a new adventure.

AFTERWORDS

What do I take from all this? I mean, this has been a ton of extreme stimulation? How do I take away and inventory all of these amazing moments and download them all and grow richer from the experience? What have I really done and what does any of it mean? RAAM was an incredible adventure and a total success, winning. Winning isn't everything, but, winning it was amazing. That is the goal of any race, right? To win you must be first. And if that is so was Pikes Peak a loss because I did not win and set a new record? How could it be that I did not win? And why couldn't I have won? It feels so good to win. Do I come away from it as if it was a loser? I can't. I just do not see it as loss. Why do we humans (the racer type of human, like me) have such a narrow perspective of success and achievement? Yes, we all want to win and that will always stay the same. First is first. We will always strive to win no matter what. That is the ultimate goal. But is it what is most important? In life is the actual winner always the real winner? And is it the only way to be a winner? This is a new place for me to be in. I do not know anything else that has been a part of my life other than striving to win. A racer is made to win. That has been all that has made sense. It has been so easy. The winner is the best. That has been it. Nothing else has really even mattered. At least it has not mattered until now.

I am well-worn out of "Win or Die." I just do not feel the same about it as I was once taught to feel about it. I do believe now that that mentality is all a big lie. Just a front to hide the fact that life is bigger than the winner. Is there a time when the win is just in being in the event itself? In being able to compete and race your very best? I think so. I know so. I know that I never took an easy shift. I never gave less than 100%. I did put all I had into my efforts, risked it all and put myself on the line. I think that we can feel like winners for being like winners. Putting 100% into being our best, into our planning and training, the race, the events and most importantly our deepest thoughts and actions. We give all we have. We do our very best. We make no excuses, we push ourselves to the limit and then some. I like thinking that makes you a WINNER!!! Or in the case of this set of events, it may be just too simply finish period, to survive the challenge. I do believe that in finishing RAAM you have achieved something special. That medal that is draped around your neck really means something. Official finisher of RAAM. I am proud to have one. And yes, I know what it takes to earn one and that is why I am proud to have it and it means so much

As for Pikes Peak, I thought that I had totally lost my love for it. I thought that I might never want to ride a motorcycle there ever again. I felt short of my goal, but at the same time I felt content with my effort. I worked very hard all week to get better, to be rested and ready. I spent as much time as possible prior to the race to be ready. I kept looking for more speed from the bike, from the road and from myself. I truly pushed very hard, even too hard a few times. After the death of Bobby Goodin and the quiet suppression of his death, I was sure I had had enough of Pikes Peak. How can I justify risking so much to be the King of the Mountain, that if I die trying they will sweep me under the base with no mention? Why would I want to ever go back now? Well, after a little time had passed I started to feel differently about it. I began to see the shiny silver lining that does exist there. I know the organization and the people really just were not ready to deal with Bobby Goodin's death in the moment. They are good people and I do believe in them. I see the impact it has had on them and how they are making changes to improve safety and general protocols for future accidents. They have taken on a campaign to remember and honor all the racers who have given their lives to race the mountain. They do love and respect all who race the mountain. I am once again missing the amazing moments I have had and I want to have again. I do love it there. And finally, my foolproof denial that nothing like that, that nothing bad will ever happen to me, has also returned.

I understand now that I was so tired, mentally and physically to a point reaching into my emotional limits that I could not perform or focus anywhere near my best. Also, understanding what I know now could have made a difference. I was not clear in my head enough to manage much more than just ride and rest. To prepare to make the needed changes at those moments was just not possible for me. I could have fought harder for an engine brake that was better. I could have had enough presence of mind to have changed to a harder compound tire,. I was unable to adjust on the fly or just plain too scared to make any last minute changes, and that hurt my result. Now these are just the things we learn from our races so that next time we are better. It was too much to ask of my body and my mind to race RAAM and Pikes Peak back to back and be at my best at Pikes Peak. There was no time to recover and no time to mentally recalibrate and then succeed at a point of peak performance. Impossible. In itself to do this crazy thing together was an extreme challenge of human endurance. Yes, that is what it was. It was totally crazy hard period. I was mentally fragile to point of extreme insecurity. Can you imagine the expectations for next time if I had won both of these events back to back? The bar would have been set at an impossible level. But, that would have been awesome!

Looking back to RAAM and Pikes Peak together as one big event is sort of strange. Sort of strange to have been involved with these two very different events period, let alone as a back to back. Back to back or together even seems ridiculous at times when I replay it in my head. I may not ever convince strangers that I have done these two events together, back-to-back,. Forget it, they'd just look at me like I am full of shit. So this book will be my true word. I have a new plan for the full time normal life or the main focus of my life and I have actually begun to dream about solo RAAM again. Yeah, I have already started to imagine it. How am I going to make it happen? Brenda has asked me to wait another year before I take it on and I have agreed. 2016 or 2017 is the plan for a second RAAM as a solo or a team repeat. I am not sure at the moment which one it will be. I really love the idea of doing it solo. I really do. And so training has begun. My 2015 cycling goals started slowly. Just ride a lot was enough for a few weeks. That's how it started. 150 or so miles a week and climbing lots of feet. Well, in January that got bumped up to 200 miles a week. And the climbing goal was increased to 1 million feet of climbing for the year. I see climbing 1 million feet as a pretty tough goal.

1 year has passed. In 2015 The Legends of the Road went off separately to do other projects. There would be no repeat of RAAM. Bostrom and Mirra dedicated their focus on The Ironman in Kona Hawaii. m The two of them went out to qualify for Kona at two different triathlons in different states on the same day. Ben was in Colorado and Dave was in New York. They had picked two extremely tough events that were both at high altitude. Not surprising I guess considering what kind of guys I knew them to be. Sadly during the events they both were subject to having bad days and neither one made a good enough time needed to qualify. DZ is still riding. He had taken on the Leadville 100 mountain bike race just for fun. We saw each other in Southern California at the Mike Nosco Memorial ride In November. He won the 100 mile, altitude overloaded event that it is. It was nice to see him even though we did not get to ride together much. And for me, I did complete the million feet of climbing in 2015 and an assortment of other

cycling events for the year and some motorcycle races. I also started doing a Supermoto school in Southern California. No Pikes Peak in 2015. Another motorcycle rider was killed in 2015. He crashed while practicing on the course on the Thursday before the race. Now the motorcycle division at Pikes Peak may be in danger of being discontinued. This is not good. I do want very badly to go back and race again.

Work has changed for me as well. All Access is now my most-of-the-time job. Not quite full time, but very close. Along with ah a few other All Access guys we do jobs like building the stage for the Super bowl half time show with Beyoncé, Bruno Mars and Cold Playas the performers. Work is good and I am lucky to have the work, but work is making it very hard to plan my cycling or motorcycle goals so I just focus on work for now. It is a building time and my job is sort of necessary, if you know what I mean. How will I afford to take on RAAM again without money?

I tried quite a few times to re-unite the Legends of the Road for another RAAM 4-man team in 2016. All of these attempts were only slightly entertained by the guys as they seemed unsure of making that commitment again. All three were humorous in their responses. DZ called the last one in 2014 "the ball breaker that almost broke his manhood." The only thing that my emails did get was good laughs and group communication.

DAVE MIRRA,
FEBRUARY, 4, 2016

I was working on the halftime show in Santa Clara, California when I got some very bad news. I was under the stage as the band and artists rehearsed and my phone started blowing up. A call from my friend Brian Manly came through. I answered with curiosity, "What's up Bri guy?" Manly sounded a bit distraught and said he'd heard some horrible news that Dave Mirra was dead! I thought it must be a mistake so I immediately called Mirra's cell phone and got no answer. I could feel this horrible thing inside me as I looked for information. The stage was bouncing and rocking all around me. Cold Play was dancing and singing right above me to the song " Viva La Vida Or Death and All His Friends." I flipped through social media on my phone and saw posts and news clippings. I was shocked and stunned. My friend, Dave Mirra had passed away. He took his own life. I was under the stage looking up through the Plexiglas floor as it bounced and rocked. Locked up inside I was left deeply saddened and confused. I knew I couldn't possibly make sense out of anything right now. All this, it seemed to come out of nowhere. It felt like a dream. A sad and horrible dream. I was not ready to accept that I would never see him again. Tears filled my eyes, sorrow tightened around my heart and throat and I broke down inside.

Today's rehearsal has the All Access crew rolling in and assembling the whole stage like a puzzle and then the artists do a full run through of the show followed with the disconnecting, disassembling and exiting of the stage. As I am walking off the field I am in shock. How can this be? How come I had no clue? Lately I had been seeing so many recent posts of inspiration from Dave. He always had so many posts about his family, his girls, his friends, and his creation of Beadadnotafad.com. "No, I just can't believe this," I said to myself. I had spoken to Dave recently and even messaged with him in the previous few days. I was not ready to believe this has happened. I phoned Brenda and asked her to find out what the hell was going on. Later that day I was able to hear the full story. Brenda helped me find the news that confirmed everything. We were able to talk with each other and we stayed on the phone for a long time. Suicide, it just scares me how little I know about the people I care about. Why couldn't I be aware of the way he was feeling? I had thought, "I know him. I think he's like me." Why didn't I know he was hurting inside like this? What am I? Totally out of touch with anyone but myself?

"Dear God, why has this happened?" And then I started to pray to God to take Dave to him, "and let him rest in you Dear God."

I was able to make it through the remainder of the day and get back to my hotel. I spent the next few hours alone in my hotel room. I sent messages to my family and friends--sending words that I do not usually say out loud to them, "I love you and I care about you." I sent a group mail to the Legends, Ben, DZ, Bishop, Robson, Wayne and as many legends crew that I could reach. I tried to answer emails and texts. Then I just kept to myself for the rest of the night. I know I am just a human man and can't understand these things. I don't know. I want to be strong and firm in my belief that God has taken him to rest. Dave has done all he can, he has suffered enough through whatever tormented him and God has him and he's now resting peacefully. That is my faith.

I was working 12-hour days, so that made it pretty hard to be alone. But most of the people I was working with on this job didn't really know me and the ones that did were being good to me and giving me some space. I got to think more and speak less. I just wanted to think more about everything from a quiet and still place. While running back to hotel to pick up some package

I remembered speaking about doing a two-man RAAM team with Mirra. Dave and I had actually talked a bit and both liked the idea of not just time-trialing flat out and having to suffer so much. We could see 2-man RAAM being more like solo RAAM with a sort of steady tempo and, 5-hour shifts of riding hard and fast, just not too hard or too fast. We would have been able to take time to look around and see America. Not too hard, not too slow, we still would want to win but, just right. Now I wish I would have made an effort to get that together. While Dave stayed at my house before the training camp we rode our bikes and trained a bunch, but we also were inseparable for three days. We road tripped, we hung out and talked about everything and nothing at all. We were teammates starting a crazy adventure. And it felt right--in chronological and universal order.

When I picked him up at the airport after a long day of traveling he was typical Dave; super polite and genuinely interested in how I was. He seemed happy to be here starting this adventure. He didn't start in telling me about what he was up to or talk only about himself. He wanted to know about me. He liked to know details. Details. He put me at ease and also put me on my toes. What I mean is he made me feel important and cared for, yet at the same time it made me feel that it was important for me to return that feeling to him. He was always kind and respectful to me. He was also Dave Mirra the unmistakable superstar that he is...or was. Every time you looked at him you recognized who he was. But he made that go away after a short time because he was always himself. He was super intense yet there was always this gleam in his eye that told me that he might be laughing at any second. He never seemed to take himself too serious. He really had a great sense of humor. We did laugh a lot. When he was serious, he was super serious. He'd rather die than let any of us down while he was on the bike during RAAM. He double shifted to help me and Ben get through the last shift of the race. Yes, Dave could be driven and he was certainly intense. He had won 24 X Games medals in two decades of competition--more medals than anyone on two wheels in X Games history. He was an animal and a fierce competitor. I was lucky to know both of these Daves. I liked both of these Dave Mirra's.

While I was sitting alone, lost in this memory, it suddenly dawned on me that I never called Manly back. So I called and talk to Brian for a while. Together we spoke of the feelings we have about Dave's suicide. I could hear in his voice that he is hurting. I tried to speak with my heart to tell Brian that I worry about him and his safety from all the tough stuff he deals with. After all, he's been through a lot. And I know he is such a high-strung guy. I have been through a lot with Manly. We (most athletes of the two-wheel kind) all seem to be so passionate, extremely high-spirited, explosively angry or deeply depressed at times. Seems to be more of this type of personality than any other. Damn, I am like this too. Anyway, I want him to know that I worry he may do something like this. I want him to know that I care that he does not think of this. Brian first laughs and says, well, he's had moments when he was really feeling shitty and got into some trouble. I remembered, he crashed his van into his house in a depression fueled outburst. Brian is a sensitive guy. He said he was given a choice to get on with life or be stuck in a padded room. He told me not to worry. He was over that now and he will not be going back to that again. Brian and I said goodbye for the moment.

Lauren Mirra, Dave's wife, had sent us Legends (Ben, DZ and I) an email (To the legends, Ben, DZ and I) about a ceremony set for the next night in Greenville, North Carolina at a church near her and Dave's home. DZ and I couldn't make the trip. Ben Bostrom and TJ Lavin (friend of Mirra and Ben) would get on a red eye flight that night from Vegas to be there. That's Ben for ya. He was there to show our support for Dave, Lauren and the girls. Ben and I talked and shared some thoughts and some memories before he left for the trip. I was happy that he could make it. Ben would carry me and DZ in spirit with him. We talked about our RAAM together, we pondered the possibility that if we had all decided to do another one, would Dave have been with us, busy and committed again as it was before? It is easy to speculate, "what If?" It comes back to a gift of time and the gift it was to spend that time with Dave. You feel as though you really get to know someone in that situation. Stuck in close quarters for 24-hour days on end; sharing space, sharing work, sharing food, sharing thoughts, tears and smiles. We will always have memories of how we got to know him through our time as the Legends of the Road. It was Dave that gave us that name for our team. The Legends of the Road... Dave came up with that.

Soon everywhere I looked there was news of Mirra; news posts, friend's posts, sponsors, magazines, X Games, celebrity posts. There were many touching tributes from so many people that admired and followed him. And it seemed there were many people that felt there must have been some connection to Chronic Traumatic Encephalopathy (CTE) for his depression and impulsive crazy behavior. I am sorry to say that I myself was just seeing a different side to Dave while he was here

[BROTHERS FROM ANOTHER MOTHER: This is from the start of 2014 RAAM. It would have been nice to do 2 man RAAM in 2016.]

Had I a clue that he may be sinking I surely would have thrown him a life preserver, but most of the time he was riding high. Usually he was lifting me up with his spirit and his excitement.

After RAAM we were not speaking that much. I had not seen him for a long time. I had little contact with him or Ben or DZ accept for a few phone calls, mails, texts or social media. I was always aware of his posts and updates. From the outside looking in things seemed pretty normal.

After an autopsy had been performed and the results were public everyone would know that Dave Mirra had been suffering from the effects of CTE. The information shot through the extreme sports world with a staggering effect. Everyone knew from what has happened to Dave that we are all at risk. Multiple concussions or head injuries are common in these sports are practically a rite of passage. It is sad to think that a price needs to be paid by those who excel at these sports and that the cost may be everything.

I received so many messages from people who were saddened and concerned. Dave had left an impression on so many. All of the Legends team, all of them mourned Dave, shed tears, felt a loss. I think we all have our special personal memories of Dave. I am so glad I have mine. I am also glad that we shared many memories as a group. He was an amazing human being. I will remember him this way. I will remember him and honor him as the authentic, generous, huge hearted and passionate awesome guy that I knew. I loved having my time with Dave and I will miss him, we will all miss him. He made us feel special, treated us important, cared enough to suffer for us and would not let us down out there. He was kind, he was generous, he was funny, and he was good to be around. Dave was a super cool guy. He was a sports superstar and had all the records and gold medals and all the accolades. But underneath all of that he was he was much more.

Dave Mirra was a special and rare soul. There is a feeling that you get from such people. The feeling is so good. It just makes you feel good to be with one. It is rare to see one in the moment and most of the time you just don't see it, you feel it. I felt it when I was with Dave. he really was one in a billion. I will miss the friendship we had just began to have . I will miss vital parts of me that are missing from that.

Dave Mirra, Legend. Rest in peace my friend.

Writing this book has become very difficult at times. It is a labor of love and it is a labor of endless work. It is a love for the remembering and cringing hate of the compromise of the true feelings that get lost in translation. I am not a super-educated man with a long list of words and choices. I love to write it all down in a style of code, using only my key words to remember. I hate to go back and edit it, but I need to so it makes sense to everyone else. "To work on my craft," as they say. Getting it finished and published has in many ways been just as grueling and enduring as the three weeks of RAAM and Pikes Peak. And so life goes on and all the more important things in life just happen. I'm 51, feeling like there is little time to tackle even smaller projects. I'm a grandpa, the kids are getting older and going through life's ups and downs--some good some bad but, all the things are just life. God has new plans for me too and in many ways. Work has changed and there will be no more Nuclear Cowboyz so I will have to find new work. A new start somewhere doing some new things with new people. It is time to re-invent myself at 51 years old. Whatever that might be I can take with me the knowledge and experience of this accomplishment. At least I do know that I dared to take the challenge, I lived it. I know that I fought the good fight and raced the good race and I, and we, finished the race, and above all I keep the faith

Made in the USA
Middletown, DE
19 October 2018